Understanding the Dynamics of Language and Multilingualism in Professional Contexts

This book is dedicated to all the pioneers in language-sensitive research, past, present and future.

Understanding the Dynamics of Language and Multilingualism in Professional Contexts

Advances in Language-Sensitive Management Research

Edited by

Philippe Lecomte

President of GEM&L, Retired Professor of International Communication, Toulouse Business School, France

Mary Vigier

Professor Emeritus, Department of Management, ESC Clermont Business School, France

Claudine Gaibrois

Professor of Global and Intercultural Management, Bern University of Applied Sciences, Business School, Switzerland; External Lecturer in Language Diversity, Research Institute for Organizational Psychology, University of St. Gallen, Switzerland

Betty Beeler

Retired Professor of Intercultural Management, Ecole Supérieure de Commerce, Saint-Étienne, France

EE Edward **Elgar**
PUBLISHING

Cheltenham, UK • Northampton, MA, USA

Published by
Edward Elgar Publishing Limited
The Lypiatts
15 Lansdown Road
Cheltenham
Glos GL50 2JA
UK

Edward Elgar Publishing, Inc.
William Pratt House
9 Dewey Court
Northampton
Massachusetts 01060
USA

Paperback edition 2024

A catalogue record for this book
is available from the British Library

Library of Congress Control Number: 2022948508

This book is available electronically in the **Elgar**online
Business subject collection
http://dx.doi.org/10.4337/9781789906783

ISBN 978 1 78990 677 6 (cased)
ISBN 978 1 78990 678 3 (eBook)
ISBN 978 1 0353 3207 6 (paperback)

Printed and bound by CPI Group (UK) Ltd, Croydon, CR0 4YY

Contents

Contributors

GUEST EDITORS

Philippe Lecomte completed his PhD at University of Paris Nanterre, France. He is President and founding member of GEM&L (Research Group on Management and Language), an international research group on management and language. He has been Associate Professor at Toulouse Business School (TBS), France, for over 30 years. He was head of the Language Department of TBS and co-director of the Major in International Management at TBS. He has co-edited two special issues on language and management in leading international management journals. His current research interest is on language in international business and management education.

Mary Vigier is Professor Emeritus and International Development Manager for English Language Programs at ESC Clermont Business School in Clermont-Ferrand, France. She obtained her PhD in Applied Linguistics at the University of Warwick, UK. Her research interests include multicultural team management, the internationalization of management education, the international student experience, and the effects of English as the mandatory language for business schools in non-English-speaking contexts to achieve international accreditations. She has published in such international journals as the *International Journal of Cross Cultural Management*, *Cross Cultural & Strategic Management*, and *Critical Perspectives on International Business*. Mary Vigier is General Secretary of GEM&L.

Claudine Gaibrois is Professor of Global and Intercultural Management at the Bern University of Applied Sciences, Switzerland, and an External Lecturer in Language Diversity at St. Gallen University, Switzerland. Her research interests include linguistic and cultural diversity, communication in organizational contexts, intercultural communication and power relations. Her work has been published in journals such as the *Journal of World Business*, the *International Journal of Cross Cultural Management* and the *European Journal of International Management*. Claudine Gaibrois is a member of the scientific committee of GEM&L.

Betty Beeler holds a PhD in Modern Languages from Duke University, USA. She is a retired Director of International Relations and Senior Lecturer in Cross-Cultural Management and Business Communication at the Saint-Etienne School of Management in Saint-Etienne, France. She is currently a member of the GEM&L Scientific Committee and her research centres on the impact of linguistic diversity on business performance from a Bakhtinian perspective.

CONTRIBUTORS

Jo Angouri is Professor in Sociolinguistics, the University-level Academic Director for Education and Internationalisation at the University of Warwick, a Visiting Distinguished Professor at Aalto University, School of Business, Finland and Affiliate (Visiting Professor) at Monash University, Australia. Jo has extensive research experience in corporate and medical contexts and is the author of *Culture, Discourse, and the Workplace* (Routledge, 2018), has co-edited *The Routledge Handbook of Language, Gender, and Sexuality* (Routledge, 2021) and *Negotiating Boundaries at Work* (EUP, 2017). Jo is a National Teaching Fellow (UK) and Subject Chair for Linguistics, Language, Communication and Media on the Scopus board.

Sercan Hamza Bağlama completed his PhD at Durham University, UK. He visited the University of California, Berkeley as a research scholar. He now works as an Associate Professor in the Department of English Literature at Çanakkale Onsekiz Mart University, Turkey. His research interests lie in Refugee Studies, Postcolonial Literatures, and Political Philosophy.

Wilhelm Barner-Rasmussen is Professor of Marketing and International Communication at Åbo Akademi University, School of Business and Economics, Finland. His research focuses on knowledge sharing and communication across different kinds of boundaries. He is particularly interested in how combinations of language, cultural skills and social capital shape individual- and group-level communication in international business contexts. His work on these issues has been published in outlets including *Journal of Management Studies*, *Journal of International Business Studies*, *Journal of World Business*, *Management and Organization Review*, and *Journal of International Management*.

Linda Cohen is a specialist in managing cultural and linguistic diversity in organizations. She chaired the Department of Language and Culture at ESCP Business School, Paris campus and has taught in French universities and business schools. Her current research areas include the use of English as a working language in international business, managing language diversity in organizations and teaching and learning in multicultural/multilingual contexts. She is currently a consultant in managing diversity in organizations.

Cihat Erbil, PhD, is currently an Assistant Professor in the Department of Business Administration at Ankara HBV University, Turkey. His research centres on organizational sociology and critical management studies. In his studies, he aims to give voice to 'others' and make them visible.

John Fiset is an Associate Professor of Management at The Sobey School of Business, Saint Mary's University in Halifax, Canada. His research interests focus on how leaders influence intragroup workplace dynamics, employee exclusion, and multilingualism at work. This research was supported by funding from the Government of Canada, Social Sciences and Humanities Research Council of Canada (grant 430-2018-00321).

Leonie Gaiser is Lecturer in Intercultural Communication based in the Centre for Translation and Intercultural Studies (CTIS) at the University of Manchester. Her research interests include urban multilingualism, language and identity, and micro-level language policy. Her PhD project, which she completed in June 2021, draws on the example of Arabic in Manchester, UK, to explore and challenge notions of 'language' and 'community' in the globalized city. She has conducted research and co-authored a series of reports and publications on linguistic landscapes, supplementary schools, and language provisions in the healthcare sector.

Marianne Grove Ditlevsen, PhD, is an Associate Professor at the School of Communication and Culture, Aarhus University, Denmark. Her main research interests relate to the two research fields of human resource communication and financial communication. Within the field of human resource communication, she has done research on onboarding and organizational socialization and identification from a critical organizational communication perspective. Her research within the field of financial communication relates primarily to investor relations communication, seen as a strategic management function, for example the equity story as a strategic investor relations management tool and integrated corporate reporting.

Kristina Humonen is Lecturer in Business Management at Newcastle University Business School, UK. She completed her fully funded PhD in Intercultural Communication at the University of Warwick and then won further ESRC funding (grant ES/V011413/1) for her postdoctoral research project: 'Managing for Inclusion in the Multilingual Workplace'. Kristina is passionate about themes related to (linguistic) diversity management, language and power, and employee voice.

Marjana Johansson is a Senior Lecturer in Organisational Behaviour at the University of Glasgow, UK. Her research interests focus on organizational inequalities, diversity and inclusion, and intersectionality. Current and recent research includes examining gendered aspects of knowledge production in language-sensitive IB research, the dynamics of class and gender in academia, and intersectional analyses of professional work. She has published in journals such as *Human Relations, Gender, Work & Organization, Organization* and *Journal of International Business Studies*.

Anne Kankaanranta is a Senior University Lecturer at the Department of Management Studies of Aalto University School of Business and Adjunct Professor, Vaasa University, Finland. Her research focuses on the role and use of English in multilingual and multicultural business contexts. In particular, she is interested in the notion of English as (a) corporate language in MNCs including BELF (English as a Business Lingua Franca). She has published in, for example, *Journal of Management Studies, Multilingua: Journal of Cross-cultural and Interlanguage Communication, European Journal of International Management, Journal of International Business Communication,* and *IEEE Transactions on Professional Communication*.

Jane Kassis-Henderson is Emeritus Professor at ESCP Business School, Paris campus. Her research interests focus on language-related factors in international management and academic contexts, particularly the consequences of the use of English as a working language in multicultural/multilingual settings. Her publications include studies of language diversity in international management teams and the implications of language boundaries on the development of trust in teams.

Peter Kastberg is a Professor of Organizational Communication and the founding Director of the Communicating Organizations research group at the Faculty of Social Science and Humanities, Aalborg University, Denmark. He is the founder and main organizer of the Dark Side conference series. He holds a BA and an MA degree in International Business Communication as well as a PhD in applied linguistics / tech comm. Among his current research interests count: philosophy of communication, the mediation of specialized knowledge across knowledge asymmetries, communication theory, as well as organizational socialization.

Dorte Lønsmann is an Associate Professor of English Language at the Department of English, Germanic and Romance Studies, University of Copenhagen. She works within linguistic anthropology and researches English in Denmark, English as a global language, linguistic diversity in workplaces, language and migration, language socialization and language ideologies. Her current research project *English and Globalisation in Denmark: A Changing Sociolinguistic Landscape* investigates the role of English in current Danish society and sociolinguistic change in relation to globalization. Dorte Lønsmann has published, alone and with co-authors, in highly regarded international journals such as *Journal of Linguistic Anthropology*, *Language in Society* and *Multilingua*.

Yaron Matras is former Professor of Linguistics at the University of Manchester, where he founded and led the Multilingual Manchester research unit (2010–2020). He is currently Honorary Professor at the Aston Institute for Forensic Linguistics. His publications include *Language Contact* (CUP, 2009/2020), *The Routledge Handbook of Language Contact* (with Evangelia Adamou, Routledge, 2020), *Contact Languages: A Wider Perspective* (with Peter Bakker, De Gruyter Mouton, 2013), *A Grammar of Domari* (De Gruyter Mouton, 2012), *Romani in Britain: The Afterlife of a Language* (EUP, 2010), and *Grammatical Borrowing in Cross-linguistic Perspective* (with Jeanette Sakel, De Gruyter, 2007).

Mustafa F. Özbilgin is Professor of Organisational Behaviour at Brunel Business School, London. He also holds two international positions: Co-Chaire Management et Diversité at Université Paris Dauphine and Visiting Professor of Management at Koç University in Istanbul. His research focuses on equality, diversity and inclusion at work from comparative and relational perspectives.

Tiina Räisänen is a Senior Lecturer at the Research Unit of Languages and Literature, University of Oulu, Finland. Her research areas include sociolinguistics, discourse analysis and ethnography and she is interested in the use of English as a lingua franca in multilingual working life settings. She has published in, for example, *International Journal of Applied Linguistics*, *IEEE Transactions on Professional Communication* and *European Journal of International Management* and co-edited *Dangerous Multilingualism: Northern Perspectives on Order, Purity and Normality* (Palgrave Macmillan, 2012) and *Shaping the North through Multimodal and Intermedial Interaction* (Palgrave Macmillan, 2022).

Guro R. Sanden is an Associate Professor at the Department of Communication and Culture at BI Norwegian Business School. Her research focuses on the role of language strategies in multinational corporations, and the relationship between national language policies and corporate law. Before entering academia, Guro held various industry positions, including management trainee in the Scandinavian insurance company Tryg. Her work has been published in outlets such as *Applied Linguistics*, *European Journal of International*

Management, and *Journal of Multilingual and Multicultural Development*. Guro is Vice President and Scientific Manager of GEM&L.

Martyna Śliwa is Professor of Business Ethics and Organisation Studies at Durham University Business School, UK. Her research interests span across organization studies and international management, and address a range of topics connected to equality, diversity, inclusivity and respect in organizations. Martyna has a particularly strong interest in linguistic diversity and multilinguality. Her work has been published in a range of journals, including the *British Journal of Management, ephemera, Gender, Work and Organization, Human Relations, Journal of Business Ethics, Journal of International Business Studies, Journal of World Business, Management Learning, Organization* and *Organization Studies*.

Janne Tienari is Professor of Management and Organization at Hanken School of Economics, Finland. His research and teaching interests include gender and diversity, feminist theory, strategy work, managing multinational corporations, mergers and acquisitions, branding, media and social media, and changing academia from a critical perspective. Tienari's work has been published in leading international journals.

Rebecca Tipton, PhD, is a Lecturer in Interpreting and Translation Studies based in the Centre for Translation and Intercultural Studies (CTIS) at the University of Manchester. She has published on interpreting in asylum settings, police interviews, conflict zones, and in social work. She is currently a Co-Investigator on the Interpreter-mediated Mental Health Act Assessments (INforMHAA) study. She is co-author (with Olgierda Furmanek) of *Dialogue Interpreting: A Guide to Interpreting in Public Services and the Community* (Routledge, 2016), and co-edited (with Louisa Desilla) the *Routledge Handbook of Translation and Pragmatics* (2019).

Foreword

The field of language-sensitive research in International Business (IB) was still nascent back in the 1990s when I was working on my doctoral dissertation. Since then, I have witnessed how this field, initially regarded as being at the margins of the IB field, has established and legitimized itself as a major area of conceptual and empirical research. Several special issues in journals, handbooks and edited volumes such as the present one have been instrumental in shepherding the increasing interest in language issues among IB scholars. Not only have these publications taken stock of previous contributions but more importantly, they have raised a number of previously unaddressed research questions and topics that have allowed the field to move forward. These positive developments, albeit not free from growing pains, have given me a deep sense of meaning and satisfaction over the years.

The present co-editor team has made an immense contribution to language-sensitive research. As boundary spanners themselves, they have broadened the scope and outreach of language-sensitive research in IB in important ways. To start with, they invited a group of scholars from several disciplines such as organization studies, sociolinguistics and organizational communication to enrich the field by contributing to this volume. These contributions introduce professional settings such as restaurant kitchens, internship programmes for refugees and healthcare clinics that IB researchers typically do not consider as research sites. In these settings, as the chapters show, management of multilingualism is at least as equally important as in multinational corporations, the dominant research site in IB. The chapters also challenge the heavy reliance on interviews in qualitative IB research by drawing on unusual sources such as ethnographic data, employee magazines and crowdsourcing platforms. I very much enjoyed reading the translations and sense-making of empirical findings by the authors of these chapters.

What also caught my attention was that many of the contributions are written by interpretive and critical management and communication scholars. They emphasize the contested nature of language use in organizations, which they regard as arenas of resistance, political struggles and power games. Several authors are very sensitive to their own roles as researchers, showing great self-reflexivity in their research accounts. Furthermore, these scholars do not shy away from accounting for emotions, uncertainty and ambivalence that often remain unaddressed in mainstream research. I would argue that the critical tone in this book is unusual given the functionalist tradition that still characterizes much of today's IB research. Perhaps because of this, the chapters provide fascinating insights into the performative effect of language and accents in organizations, downplaying the instrumental view of language that we have become so accustomed to. These contributions also approach language issues from fresh theoretical perspectives such as recognition theory, institutional logics, communication as constitutive of organizations, employee voice and identity work. To me, this suggests that what started as a phenomenon-based intellectual movement has become a rich source of theoretical insights for many scholars not only in IB but also in other disciplines.

The chapters included in this volume give voice to a number of actors who commonly feature in the margins in our research accounts, if they appear at all. These actors include refugees, blue collar workers, healthcare professionals and foreign academics. Several of the chapters are situated at the business–government–society interface, drawing attention to growing inequalities, difference and diversity in contemporary societies. I was delighted to note that many of the chapters span across multiple levels of analysis, zooming out to contemporary or historical events at the national and global levels while simultaneously zooming in on language practices at the local level. In this way, they embrace the macro when explaining multilingual practices on the ground. Overall, the novel findings presented in this book point very clearly to the societal relevance of language-sensitive research to policy makers.

The many contributions to this book also attest that the field of language-sensitive research in IB has now reached a certain stage of maturity. It does not anymore consist of a small community of scholars whose members are primarily having a conversation amongst themselves; rather, this conversation has a much broader appeal. It also shows that the boundaries of language-sensitive research are porous, open to cross-disciplinary pollination and members of diverse scholarly communities. I am excited about the pluralistic and multivocal future that the co-editor team of this volume has envisioned for us.

In Espoo, 13 April 2022
Rebecca Piekkari
Marcus Wallenberg Professor of International Business
Aalto University School of Business
Finland

Introduction to *Understanding the Dynamics of Language and Multilingualism in Professional Contexts*

Betty Beeler, Mary Vigier, Claudine Gaibrois and Philippe Lecomte

For the past 40 years, language-sensitive Organisational Studies (OS) and International Business (IB) researchers have contributed to a vision of language as a dynamic social practice, challenging the functionalist view of language as a set of formal structures. Drawing on disciplines ranging from applied linguistics, sociolinguistics, communication studies and social psychology to anthropology, they have gained insights into emerging language practices in the increasingly multilingual workplace, and are helping practitioners and scholars to understand the central role that language usage and linguistic diversity play in organisational processes. Nevertheless, many managers and researchers still tend to dismiss the importance of language in the shaping of meaning through dialogical relations, resulting in lost opportunities for organisations and for research.

PURPOSE OF THIS BOOK

In this book, we take stock of the current state of research on language practices in multilingual professional settings and point to promising paths forward, pursuing three main objectives. First, each of the chapters in this volume is designed to acknowledge the strides made by scholars up to now. In some cases, we revisit important topics such as power, agency, trust and social identity in light of new findings; in others, we explore the broader implications of geopolitical, technological and societal developments, recognising that issues affecting the multilingual workplace are not confined to the four walls of the organisation. Thanks to these contributions, we hope to reach language-oriented IB and OS scholars as well as non-specialists interested in discovering this field in order to encourage new ways of thinking about language use in the multilingual workplace.

Our second goal builds on the first one, as we seek to identify blind spots and emerging issues that are gaining traction in language-sensitive OS and IB studies. While some of the themes may be novel for scholars outside of language-sensitive studies – themes such as 'translanguaging' (Barner-Rasmussen and Langinier, 2020) or 'language repertoires' which are discussed in Parts I and III of this book – many of them will resonate with those who are adopting similar paradigms and approaches in their own fields. Process-oriented OS scholars, for example, might readily identify with the notion of language as a dialogical process in a polyphonic world of 'ceaseless change, emergence and self-transformation' (Nayak and Chia, 2011, 282). Similarly, researchers engaged in critical and postmodern studies are likely to recognise the importance of challenging neo-colonial language practices and corporate language policies which reinforce power structures. Additionally, we expect that the paradigm shift from monolingual to multilingual strategies (Angouri and Piekkari, 2018) which is underway in language-sensitive research will have special appeal for scholars interested in Bakhtin's (1981) dialogical perspective or Boje's (2018) antenarrativity theory.

The sharing of perspectives like those described above demonstrates the multidisciplinary nature of language-oriented research, pointing to the third goal of this book: up to now, cross-pollination between language-sensitive and mainstream scholars has remained largely under-developed. We hope therefore to stimulate a greater dialogue between the disciplines by exploring ways to bridge the divide and identifying common areas of enquiry. The breaking down of 'silos', as we will show, can lead to promising opportunities for collaboration between all parties.

AN OVERVIEW OF THIS BOOK

This book is comprised of four parts, each preceded by a detailed presentation. We briefly introduce the four overarching themes here in order to show the scope of our investigation. **Part I** on 'Multilingualism in a rapidly changing world: new perspectives on language differences in organisations' sets the tone for the rest of the book as it takes a fresh look at familiar issues from different angles. The authors in this section invite us to consider how language diversity might intersect with other diversity dimensions such as geopolitical or societal macro-events. In their chapter, for example, Johansson and Śliwa report their findings on the relationship between language diversity and institutional recognition which reveal that the granting or withholding of language-based recognition can have an impact on the power – and therefore, agency – exercised by members of certain language groups. Other dimensions that are examined from a language-sensitive perspective in this section are the gap between institutional logics and the logic of refugees in a Danish organisation (Lønsmann), and the effects of language diversity on dynamic, polyphonic practices in multilingual urban settings (Matras, Tipton and Gaiser). In the chapter by Matras and his colleagues, a multilingual healthcare setting provides a unique vantage point from which to observe the emergence of language repertoires and 'conversational agency'. From all three chapters we learn that a better understanding of the processes underpinning language-based power can help speakers of less recognised languages create spaces for agency in their workplace. While achieving agency is a challenge for refugees who are deprived of recognition, for example, it is a by-product of multilingual urban settings and environments where multiple language repertoires successfully co-exist.

All three chapters in **Part II** focus on 'Language practices in multilingual workplaces and implications for human resource management' and are based on empirical findings. The authors are concerned with language-related microprocesses that occur in the everyday workplace. The broad topics they address include: (1) the difference between frontstage 'official English' used primarily in written corporate discourse, and the backstage 'working language' pertaining to mixed genres, both written and oral (Räisänen and Kankaanranta); (2) the view of language as a social practice (Humonen and Angouri); and (3) employee motives for speaking non-mutually understood languages at work (Fiset). From a methodological perspective the authors in this section use ethnography (Humonen and Angouri; Räisänen and Kankaanranta), research reflexivity (Humonen and Angouri), and a critical-incident paradigm (Fiset) – empirical approaches that enable gaining a closer look at language use in situated contexts at the ground level. It is only from this standpoint that an awareness of the consequences of language use as a social reality in the multilingual workplace can be captured. By doing so, this section offers insights about specific managerial policies that could and should be implemented in a multilingual environment to make linguistic diversity a resource rather than a problem. Some practical guidelines Fiset suggests for HR managers to take into consideration include hiring processes that recognise language skills, training and leadership development that enhance multilingual practices, and the use of multiple languages to communicate key information.

Part III explores the theme of 'Organisations as discursive, polyphonic spaces: a multidisciplinary approach'. The authors in this section discuss a number of opportunities for collaboration between language-oriented OS scholars and their colleagues who tend to dismiss the relevance of language practices and natural languages to their own work on language. While these mainstream OS scholars are advancing research on important topics such as discursivity, narrativity, polyphony and organisational communication, many of them have yet to look at issues such as power, social identity, diversity and dialogical relations through a linguistic lens (Tietze, 2008). In the first chapter of this section, Johansson and Barner-Rasmussen draw on language-oriented

IB and OS research to recommend areas of mutual interest to both parties such as the concept of the Communicative Constitution of Organisations (CCO) developed by OS scholars (Cooren et al., 2011). Using an intersectional perspective which is familiar to the OS community, Cohen and Kassis-Henderson discuss their findings on 'language repertoires' which are the result of the fluidity of the multiple identities which we have at our own disposal. In their chapter, they show the consequences on organisational performance of neglecting people's intersecting language skills. Finally, Erbil, Özbilgin and Bağlama use a critical approach to show how the hierarchisation of languages in post-colonial contexts can lead to symbolic violence and suggest ways to achieve a paradigm shift from a monolingual mindset to plurilingual openness.

Finally, **Part IV** provides 'Different critical perspectives on the power of language in international business'. One approach presents the recognition of linguascapes consisting of both macro-policies and microprocesses and how they intersect within the same multilingual workplace environment (Sanden). This approach highlights the power implications related to the discrepancy between official 'de jure' language decisions implemented by the organisation, and 'de facto' language use constructed by users to manage language policies on a pragmatic basis. A second approach critically examines how power manifests itself through the concepts of voice and voicer (Kastberg and Ditlevsen). From the point of view of CCO (Cooren et al., 2011), voice and voicers are portrayed as instruments of power which shape organisational reality by constructing, regulating and controlling social identity, whereby not every voice/voicer is legitimate. A third approach of viewing language and power is illustrated through a management scholar's personal testimony about juggling several languages simultaneously: English in academic writing and publishing, and Swedish and Finnish to operate in a multilingual context (Tienari). This portrayal exemplifies the power games at play between the monolingual academic language of management research dominated by the hegemonic English language vs. the national bilingualism in specific contexts in Scandinavia.

CONCLUSION

This book is for management researchers interested in the role of language as well as sociolinguists and business communication scholars looking for new perspectives on management in a globalised world. This includes those who recognise the central role of language in international business and management as well as those who hold conventional assumptions about language as a technical tool. This volume should also be of interest to advanced business students since the role of language and language diversity in work and business is rarely discussed in the curricula of business schools. Management practitioners, Human Resources Directors, and Diversity, Equity and Inclusion

(DEI) Officers might find valuable inspiration for managing an increasingly complex workforce in the era of globalised business, migration and virtual communication.

It would not be possible to cover all aspects of language in the multilingual workplace in one volume, of course, nor would such a goal make sense in a constantly evolving world. We have chosen instead to put the spotlight on issues which exemplify current thinking on the multifaceted nature of language in professional contexts. If the contributions help language-sensitive scholars to envision the road ahead while generating an awareness of the need for cross-pollination between language-oriented and mainstream IB and OS scholars, we will have accomplished our mission.

REFERENCES

Angouri, J. and R. Piekkari (2018), 'Organising multilingually: Setting an agenda for studying language at work', *European Journal of International Management*, **12** (1/2), 8–27.

Bakhtin, M. M. (1981), *The Dialogic Imagination: Four Essays*, Michael Holquist (ed.), Austin, TX: University of Texas Press.

Barner-Rasmussen, W. and H. Langinier (2020), 'Exploring translanguaging in international business. Towards a comparison of highly context-embedded practices: Evidence from France and Finland', in Sierk Horn, Philippe Lecomte, and Susanne Tietze (eds), *Managing multilingual workplaces: Methodological, empirical and pedagogic perspectives*, New York: Routledge, pp. 105–121.

Boje, D. M. (2018), *Organizational research: Storytelling in action*, New York: Routledge.

Cooren, F., T. Kuhn, J. P. Cornelissen and T. Clark (2011), 'Communication, organizing and organization: An overview and introduction to the special issue', *Organization Studies*, **32** (9), 1149–1170.

Nayak, A. and R. Chia (2011), 'Thinking becoming and emergence: Process philosophy and organization theory', in Haridimos Tsoukas and Robert Chia (eds), *Philosophy and organization*, Bingley, UK: Emerald Group Publishing, pp. 281–309.

Tietze, S. (2008), *International management and language*, London: Routledge.

PART I

Multilingualism in a rapidly changing world: new perspectives on language differences in organisations

1. Introduction to *Multilingualism in a rapidly changing world: new perspectives on language differences in organisations*

Claudine Gaibrois

How can we provide researchers from inside and outside the language-sensitive Organisation Studies (OS) and International Business (IB) communities with fresh inspiration and novel insights into certain 'blind spots' in the field? How do scholars at the forefront of language-sensitive research in management and organisational studies advance our understanding of the processes underlying collaboration across boundaries? Part I of this book seeks to provide some answers to these questions by questioning our common understanding of why language diversity is relevant for whom, and by offering several proposals for the exploration of new empirical and conceptual terrain in this regard.

By so doing, it aims at complementing the findings of language-sensitive International Business (IB) literature, which has mainly addressed language diversity on the individual level. Even when research is situated at the level of organisations, the implicit assumption frequently is that language diversity is a sum of individual-level language skills. Also the significant strand of research that investigates the power effects of language diversity tends to focus on individual-level consequences of language skills or of the lack thereof (Tietze et al., 2016). This important research has shown that language skills can be interpreted as empowering or disempowering resources (Vaara et al., 2005), and as a source of individual power and influence (Tietze et al., 2003; Janssens et al., 2004; Barner-Rasmussen et al., 2014; Peltokorpi and Vaara, 2014). Therefore, foreign language proficiency represents an important part of 'employee career capital' (Peltokorpi, 2015, 164). Employees might be able to rise in the hierarchy due to their valuable language skills (Logemann and Piekkari, 2015), or even to find themselves 'in more powerful positions than would normally be the case' (Marschan-Piekkari et al., 1999, 436).

However, language is a diversity dimension which is not only relevant on the individual, but also on the group level. This section therefore aims at further raising our awareness to the fact that it is thus important to also investigate the position of members of language *groups* in organisations, and to explore how this position relates to the institutional set-up of the organisation and its environment. Furthermore, as Bourdieu (1991) has pointed out, not all languages share the same value on the market of languages. The section thus seeks to add to the group-level perspective that has already been adopted by studies which found that native speakers – especially of English, which is often adopted as a corporate language – are put in an advantageous position (Marschan-Piekkari et al., 1999; Feely and Harzing, 2003; Tietze et al., 2003; Harzing and Pudelko, 2013; Neeley, 2013), which might even result in a 'hierarchy of privilege' (Gaibrois and Nentwich, 2020).

Some studies have also investigated the effects of macro-level developments on members of multilingual organisations. One example is research on language policy informed by theories of imperialism and colonialism (Vaara et al., 2005; Śliwa, 2008; Boussebaa et al., 2014; Boussebaa and Brown, 2017), or on the linkages between global English and neoliberalism (e.g. Śliwa, 2010). However, the broader societal and political context of International Business would deserve much more attention in language-sensitive research in IB. As an example, the perspective of migrants, who in many countries represent a significant part of the workforce, is largely absent from the literature. This is even more the case for refugees, in spite of the recent refugee crisis in Europe in the wake of the civil wars in Syria and Afghanistan, or the war in Ukraine that was going on at the time of writing after the Russian invasion in February 2022. In general, there is a need to take into consideration how language diversity might intersect (Crenshaw, 1991) with other diversity dimensions.

The rapid change of languages driven by migration, globalisation and globe-spanning communication technologies also calls for a revision of the general tendency to emphasise national languages in language-sensitive IB literature (Tietze et al., 2016). Often, language has been implicitly equated with national languages, and multilingualism has been understood as a sum of national languages. The understanding of communicating in a multilingual professional context implicitly mostly relies upon the native speaker ideal. Only recently have scholars started to reflect upon more dynamic notions of language and multilingualism. Conceptual contributions suggested to consider linguistic performance within global work settings as a hybrid process (Janssens and Steyaert, 2014; Gaibrois, 2018).

This section therefore offers new perspectives on language differences in organisations by investigating the consequences of belonging to a specific language group, and by focusing on the role of the broader societal and political context. The authors of the section show how current societal and geopolitical developments affect members of multilingual organisations and analyse language practices in different national and institutional contexts, investigating how macro-level events as well as institutional logics affect certain language groups, while at the same time showing how these language groups at least in some cases carve out spaces for agency.

In the first chapter of this section, **Marjana Johansson** and **Martyna Śliwa** contribute to further develop our understanding of the power effects of language diversity by proposing recognition theory as a new lens for investigating language differences in multilingual organisations. Recognition work encompasses individual and organisational acts of bestowal or denial of recognition, to account for how recognition does not only take place between individuals but, significantly, also involves institutions such as the workplace (Cox, 2012). Johansson and Śliwa's study of non-native English-speaking international staff at universities in the UK gives insights into instrumentality as a significant aspect of misrecognition of international staff. As their study shows, there were forms of institutional recognition which, on the one hand, highlighted the value of international academics for the organisation. However, these forms of recognition remained void of meaning for individuals who were part of this category, for example because international staff were not given the support they needed in order to overcome disadvantages associated with not being a native English speaker. As a result, this institutional recognition was dismissed as inauthentic.

As the authors show, recognition theory can help analyse and understand patterns of recognition as relations and hierarchies of power in multilingual contexts, and hence generate insights into how power works in these contexts. At the same time, they highlight the potential for creating agency for both individuals and institutions that this new theoretical lens provides. As they conclude, recognition theory can also provide the means for engaging with the described patterns and hierarchies with a view to changing them and redressing language-based, and indeed other types of inequalities and disadvantages.

Next, **Dorte Lønsmann** investigates the effects of geopolitical events on members of multilingual organisations, focusing on refugees as the people who are most directly concerned by them. The refugee wave caused by the war in Ukraine that was going on at the time of finalising this book has sadly shown how urgent it is to broaden our horizon beyond managers and white collars in International Business and management. In her study of language internships for refugees in Denmark, Lønsmann presents the refugees, the employers and the municipalities as actors with (to some extent) incompatible interests. As the author shows, the lack of success of these integration programmes was based on conflicting institutional logics that resulted in mismatched expectations, particularly regarding employment opportunities. The private company who offered the refugees the internships worked primarily within a diversity logic in which the internships were about helping people by socialising them into Danish workplace culture, and not about hiring large numbers of new employees. In contrast, the interns themselves saw the internships primarily as opportunities for obtaining paid employment. On yet another level, the municipal activation logic caused the refugees to be sent into one internship after another.

This mismatch of expectations based in the different institutional logics led to one of the biggest problems from the perspective of the company managers: the interns' lack of motivation for the internships. Drawing on neoliberal logics, the company managers talked about the importance of 'motivation', 'the right attitude' and 'interest', but they also recognised that in many cases motivation decreased when successive internships made it clear that the intern could not expect permanent paid employment at the end of the internship. When we consider that from the refugee perspective the internships were seen as the road to paid employment, it is quite easy to see how an internship programme designed through an activation logic and executed from within a diversity logic failed to motivate the interns and how the programme could have become a heavy drain on resources for the employer.

In the final chapter of this section, **Yaron Matras**, **Rebecca Tipton** and **Leonie Gaiser** explore language practices in the healthcare system of Manchester, which has risen to prominence as 'Britain's City of Languages', where over 200 languages are spoken (The University of Manchester, 2013). The authors show how staff create communicational agency by drawing on a wide range of language resources that the multilingual city they work in offers. They present a case where decisions, actions and initiatives draw on the kind of urban, super-diverse repertoire described by Busch (2012) and by Blommaert and Backus (2013). The multilingual urban setting is thus a key source of knowledge about language practices, provisions, options for support in heteroglossic encounters and about language itself. Experience in the linguistically diverse city allows actors to gauge their knowledge and course of action against their own and others' expectations and aspirations and empowers them to take the initiative and to narrate explanations and justifications for their own initiatives.

This approach problematises the notion of 'language' as a pre-defined set of structures and replaces it with the view that language and communication experience constitute a dynamic pattern of practices, potentially detached from pre-defined groups or speech communities and placed instead within emerging and evolving networks of practice. Crucially, it views language repertoires not just as language skills in the conventional sense of fluency and lexical and grammatical competence but also as the sum of impressions and experiences gained through a variety of encounters within such networks of practice. The study also highlights how healthcare staff create agency by developing their own practices of language use. Agency arises, as Emirbayer and Mische (1998, 984) suggest, 'as actors attempt to reconfigure received schemas by generating alternative possible responses to the problematic situations they confront in their lives'. Power relations are derived not just from institutional roles; rather, in an environment that is highly de-regulated and where there are often different options to manage encounters, actors rely, to a considerable degree, on accumulated knowledge. This includes local knowledge, gained passively by virtue of being immersed in the everyday locale, as well as first-hand experience gained from accumulated interactions in the work environment of public service in a diverse city.

REFERENCES

Barner-Rasmussen, W., Ehrnrooth, M., Koveshnikov, A. and Mäkelä, K. (2014), 'Cultural and language skills as resources for boundary spanning within the MNC', *Journal of International Business Studies*, **45** (5), 886–905.

Blommaert, J. and Backus, A. (2013), 'Superdiverse repertoires and the individual', in Ingrid de Saint-Georges and Jean-Jacques Weber (eds), *Multilingualism and multimodality: The future of education research*, Rotterdam: Sense Publishers, pp. 11–32.

Bourdieu, P. (1991), *Language and symbolic power*. Translated by Gino Raymond and Matthew Adamson, Cambridge: Cambridge Polity Press.

Boussebaa, M. and Brown, A-D. (2017), 'Englishization, identity, regulation and imperialism', *Organization Studies*, **38** (1), 7–29.

Boussebaa, M., Sinha, S. and Gabriel, Y. (2014), 'Englishization in offshore call centers: A postcolonial perspective', *Journal of International Business Studies*, **45** (9), 1152–1169.

Busch, B. (2012), 'The linguistic repertoire revisited', *Applied Linguistics*, **33** (5), 503–523.

Cox, R. (2012), 'Recognition and immigration', in Shane O'Neill and Nicholas H. Smith (eds), *Recognition theory as social research: Investigating the dynamics of social conflict*, Basingstoke: Palgrave, pp. 192–212.

Crenshaw, K. (1991), 'Mapping the margins: Intersectionality, identity politics, and violence against women of color', *Stanford Law Review*, **43** (6), 1241–1299.

Emirbayer, M. and Mische, A. (1998), 'What is agency?', *American Journal of Sociology*, **103** (4), 962–1023.

Feely, A. and Harzing, A.-W. (2003), 'Language management in multinational companies', *Cross-Cultural Management: An International Journal*, **10** (2), 37–52.

Gaibrois, C. (2018), 'It crosses all the boundaries: Hybrid language use as empowering resource', *European Journal of International Management*, **12** (1/2), 82–110.

Gaibrois, C. and Nentwich, J. (2020), 'The dynamics of privilege: How employees of a multinational corporation construct and contest the privileging effects of English proficiency', *Canadian Journal of Administrative Sciences*, **37** (4), 468–482.

Harzing, A.-W. and Pudelko, M. (2013), 'Language competencies, policies and practices in multinational corporations: A comprehensive review and comparison of Anglophone, Asian, Continental European and Nordic MNCs', *Journal of World Business*, **48**, 87–97.

Janssens, M., Lambert, J. and Steyaert, C. (2004), 'Developing language strategies for international companies: The contribution of translation studies', *Journal of World Business*, **39** (4), 414–430.

Janssens, M. and Steyaert, C. (2014), 'Re-considering language within a cosmopolitan understanding: Toward a multilingual franca approach in international business studies', *Journal of International Business Studies*, **45** (5), 623–639.

Logemann, M. and Piekkari, R. (2015), 'Localize or local lies? The power of language and translation in the multinational corporation', *Critical Perspectives on International Business*, **11** (1), 30–53.

Marschan-Piekkari, R., Welch, D. and Welch, L. (1999), 'In the shadow: The impact of language on structure, power and communication in the multinational', *International Business Review*, **8** (4), 421–440.

Neeley, T. B. (2013), 'Language matters: Status loss and achieved status distinctions in global organizations', *Organization Science*, **24** (2), 476–497.

Peltokorpi, V. (2015), 'Language-oriented human resource management practices in multinational companies', in Nigel Holden, Snejina Michailova and Susanne Tietze (eds), *The Routledge companion to cross-cultural management*, London, UK: Routledge, pp. 161–180.

Peltokorpi, V. and Vaara, E. (2014), 'Knowledge transfer in multinational corporations: Productive and counterproductive effects of language-sensitive recruitment', *Journal of International Business Studies*, **45** (5), 600–622.

Śliwa, M. (2008), 'Understanding social change through post-colonial theory: Reflections on linguistic imperialism and language spread in Poland', *Critical Perspectives on International Business*, **4** (2/3), 228–241.

Śliwa, M. (2010), '"Catching up with civilisation": Reflections on language spread in Poland', *Journal of Organizational Change Management*, **23** (6), 689–709.

The University of Manchester (2013), 'Manchester is Britain's city of languages', accessed 8 April 2022 at https://www.manchester.ac.uk/discover/news/manchester -is-britains-city-of-languages.

Tietze, S., Cohen, L. and Musson, G. (2003), *Understanding organizations through language*, London: Sage.

Tietze, S., Holden, N. and Barner-Rasmussen, W. (2016), 'Language use in multinational corporations: The role of special languages and corporate idiolects', in Victor Ginsburgh and Shlomo Weber (eds), *The Palgrave handbook of economics and language*, Basingstoke: Palgrave Macmillan, pp. 312–341.

Vaara, E., Tienari, J., Piekkari, R. and Säntti, R. (2005), 'Language and the circuits of power in a merging multinational corporation', *Journal of Management Studies*, **42** (3), 595–623.

2. Recognition theory: a new lens for investigating language differences in multilingual organisations

Marjana Johansson and Martyna Śliwa

INTRODUCTION

People go through life struggling for recognition. We want to be accepted and respected for who we are, regardless of our gender, ethnicity, sexual orientation or any other category of social difference that we embody. In multilingual contexts, language differences constitute one way in which people differ from one another. Coupled with the universal human need for recognition, this means that whether and how people are judged by others on the basis of their competence in a particular language – for example, the official language of the organisation they work for – will have an impact on their sense of self: whether and how they feel recognised and respected as human beings. With multilinguality and linguistic diversity being common features of contemporary society and organisations, approaching issues related to language difference from a place of respect and consideration for the other is a key societal and organisational challenge.

To date, studying language differences in organisational contexts remains firmly within the domain of language-sensitive IB research. This body of work has provided us with insightful and persuasive studies addressing the importance of language-related issues from the perspective of organisational performance, communicational effectiveness and power dynamics occurring at different levels of analysis (e.g. Brannen et al., 2014; Sanden, 2020; Tenzer et al., 2017). In this chapter, we introduce to language-sensitive IB research a new theoretical perspective on language differences in organisations, informed by research within organisation studies that attends to the political aspects of organisational processes related to difference, diversity and inclusion (Ahonen and Tienari, 2015; Tyler, 2019).

We draw on identity- and status-based recognition theory (Taylor, 1994; Honneth, 1995, 2001; Fraser, 2000; Zurn, 2003). An identity-based approach to recognition emphasises the fundamental human need for reciprocal social validation, whereby 'the integrity of human subjects' is dependent upon 'their receiving approval and respect from others' (Honneth, 1992, 188). Following this, *mis*recognition is an injurious act that denies self-realisation. A status-based approach, on the other hand, addresses the perceived lack of power of the identity-based model through a focus on the pursuit of social justice, framing recognition as concerned with 'the status of individual group members as full partners in social interaction' (Fraser, 2000, 113). Misrecognition in the case of the latter, therefore, implies 'a form of institutionalized status subordination' (McNay, 2008, 22) rather than psychological injury only. Within a multilingual organisational context these perspectives enable us to examine (a) the dynamics of relations of recognition, with an emphasis on the role of language differences, on an individual level and (b) how those dynamics are embedded in organisational power relations and practices of giving recognition to individuals and groups, in particular to the non-native speakers of the organisation's official language.

We also introduce the concept of *recognition work*, and apply it in theorising about actions performed towards, as well as by, staff from international, non-native English-language backgrounds in a linguistically diverse but officially anglophone context: UK universities.[1] Recognition work encompasses acts undertaken by individuals as well as those undertaken by institutions through, for example, the implementation of guidelines and policies. The concept of recognition *work* draws attention to the continual creation, maintenance and withdrawal of recognition that underpins social value hierarchies, as parties who undertake recognition work have varying degrees of access to resources, reflected in relations of power.

In what follows we first introduce recognition theory as an important theoretical lens for analysing issues of language differences in multilingual settings. We then present the methodology underpinning our study, before analysing the processes of (mis)recognition and recognition work performed in relation to international, non-native English-speaking staff. We then discuss the contributions and implications of our study for language-sensitive IB research.

INTRODUCING RECOGNITION THEORY TO THINKING ABOUT LANGUAGE DIFFERENCES IN MULTILINGUAL SETTINGS

Originating in a Hegelian phenomenology of reciprocal subject relations and a critical tradition of emancipatory justice, recognition 'is proving central to efforts to conceptualize today's struggles over identity and difference' (Fraser et al., 2003, 1). Recognition theory seeks to understand how an individual's sense of self is grounded in relational forms of recognition, and what the conditions of social justice are with regard to parity of participation in social life. Recognition has recently begun to receive attention from scholars interested in workplace organisations (e.g. Grover, 2013; Hancock, 2015; Renger et al., 2020; Tyler and Vachhani, 2021). A small number of studies refer to organisational diversity, specifically how diversity management objectifies people as economic resources (Hancock, 2008), and how it reinforces an understanding of minorities as 'deviant, as deficient, and as less valuable labour' (Holck and Muhr, 2017, 9). To date, however, recognition theory has not been applied to our thinking about multilinguality and language differences in organisations. This, in our view, is an important omission. We see great potential in bringing this lens to our theorising about language because recognition theory enables us to see how differences – including language differences – are articulated at an individual level, and how expressions of felt (mis)recognition are embedded in institutional and organisational regulations and practices, including policies and approaches towards multilinguality and linguistic diversity in organisations. Below, we briefly consider identity- and status-based approaches to recognition, before moving on to demonstrating, through empirical illustrations, their relevance to our theorising about language in multilingual organisational contexts.

Identity- and Status-Based Approaches to Recognition

The identity-based model is grounded in the intersubjectivist tenet that 'individual identity is formed only in and through social relations of recognition' (Zurn, 2003, 519). Being recognised through the evaluative acknowledgement of others is seen as necessary for the formation of an 'intact sense of self' (ibid.). According to Honneth (1995), a key proponent of identity-based recognition theory is when individuals experience a sense of dignity and self-esteem, insofar as they are recognised as being 'worthy of concern and acknowledgement' (Islam, 2012, 39). Following a relational model, the party who performs the recognitive act must also be judged as being capable of doing so by the 'recognisee', meaning that 'a genuine instance of recognition requires that we authorise someone to confer recognition' (McQueen, 2015, 19). Hence, processes of genuine recognition are predicated upon legitimacy afforded to the recogniser by the recognisee. The identity-based model of recognition draws attention to how acts of (mis)recognition shape individual experiences of being valued or mistreated, and thereby presents a valuable micro-level analytical lens. In the context of language-sensitive research it also enables us to conceptualise how others' evaluations of the linguistic competence of an individual is tied to that individual's sense of self and social worth (see also Śliwa and Johansson, 2014).

However, in bringing in a status-based perspective, Fraser (2000) argues that one must also look beyond individually focused effects on the self, to conceive of recognition as a matter of social status understood as parity of participation in social life. Fraser thus wants to connect the identity-based psychological aspect of recognition to a status-based perspective on recognition, which attends to social hierarchies and institutions. In other words, recognition does not only occur at the level of 'discrete individuals' (Smith, 2012, 7) but is also situated within 'institutions such as… the workplace [which]… produce or deny recognition' (Cox, 2012, 195). Conversely, 'misrecognition is relayed not through deprecatory attitudes… but rather through social institutions' (Fraser et al., 2003, 29). Relations of (mis)recognition take place within socio-cultural and political structures which facilitate or foreclose particular forms of recognition. Although recognition may 'empower subjects to make self-assertions of pride' (Wagner, 2011, 350), it may also fix relations of domination to the detriment of the 'recognised' subject. If recognition can be achieved through adhering to dominant norms, individuals may subject themselves to these even when these norms appear unfavourable or hurtful (Kenny, 2010). This is not necessarily a reluctant act; 'voluntary subordination' (Honneth, 2007, 326) occurs through the internalisation of patterns of social acceptance. In sum, recognition theory enables an analysis of the effects of interpersonal and institutional practices on individuals and groups, which, we argue, is of value to language-sensitive IB research.

Relevance of Recognition Theory to Language-Sensitive IB Research

We introduce recognition theory to language-sensitive IB research, as it allows us to draw attention to language differences and multilinguality as an important organisational and societal challenge. As such, recognition theory provides a means for advancing language-sensitive IB research which examines languages and multilingualism in relation to power, status, privilege and marginalisation in organisations (e.g. Gaibrois and Nentwich, 2020; Marschan-Piekkari et al., 1999; Neeley, 2013; Neeley and Dumas, 2016; Śliwa and Johansson, 2014; Tenzer and Pudelko, 2017). Specifically, we conceptualise the production of (mis)recognition as recognition work, which denotes acts of bestowal, refusal and contestation of recognition undertaken within relations of recognition, in this case on linguistic grounds. Hierarchical positions are shaped by organisational power relations that enable certain forms of recognition, and individuals and groups associated with them – in particular, the 'native speakers' in a given multilingual organisational context – to hold a privileged position (Gaibrois and Nentwich, 2020). In other words, they have legitimacy to be recognisers, while others – in this case, non-native speakers of the official language of the organisation – struggle to be recognised, and to achieve parity of participation in organisational life.

Recognition theory provides a valuable lens for examining the constitution and effects of differences in organisations, including language differences. First, it enables an inquiry into how and in which situation differences emerge and how they are articulated. (Mis)recognition is contextual and dynamic, meaning that a particular context can produce recognition for some and misrecognition for others, and that the same individual may experience recognition or misrecognition depending on what differences become salient in any given context, brought into being through the relational dynamic between recogniser and recognisee. This means that differences, be it of a linguistic or other nature, are not essential or static, but relational and dynamic. The forms of recognition that are required in any given case depend on the forms of misrecognition to be redressed – recognition can either address distinctiveness ('difference') or commonality ('sameness'). Misrecognition may occur through 'burdening [some people] with excessive ascribed "difference" *or* by failing to acknowledge their distinctiveness' (Fraser et al., 2003, 36, added emphasis). This underscores that, when examining organisational differences with regard to language use, we must be mindful of the assumed, politically informed grounds for *sameness* – here, with regard to certain types of language use or degrees of competence – which underpin social relations (cf. Ghorashi and Sabelis, 2013). This is especially pertinent in relation to dominant groups, such as the 'native speakers' of the official language of the organisation, whose characteristics are presumed to be universalist due to their distinctiveness having become construed as the norm. Further, recognition theory enables us to explore discrepancies between organisational policy in relation to language(s) and organisational members' accounts of their effects. For genuine recognition to occur it must be viewed as credible, including being supported by material changes which aim to redress inequalities.

Moreover, recognition is not about merely acknowledging already existing differences; rather, recognition is 'a constitutive act' (Honneth, 2007, 331) which *produces* that which it (mis)recognises. From this follows that being recognised can include expectations regarding how 'someone ought to act in a certain way by virtue of being recognised' (McQueen, 2015, 20). Power is thus inherent in processes of recognition: 'one becomes an individual subject only in virtue of recognising, and being recognised by, another subject' (Fraser et al., 2003, 10). This reciprocal relation opens up the possibility for analysing, in the context of language differences in multilingual organisations, the complexities of power relations through both considering how particular individuals and groups are granted or denied recognition and how individuals and groups are granted or denied the position of being a recogniser, for subsequent (mis)recognition to occur. We conceptualise these processes as facets of recognition work, which is performed both at an individual and organisational level, within wider structures. To achieve recognition is not equally possible for all; rather, it is something that is negotiated, demanded, granted or denied, depending on power relations. As recognition is crucial for self-enhancement and organisational participation, and (mis)recognition is hence impossible 'to behave indifferently toward' (Wagner, 2011, 355), there is considerable investment by individuals into achieving and maintaining recognition. In our empirical analysis and discussion, we demonstrate how these ideas can enrich our theorising about language differences within language-sensitive IB research.

METHODOLOGY

Sample and Data Collection

The research design reflected the tenet of recognition theory according to which social struggle can be understood through exploring 'experiences that shape [people's] agency' (Smith, 2012, 7). We conducted 54 professional life history (Maclean et al., 2012) interviews with non-native English-speaking full-time employed academics in 19 business schools in the UK, including 31 women and 23 men aged between 29 and 50, and representing all levels of seniority, from Lecturer to Professor. The participants originated from 22 countries; most of them were European (see Table 2.1), reflecting the overall profile of UK academia where the majority of non-national faculty are from the EU. Participants were recruited through university websites and professional contacts, with subsequent snowball sampling.

To preserve anonymity, continents rather than countries are mentioned in relation to interview extracts, and the participants are divided into age groups in the table. We have chosen Anglophone pseudonyms to avoid indicating specific regions or countries. The interviews lasted between 46 minutes and two hours, and were recorded and transcribed.

Our key criterion behind sample selection was a distinction between native UK-born (native English-speaking) and 'international' (i.e. non-UK born and non-native English-speaking) academics. We are aware that by applying the criterion 'international academic' we become complicit in reproducing a potentially essentialising category. However, we view the demarcation UK-born/international academics as analytically relevant for this chapter. We therefore apply this category here while acknowledging that it represents a wide variety of individuals and experiences. Meanwhile, the criterion of selecting non-native English speakers meant that all participants had this aspect in common. As English is the dominant language in the UK context and

Table 2.1   *Overview of participants*

		Number of participants
Academic position	Lecturer	33
	Senior Lecturer	9
	Reader	2
	Professor	8
	Other	2
Region of origin	Africa	4
	Asia (incl. Russia)	12
	Europe	36
	South America	2
Age group[1]	25–29	1
	30–34	14
	35–39	17
	40–44	13
	45–49	7
	50–54	1

Note: [1]One participant preferred to withhold their age.

our theoretical framing emphasises struggles for recognition, we chose not to include native English speakers in our sample.

Our own experiences as international faculty in UK academia were useful for conducting the research in that we had the sense that commonalities existed – such as having experiences of moving countries, and learning to navigate a new social, cultural and professional context, as well as not having English as our first language – which helped us establish rapport with the participants. The shared articulated experiences of how one's accent is noticed and sometimes evaluated, and the differing degrees to which individuals feel confident in expressing themselves in speech and writing provided common ground. We were interested in accounts of instances in the workplace where, for some reason or other, the participants described the situation as having to do with difference; of being positioned as different, for example, or of any form of difference surfacing as meaningful in some other respect. Although we were specifically interested in the participants' experiences of working in UK academia, the interviews began by exploring their educational background and their reasons for coming to and staying in the UK, before addressing their career progression.

Data Analysis

Data analysis began by individually reading the transcripts and noting instances where 'difference' – be it directly related to an individual's positioning as a person of non-UK origin, or in relation to other aspects such as gender – emerged. We noted all instances which, following the relational focus of recognition theory, included some form of counterpart; either between the participants and other individuals or groups in concrete interactions, or between the participants and some institutional entity such as 'the university'. This first reading generated a 'list of incidents' (van Laer and Janssens, 2011, 1210) indicating which notions of difference came to the fore in particular contexts, including being downplayed or dismissed. Differences included gender, race, nationality, and language. We then brought our descriptive 'lists' together for continued analysis. In the second phase we focused on the participants' interpretations, responses and expressed felt effects, and assigned refined themes to each 'incident'. The iterative, dialogical analysis process enabled us to confirm or question our individual readings of the data and produce a co-constructed analysis (see Gilmore and Kenny, 2015). During the next phase we moved back and forth between data and the literature to theoretically make sense of the emerging themes. Through this process we related overlapping themes with particular theoretical dimensions, which then informed the structuring of the analysis.

ANALYSIS

Institutional (Mis)Recognition of 'International Academics'

In the participants' accounts, an international staff composition emerges as a common feature of present-day UK business schools. While the variety of nationalities and language backgrounds is viewed as a commonplace and often valuable aspect of the workplace, English proficiency is highlighted as a universal criterion for international academics' ability to be accepted within the organisation:

> This is an international university so nobody really minds whoever you are and wherever you're from or what nationality you are. As long as you can speak English and you can communicate. (Robert, 32, Lecturer, Europe)

The presence of a number of international staff and the fact that 'nobody minds', provided that English-language competence requirements are met, was generally seen as offering a comfortable work environment where difference represented by nationality is accepted, and identity-based recognition can be achieved. From an institutional perspective, having an international staff base serves marketing purposes: international diversity becomes celebrated and used in public relations (PR) materials aimed at attracting international students. Whilst such celebration of international staff can be seen as recognition work undertaken by the organisation, through the practices by which the category is framed it becomes infused with particular ideas of value: recognition is bestowed from a market-based position of identifying a competitive resource. In this sense, a person's linguistic background and skills are only recognised if they are considered useful for the organisation's competitiveness.

Liam (40), a Professor from a country in continental Europe, framed the employment of international staff as 'a big selling point for the UK', expanding on the point further:

> I've actually found out that one of the reasons we've got, like, 36% in this business school, of foreign academics, is because this is the only way to meet the EQUIS[2] criteria or something. So, to be a top league university, you have to have foreign academics as well. So, fair enough, I'm ticking one box for them.

Liam frames the institutional recognition of international staff in calculative terms and while he acknowledges the recognition afforded by the organisation, he also views his role as 'ticking a box'. Relationally this is a dismissal of the other as a bestower of identity-based recognition, as the relation is framed as a purely transactional exercise rather than grounded in respect. Although these organisational measures render a particular difference, including the fact of not being a native English speaker, visible (Ahonen and Tienari, 2015), they do not necessarily result in a *meaningful* kind of recognition (McQueen, 2015), especially as in other contexts this category does not seem to warrant concrete institutional measures:

> It would be nice if we had a little bit more encouragement or acknowledgement about the difficulties we can face as foreigners... we [employing university] have this international emphasis, we employ people from many different countries, but there is no training offered, for example, in English writing, any kind of support, or maybe even just speech training. There is nothing there. (Emma, 35, Lecturer, Europe)

While international academics merit institutional recognition on the grounds that they enhance the market profile, this is not considered a 'relevant' difference in the context of staff development, especially for creating effective structures of support and dedicating resources to help international staff improve or facilitate their professional linguistic performance in English. As such, the symbolic recognition is not reflected in material measures that might redress inequalities. It is also a telling example of how a category is mobilised for particular institutional purposes in some contexts, while the same cate-gory does not merit institutional recognition in relation to another situation. This produces misrecognition, in that some expressed needs do not result in organisational intervention, thus potentially denying some full participation, for example, due to a level of competence in English that is lower compared to that of native speakers. Specifically, language differences and the associated support needs are either ignored or treated as an issue that the individuals should address themselves, without institutional support. These illustrations show that power works through what differences gain recognition, and under what conditions.

Not having English as one's native language is also reflected in organi-sational hierarchies. Emma points to hierarchical patterns in relation to the organisational positions of international academics:

> In my department it's very clear that the Management Committee is dominated by white, male, British people… there are no foreigners on the committee… And the rest of the department is international and… it's very difficult to put your finger on it because it's done in such a subtle way it will never be made explicit, it's just very hidden when it happens… it's something I know now it does have an impact on my career.

Emma does not explicitly refer to language difference, but notes how the cat-egories of gender, race and nationality are reflected in the hierarchical pattern of the distribution of power in her department. She also sees a connection between the existence of that gendered and racialised power structure and her own career progression. Language, however, is an implicit dimension of this pattern, since the juxtaposition of the categories 'British people' and 'foreigners' points to the distinction between 'native' and 'non-native' English speakers. Emma, similar to other participants who have noted the same issue in the departments they work for, is unable to articulate how the system of academic employment and progression, which is built on meritocratic prin-ciples and within which equality of treatment is legally guaranteed, produces this particular pattern. What this shows is that institutional processes produce individually felt (mis)recognition, and that the two dimensions are intertwined.

Processes of 'Saming'

A significant part of our data related to how participants expressed their relation to a perceived norm, and the means by which they could potentially be recognised as belonging to it. In several cases there was an emphasis on seeking similarity, which we refer to as processes of 'saming': an ongoing form of recognition work which takes different forms and draws on different resources. For example, Thomas (34, Senior Lecturer, Asia) expressed sameness with a perceived dominant norm as follows:

> The thing that plays for me in this environment is that it is probably more difficult…
> to single me out… I don't stand out in terms of the colour of my skin […] the shape
> of my face […] I kind of merge with the background very nicely.

Thomas's whiteness, understood in terms of skin colour and facial features, is understood by him as an advantage as it allows him to pass on the basis of his looks. This simultaneously serves as the basis for recognition work (emphasising similarity to the norm) and performs misrecognition towards those who are more visibly different. It also indicates the power of 'race' as a key signifier of differentiation (cf. Ahmed, 2012), and equates the dominant norm with whiteness. In Thomas's case, the notion of 'merging nicely with the background' versus fearing being misrecognised through being singled out demonstrates awareness of the existence of a norm, of one's standing relative to it, and the possible misrecognition resulting from a distance from the norm. The potential reward to be reaped from being recognised within the dominant norm (Kenny, 2010), or at least avoidance of devaluation resulting from being positioned outside it, means that individuals in different ways seek to position themselves as being part of, or close to it. Therefore, to be negatively evaluated for not corresponding to an expected norm results in trying to counteract such evaluations:

> I had complaints [from students] … One of the complaints was that 'the teacher
> speaks with huge accent, with a very strong accent. I don't understand the teacher'.
> I don't believe it. I know some other people who have a stronger accent than I have.
> (David, 39, Lecturer, Asia)

David feels professionally misrecognised as a result of a student complaint about his accent, and refuses to accept the anonymous student as somebody who can legitimately act as a recogniser. Instead, David positions himself closer to the norm compared to other colleagues who, according to him, have a stronger accent. Recognition work aimed towards becoming closer to the norm involves being aware of its key characteristics, assessing if and to which extent one might be recognised as fitting within it, and taking action to achieve a fit. A primarily British composition of students – particularly MBA cohorts – was raised as a context that presented challenges for some and that led to work being undertaken by the individual to redress the felt misrecognition. In particular, several women academics in our study expressed concern about potentially being stereotyped by students as not professional and knowledgeable enough, and about having their presence interpreted as not 'natural' in a professional context of this kind, due to their gender, skin colour, and the way they speak English.

The data also suggest that recognition work undertaken to position oneself as being closer to the norm can take the form of embodied self-modification. In such cases, one's way of speaking becomes integrated into a range of dimensions of such self-modification. Below, Beatrice reports on how she purposefully changed her voice, accent and posture to better meet what she perceived were implicit expectations when teaching MBA students:

> A certain type of student, for example the MBA, expects a male, possibly oldish, possibly pretty tall, with a posh voice, and with a very strong, clear voice. I'm sure about that because I have, actually, tried to experiment, whereby I taught an MBA class, speaking with a lower voice. I coached myself, I actually did it and my feedback went up. So it's true. I did a little test... I tried to experiment with changing my accent and changing the tone of voice and posture. All of it. And it resulted in a higher feedback. (Beatrice, 35–39, Senior Lecturer, Europe)

Being perceived as part of the social norm provides the opportunity to achieve recognition in terms of 'solidaristic acceptance' (Honneth, 2001, 49) and hence social inclusion. To be socially 'worthy' might mean to show likeness with the norm, including the norm of speaking English with a native English accent, presumed to be used by 'posh' men in the UK. Such practices of 'behavioural saming', however, leave the underlying recognition regime unquestioned and thus serve its continued reproduction. Further, by engaging in recognition work of 'saming', for example through lowering their voice and mimicking 'posh English men's' accent, individuals may partake in misrecognition of others by reinforcing a perceived – and exclusionary – norm.

DISCUSSION

The aim of this chapter has been to demonstrate the value of recognition theory for advancing theorisation about language differences in multilingual organisations. We contribute to language-sensitive IB literature through offering a perspective on language differences which is grounded in relations of recognition. Existing language-sensitive IB research which focuses on how language shapes organisational inclusion and exclusion partly addresses similar issues, but recognition theory brings a two-pronged perspective which analytically distinguishes between individual identity-based recognition and institutional status-based recognition, but also shows how they are linked. Below we outline the key insights gained through our analysis.

Multilingualism and Recognition Work

The attribution of difference, including language difference, shapes the possibilities of individuals and groups (Ahonen and Tienari, 2015). In this chapter, we have introduced the concept of recognition work to consider acts of agency in relations of recognition in the context of language differences. Recognition work encompasses individual and organisational acts of bestowal or denial of recognition, to account for how recognition does not only take place between individuals but, significantly, also involves institutions such as the workplace (Cox, 2012). This enables us to, for example, enrich research which focuses on the implementation and effects of corporate language policies in terms of inclusion and exclusion (e.g. Sanden, 2020). Viewing such policies through a recognition theory lens draws into focus how such policies do not simply bring out already existing differences, but that they *produce* particular forms of (mis)recognition (Honneth, 2007) along linguistic lines. Our findings highlight how both formal and informal organisational relations result in affirmation or dismissal related to a person's language use – for example, their competence in the official language of the organisation or the accent with which they speak. Being set in an officially anglophone working context, our research, which specifically includes participants who are not native speakers of English, brings out interesting aspects of language-specific (mis)recognition.

The recognition work that is required in any given case depends on the forms of misrecognition to be redressed – it can either address distinctiveness ('difference') or commonality ('sameness'). In terms of individual recognition work we gave examples of 'saming' – a notion that draws attention to the ongoing, varying means by which closeness to particular aspects of a perceived norm – such as a specific tone of voice or accent with which the official language of the organisation is spoken – is strived for, rather than conceiving of sameness as monolithic and binary. The work of 'saming' might enhance one's position as close to the norm but it also contributes to the distancing of others from it, by reproducing the dominant norms of recognition (Wagner, 2011), such as consideration of native speakers in multilingual organisations as superior and non-native speakers as inferior (see e.g. Gaibrois and Nentwich, 2020).

Instrumentality and Institutional Bases for Recognition

Our study gives insights into instrumentality as a significant aspect of misrecognition of international staff. As discussed in the findings, there were forms of institutional recognition which, on the one hand, highlighted the value of international academics for the organisation. However, these forms of recognition remained void of meaning for individuals who were part of this category, for example because international staff were not given the support they needed in order to overcome disadvantages associated with not being a native English speaker. As a result, this institutional recognition was dismissed as inauthentic. The reason for this can be understood in terms of its instrumentality, which is related to the conditions through which recognition is bestowed. The category is meaningful for the institution in that it fits the contemporary market-based logic of the marketisation of higher education. The market-based impetus for the recognition renders it a calculative practice, the object of which is not the individual encompassed by the category, but ultimately the institution itself through enhanced market strength and reputation. This can be understood as instrumental recognition for economic purposes (Hancock, 2008). Such practices, and resultant relations of recognition, are shaped by the wider societal context. With regard to UK academia, New Public Management (NPM) practices informed by neoliberal principles of marketisation, managerialism and internationalisation are prevalent (Bamberger et al., 2019). These principles produce particular institutional forms of recognition – for example market-based forms – which have a bearing on individuals' identity-based recognition (such as 'ticking a box').

CONCLUSION

We have introduced recognition theory as a new theoretical lens for analysing issues related to language differences in multilingual organisations. The chapter contributes to understanding and addressing an important contemporary challenge facing multilingual society and organisation, that is, the need for developing sustainable, constructive and positive relationships between actors in multilingual contexts. Recognition theory complements the ideas about how to address this challenge that have previously been proposed within language-sensitive IB research. Specifically, it reminds us that in their everyday lives – including as citizens and employees – people struggle for recognition. Recognition theory gives rise to the realisation that language differences have an impact not only on organisational communication, performance or power relations, but also on the sense of self and the feeling of being (mis) recognised by staff in multilingual organisations, especially those for whom the official language is not their native language.

Introducing recognition theory to language-sensitive IB research allows for carving space within the latter for attending to issues of social justice, respect and parity of participation among staff from different linguistic backgrounds and with different levels of competence in the official language of the organisation. Recognition theory can help analyse and understand patterns of recognition as relations and hierarchies of power in multilingual contexts, and hence generate insights into how power works in these contexts. It can also provide the means for engaging with those patterns and hierarchies with a view to changing them and redressing language-based, and indeed other types of inequalities and disadvantages. Future research might therefore draw on recognition theory to also attend to how, for example, gender and race intersect with language-specific forms of (mis)recognition, possibly also addressing contexts characterised by the dominance of languages other than English.

NOTES

1.   Although our research is conducted in an anglophone context we refer to multilingual organisations to emphasise that organisations may be officially monolingual, yet multilingual by virtue of the variety of native languages amongst staff. The 'unofficial' status of different languages adds a further dimension to processes of (mis)recognition.
2.   EQUIS is a major quality assessment accreditation often sought by business schools.

REFERENCES

Ahmed, S. (2012), *On being included: Racism and diversity in institutional life*, Durham and London: Duke University Press.

Ahonen, P. and Tienari, J. (2015), 'Ethico-politics of diversity and its production', in Alison Pullen and Carl Rhodes (eds), *The Routledge companion to ethics, politics and organization*, London: Routledge, pp. 271–287.

Bamberger, A., Morris, P. and Yemini, M. (2019), 'Neoliberalism, internationalisation and higher education: Connections, contradictions and alternatives', *Discourse: Studies in the Cultural Politics of Education*, **40** (2), 203–216.

Brannen, M.Y., Piekkari, R. and Tietze, S. (2014), 'The multifaceted role of language in international business: Unpacking the forms, functions and features of a critical challenge to MNC theory and performance', *Journal of International Business Studies*, **45** (5), 495–507.

Cox, R. (2012), 'Recognition and immigration', in Shane O'Neill and Nicholas H. Smith (eds), *Recognition theory as social research: Investigating the dynamics of social conflict*, Basingstoke, UK: Palgrave, pp. 192–212.

Fraser, N. (2000), 'Rethinking recognition', *New Left Review*, **3**, 107–120.

Fraser, N., Honneth, A. and Golb, J. (2003), *Redistribution or recognition? A political-philosophical exchange*, London: Verso.

Gaibrois, C. and Nentwich, J. (2020), 'The dynamics of privilege: How employees of a multinational corporation construct and contest the privileging effects of English proficiency', *Canadian Journal of Administrative Science*, **37** (4), 468–482.

Ghorashi, H. and Sabelis, I. (2013), 'Juggling difference and sameness: Rethinking strategies for diversity in organizations', *Scandinavian Journal of Management*, **29** (1), 78–86.

Gilmore, S. and Kenny, K. (2015), 'Work-worlds colliding: Self-reflexivity, power and emotion in organizational ethnography', *Human Relations*, **68** (1), 55–78.

Grover, S.L. (2013), 'Unraveling respect in organization studies', *Human Relations*, **67** (1), 27–51.

Hancock, P. (2008), 'Embodied generosity and an ethics of organization', *Organization Studies*, **29** (10), 1357–1373.

Hancock, P. (2015), 'Recognition and the moral taint of sexuality: Threat, masculinity and Santa Claus', *Human Relations*, **69** (2), 461–481.

Holck, L. and Muhr, S.L. (2017), 'Unequal solidarity? Towards a norm-critical approach to welfare logics', *Scandinavian Journal of Management*, **33** (1), 1–11.

Honneth, A. (1992), 'Integrity and disrespect: Principles of a conception of morality based on the theory of recognition', *Political Theory*, **20** (2), 187–201.

Honneth, A. (1995), *The struggle for recognition: The moral grammar of social conflicts*, Cambridge, MA: Polity Press.

Honneth, A. (2001), 'Recognition or redistribution? Changing perspectives on the moral order of society', *Theory, Culture & Society*, **18** (2–3), 43–55.

Honneth, A. (2007), 'Recognition as ideology', in Bert van den Brink and David Owen (eds), *Recognition and power: Axel Honneth and the tradition of critical social theory*, Cambridge, UK: Cambridge University Press, pp. 323–347.

Islam, G. (2012), 'Recognition, reification, and processes of forgetting: Ethical implications of Human Resource Management', *Journal of Business Ethics*, **111** (1), 37–48.

Kenny, K. (2010), 'Beyond ourselves: Passion and the dark side of identification in an ethical organization', *Human Relations*, **63** (6), 857–873.

Maclean, M., Harvey, C. and Chia, R. (2012), 'Sensemaking, storytelling and the legitimization of elite business careers', *Human Relations*, **65** (1), 17–40.

Marschan-Piekkari, R., Welch, D.E. and Welch, L.S. (1999), 'In the shadow: The impact of language on structure, power and communication in the multinational', *International Business Review*, **8**, 421–440.

McNay, L. (2008), *Against recognition*, Cambridge, UK: Polity Press.

McQueen, P. (2015), *Subjectivity, gender and the struggle for recognition*, Basingstoke, UK: Palgrave.

Neeley, T.B. (2013), 'Language matters: Status loss and achieved status distinctions in global organizations', *Organization Science*, **24** (2), 476–497.

Neeley, T.B. and Dumas, T.L. (2016), 'Unearned status gain: Evidence from a global language mandate', *Academy of Management Journal*, **59** (1), 14–43.

Renger, D., Miché, M. and Casini, A. (2020), 'Professional recognition at work: The protective role of esteem, respect and care for burnout among employees', *Journal of Occupational and Environmental Medicine*, **62** (3), 202–209.

Sanden, G. R. (2020), 'The reasons why corporate language policies can create more problems than they solve', *Current Issues in Language Planning*, **21** (1), 22–44.

Śliwa, M. and Johansson, M. (2014), 'How non-native English speaking staff are evaluated in linguistically diverse organizations: A sociolinguistic perspective', *Journal of International Business Studies*, **45** (9), 1133–1151.

Smith, N-H. (2012), 'Introduction: A recognition-theoretical research programme for the social sciences', in Shane O'Neill and Nicholas H. Smith (eds), *Recognition theory as social research: Investigating the dynamics of social conflict*, Basingstoke, UK: Palgrave, pp. 1–18.

Taylor, C. (1994), 'The politics of recognition', in Amy Gutmann (ed.), *Multiculturalism: Examining the politics of recognition*, Princeton, NJ: Princeton University Press, pp. 25–73.

Tenzer, H. and Pudelko, M. (2017), 'The influence of language differences on power dynamics in multinational teams', *Journal of World Business*, **52** (1), 45–61.

Tenzer, H., Terjesen, S. and Harzing, A.-W. (2017), 'Language in international business: A review and agenda for future research', *Management International Review*, **57** (6), 815–854.

Tyler, M. (2019), 'Reassembling difference? Rethinking inclusion through/as embodied ethics', *Human Relations*, **72** (1), 48–68.

Tyler, M. and Vachhani, S. (2021), 'Chasing rainbows? A recognition-based critique of Primark's precarious commitment to inclusion', *Organization*, **28** (2), 247–265.

van Laer, K. and Janssens, M. (2011), 'Ethnic minority professionals' experiences with subtle discrimination in the workplace', *Human Relations*, **64** (9), 1203–1227.

Wagner, G. (2011), 'The two sides of recognition: Gender justice and the pluralization of social esteem', *Critical Horizons: A Journal of Philosophy and Social Theory*, **12** (3), 347–371.

Zurn, C.F. (2003), 'Identity or status? Struggles over "recognition" in Fraser, Honneth, and Taylor', *Constellations*, **10** (4), 519–537.

3. Diversity, activation and self-support: clashing institutional logics around the inclusion of refugees on the labour market

Dorte Lønsmann

INTRODUCTION

Today, businesses are increasingly part of a global labour market with workplaces operating in conditions characterised by mobility and migration. At the same time, national culture, language and legal frameworks play a big part in determining local labour market conditions. At this intersection between the global and the local, boundaries are challenged when previously local businesses are increasingly influenced by transnational flows of people, money and goods. Transnational labour mobility takes many different forms, from workers making the most of the free labour mobility within the EU, transnational knowledge workers taking opportunities for new experiences across the world and refugees seeking to access the labour market in the host country. One consequence of this mobility is that previously local, and largely monolingual, labour markets become culturally and linguistically diverse. Under these conditions, linguistic resources become a valuable tool for determining who has access to local labour markets.

In many countries, particularly in Western Europe, migration and the integration of migrants have become key political and societal concerns. One challenge relates to the inclusion of refugees into the local labour market. Here, competence in the local language is often framed as the key to labour market access. Consequently, several European countries have introduced obligatory integration programmes that provide refugees with language classes while also mandating participation in internships in private companies. The internships typically have the double aim of socialising refugees into local labour market practices and providing opportunities for using the local language. In Denmark, these programmes have been criticised for using refugees as free labour (Buch, 2017), as well as for failing to provide opportunities for practising the local language (Lønsmann, 2020). From a business perspective, the internships require an investment on the part of the organisations who have to provide training and mentoring for the interns. While the internship schemes ideally are a way for businesses to contribute to the inclusion of refugees on the labour market, the question is to what extent the schemes benefit either the companies or the refugees. Consequently, this chapter investigates how different actors in internship schemes for refugees in Denmark perceive the internships both in terms of opportunities for language learning and in terms of job opportunities for the refugees. Based on a linguistic ethnographic study of language and integration in Denmark, the analysis contrasts the perspectives of managers in a big retail chain that has hosted large numbers of refugee interns with the perspectives of refugees who have participated in internships in this and other organisations. The central questions are: What logics do the participants draw on when they discuss the internships? And what are the consequences of these sometimes conflicting logics? The study aims to explore the link between language, business and the inclusion of refugees from a critical perspective, arguing also that this area of research could, and perhaps should, be a focus area for future studies in language-sensitive IB research.

Previous studies of language in international business have tended to focus on particular types of workplaces, often multinational corporations with white-collar employees. However, under the current conditions of global mobility, other types of workplaces deserve our attention too. While linguistic diversity in international organisations has gained attention in IB research (and attendant fields) in the past decades (see e.g. Angouri and Piekkari, 2018, Karhunen et al., 2018; Lecomte et al., 2018 for recent contributions), the impact of forced migration on business and vice versa has not yet been studied in depth in this field. At a time where migration flows impact societies across the globe, internationalisation 'at home' in the form of the influx of migrants is inescapable. In previous investigations of language in international business, the role of English as an international language has been in focus, as have multilingual practices in international workplaces. By expanding the scope of language in international business to also focus on instances of international-isation 'at home', we can add the use and valuation of local languages to our discussions of language in international business.

BUSINESS, LANGUAGE AND THE INCLUSION OF REFUGEES INTO LOCAL LABOUR MARKETS

Recently, studies within business and human rights have begun to investigate the role of business in relation to migrant flows and the inclusion of migrants into local labour markets. From this perspective, the private sector is a fun-damental actor in addressing the human rights problems posed by growing migration flows (Goethals et al., 2017). Work in this field has focused on private sector responsibility in relation to workers' rights and exploitation of migrant workers in regions with a high demand for migrant labour. In contrast, in Western European welfare societies, the challenge for forced migrants is to access the labour market at all (Betts and Buith, 2017). Here, the role of business in dealing with forced migration is frequently conceptualised as a part of corporate social responsibility (Wang and Chaudhri, 2019). While hiring refugees may be attractive in order to counter labour shortages, businesses more often have CSR-related motivations for engaging with refugees (OECD and UNHCR, 2016). This means that while private companies are willing to take in refugees in internships and mentor programmes, they are less willing to hire refugees in paying positions. From a refugee perspective, the lack of economic incentives to participate in internship and training schemes makes these unattractive, and many prefer to develop their language skills further instead (Betts and Buith, 2017). In addition to this mismatch between employer and refugee goals, both parties name limited language skills as one of the main barriers for refugee access to the labour market (OECD and UNHCR, 2016). Somewhat surprisingly, even refugees who report speaking the host language well consider language to be a barrier (Betts and Buith, 2017), which could be taken as an indication of discrimination of second language speakers.

Recent critical sociolinguistic studies of the role of language in relation to labour market inclusion of migrants focus on the effects of neoliberal logics. One key aspect of neoliberalism is that workers are seen as "bundles of skills" (Urciuoli, 2008, 224). Within this framing, unemployment is constructed not as contingent on structural conditions, but as a matter of workers lacking the necessary skills to be employable. This discourse of 'employability' (Rosén and Bagga-Gupta, 2013) entails that workers are responsible for 'upskilling' to ensure their own employment. Other aspects of the neoliberal employability logic emphasise responsibility and initiative as desirable in migrants (Allan and McElhinny, 2017, 85), and construct migrant motivation as the single most important element for successful reintegration into the labour market (Flubacher et al., 2017, 63). Under this neoliberal logic, migrants are seen as responsible for their own integration, including the acquisition of the language skills that they need to access the host country labour market. When employability is linked with language competence in the local language, language education is constructed as the key for migrants to gaining employment (Rosén and Bagga-Gupta, 2013), as well as the key to becoming integrated into the receiving society (Henry, 2016). While language skills have been found to be essential for granting access to the labour market (Duchêne and Heller, 2012), the framing of language competence in terms of skills and employability is problematic. First, this framing is based on the widespread and problematic assumption that language education is a quick fix, that is, that it is possible to learn a language within a few months if only the learner is motivated. From this perspective, lack of language competence equals a lack of effort and a lack of motivation to integrate. While both employers and refugees point to lack of language skills as a main barrier to employment, it is important to keep the ideological underpinnings of this discourse in mind. The common-sense ideology that language courses lead to speaking the language – and then to employment (Flubacher et al., 2017, 60) – is an ideology nested in neoliberal logics. This becomes particularly apparent in studies that show that local language skills cannot overcome barriers such as structural unemployment and discrimination against second language speakers (e.g. Creese and Kambere, 2003). This suggests that the focus on language overlooks other factors that influence migrants' access to the local labour market (Allan and McElhinny, 2017, 88–89), and also that while local language skills may be an advantage for accessing the labour market, language skills alone do not secure refugees a job.

LANGUAGE AND THE POLITICAL ECONOMY

Following on from these findings within critical sociolinguistics, this chapter analyses interview data from the theoretical perspective of language and the political economy. This perspective shares with linguistic anthropology the view of language as social action, but crucially takes a broad perspective that views language and language users as connected with language ideologies and language policies, and as connected with societal, economic and political structures. In international business, language tends to be seen as a tool for facilitating an increasingly multicultural and multilingual workforce. The implementation of language policies that regulate the linguistic aspects of work, often with the aim of increasing productivity, is built on a logic that views language as an economic resource. The critical perspective of language and political economy challenges this understanding by asking how the view of language as an economic resource affects the speakers – speakers who in late capitalism are "increasingly classified and hierarchized according to their capacity to be productive" (Del Percio et al., 2018, 59). In other words, productivity and employability are key logics in late capitalism. Del Percio et al. (2018, 55) define the field of language and political economy as "an inquiry into the way language emerges as a key site of possibility/impossibility where speakers can gain access to the valuation as well as to the production, distribution, and consumption of symbolic and material resources (Bourdieu, 1977; Gal, 1989)". This focus allows for an analysis of how language is located in larger societal structures of inequality and difference, including how language regulates people's access to resources. In the context of work and migration, it is particularly interesting to investigate how the local language is linked with speakers' access to symbolic and material resources. Within the field of language in international business, the perspective of language and political economy allows for a focus on how linguistic resources and language ideologies regulate access to the workforce, but also how language and inclusion are tied up in a complex web of logics that govern not just language use, but also access to material resources, and the assignment of status and position to different participants in workplace hierarchies and in society.

INTEGRATION AS PUBLIC–PRIVATE COLLABORATION

When an asylum seeker is granted asylum in Denmark, they become part of a five-year integration programme with the aim of becoming self-supporting, that is, getting permanent paid employment. They are transferred to a local municipality which is responsible for providing them with a place to live, language classes, integration benefits and 'employment-directed offers'. Despite the name, the employment-directed offers, which usually take the form of internships in private or public workplaces, are obligatory, as is participation in the Danish language classes.

While internships for refugees had been common before, the number of internships needed increased drastically in 2015–2016 when a large number of Syrian refugees arrived. One estimate says that 14,000 refugees needed internships in 2016 (Svansø, 2016), and that the private sector would contribute approximately one third of the internships. Several large companies in the production and service sectors created tailormade programmes where they welcomed large numbers of refugees in short-term projects combining internships and language teaching in the company. Subsequently, these programmes met with criticism in the media when it became clear that only very few of the internships led to permanent employment. The companies were accused of exploiting the refugees for free labour (Buch, 2017) and were asked to account for the low number of jobs for the interns (Kamil, 2016). This meant that some of the private employers took to the press to defend the initiatives and their own part in them (Salling Group, 2017). It seems then that the public–private collaboration around the internships was not an unqualified success. The municipalities failed to meet their targets as the employment rate among refugees remained low (Confederation of Danish Employers, 2019), some refugees felt exploited, and the companies were subject to criticism. Based on this, it is relevant to investigate how the different logics surrounding the internships have influenced the seeming lack of success, with neither refugees nor companies seeming to benefit.

METHODS

In order to investigate these logics, I draw on fieldwork conducted in 2016 and 2017 as part of the Transient Multilingual Communities project (see more at https://tmc.ku.dk/). The first data set is from a one-year ethnographic study of a language classroom for refugees in a municipality north of Copenhagen. This data set includes observations and recordings from the classroom, interviews with students, teachers and case workers, as well as various documents. The refugee participants all have experience with internships, some of them in the same retailer where the second data set was collected. The internships are frequently talked about in the classroom recordings because this particular language classroom was set up as a project integrating Danish classes with internships. This meant that the students alternated between 2–3 weeks in the classroom and 2–3 weeks in their internships. The refugee participants were mostly from Syria, but also from Azerbaijan, South Sudan, Chechnya and Iran. They had a variety of language backgrounds, including Kurdish, Arabic and Farsi. The youngest participant was in her early twenties while the oldest were in their fifties. Most of the participants had been in Denmark between one and three years when the fieldwork started, and had been learning Danish for most of this period. They were half-way through the Danish language education pro-gramme, working to pass levels three and four out of six during my time with them. The first data set provides an opportunity to investigate how a group of refugees perceive internships in terms of opportunities for language learning and job opportunities, as well as the underlying logics they draw on in their evaluations.

The second data set focuses on the business perspective and includes inter-views with managers in a large supermarket chain, for which I will use the pseudonym Super. Here, diversity efforts focused on recently arrived refugees for whom Super had created a language internship programme in collaboration with local municipalities across Denmark. Typically, 8–12 interns would be placed in the same store. They would work on the floor in the mornings, typically stocking shelves, and learn Danish on the premises after lunch. The internships had a duration of 13 weeks, with regular evaluation meetings with the refugee, the manager and a case worker from the municipal job centre. In some cases, if the candidate showed progression and potential, they would be offered an extension of the internship for another 13 weeks. In problem-atic cases, the internship was terminated before the end of the 13 weeks, for instance if the intern had problems being on time or in other ways did not live up to what was expected. This data set consists of four interviews, two with managers in the shops, and two with diversity managers at the corporate level. While the aim was to also gather observation and recording data from

Table 3.1   Interview participants

Pseudonym	Work identity/experience
Rima	Tailor, worked with children
Shadia	Bank employee
Suzan	Housewife
Yara	Housewife
Marwa	Doctor
Abdullah	Farmer, bus driver
Farnaz	Teacher
Fawzi	University student
Yasmin	University student
Sirin	Housewife
Issam	Guard
Ahmed	Electrician
Mary	Worked with children
Lise	Group level diversity manager
Signe	Group level diversity manager
Michael	Warehouse manager
Bertha	Warehouse diversity coordinator

this programme, the retailer ultimately decided against allowing ethnographic fieldwork on their premises.

The primary data for the analysis are the interviews with the 13 refugees and the four managers (Table 3.1). In addition, I draw on fieldnotes and classroom recordings. Where the manager interviews each are approximately one hour long, the refugee interviews are by comparison relatively short, between eight and 40 minutes, and to some extent influenced by a lack of shared linguistic resources. All interviews began in Danish, but the interviews with Mary, Farnaz, Yasmin and Fawzi were conducted in a mix of Danish and English. The manager interviews focused on experiences with the language internship programme. The refugee interviews focused on participants' experiences in internships and their plans for future employment in Denmark. According to participants' choices, some interviews were individual, and some were in groups.

By drawing on ethnographic data and interviews, the aim has been to provide an emic perspective on the language internships. The analysis focuses on understanding the life worlds of the participants in order to understand the problems in the public/private partnerships around the language internships. The interviews were transcribed, and the fieldnotes, interview data and observation data were coded thematically, using principles of grounded theory (Strauss and Corbin, 2003). I listened through the interviews repeatedly, taking notes and coding excerpts as I went along. In later rounds, the codes were refined and combined into overarching categories, which led me to the different logics surrounding the language internships: diversity, activation and the road to a job.

DIVERSITY, ACTIVATION OR THE ROAD TO A JOB: A CLASH OF LOGICS AND EXPECTATIONS[1]

The analysis reveals that there are several different interpretations of what the internships are and what the intended outcome should be, to some extent corresponding to the different stakeholders. I argue that these conflicting logics are part of what has caused challenges in the public–private collaboration around the internships.

The Language Internships as Diversity Work

From the perspective of the Super managers, the internships are part of their diversity work. The company has for many years worked with diversity by hiring employees with a wide range of special needs. Diversity is about 'doing something for people' and 'taking responsibility' as diversity manager Signe puts it. From this perspective, the refugee internships are constructed as a 'stepping stone' or 'practice run' where the interns, who are seen as people who lack relevant training and work experience, can get to know Danish workplace culture. From a diversity logic, it is problematic that the interns come from very different educational and work backgrounds. Some are not literate while others have completed higher education in their home countries. Some have wide experience from the service sector, while others have never had a job. Manager Michael reflects on the differences between trying to train "relatively well-educated" Syrians who have had their own shops and have work experience and those "mostly from African countries ... where some of them simply have never had a job". Also, the fact that the interns are refugees with often very traumatic experiences in their past can be a challenge. As Michael emphasises, he as employer does not have any training in dealing with traumatised staff and is often not even informed about past experiences that may impact work performance.

From a diversity perspective, the interns are frequently constructed as 'cultural Others', in contrast with and different from Danes, and consequently unemployable and in need of socialisation into Danish workplace culture. The cultural, linguistic and religious differences between the interns and the Danish employees are constructed as problematic by the Super managers, who all report problems with 'culture' ranging from unwillingness to touch pork over lack of personal hygiene to being late for work. The majority of the examples, however, centre on communication. All the managers mention the same problematic communication patterns: The interns fail to live up to the expectation we have "here in Denmark" that "our employees question and challenge (.) are present and independent and take initiative", as Signe puts it. Similarly, Michael frames it as "cultural things that cause funny things to happen", for instance that interns do not speak up if there is an instruction they have not understood. "We struggle with that a lot", says Michael. Not asking questions and not taking initiative are mentioned repeatedly in the data as major issues. In addition, the managers also note that the interns keep to themselves during breaks. While keeping to oneself or a lack of initiative could be a matter of personality or a language issue, it is consistently constructed as a cultural issue which can (and should) be overcome through socialisation into the Danish workplace culture.

Seeing the internships primarily as part of CSR efforts to socialise currently unemployable refugees into Danish workplace culture also means that there is no expectation of hiring large numbers of the interns (and only 4% were hired (TV2, 2017)), or even of training them to do the job in full. In fact, Michael says that he is happy if they manage to learn 25% of the tasks included in a sales job.

The Language Internships as Activation

The public stakeholders' interests are guided by a different logic. The municipalities, who are responsible for carrying out the national integration policy, work within an activation logic.[2] In this logic, the language internships are meant to serve the long-term goal of getting the refugees integrated into the labour market as self-supporting workers. In the short term, however, the goal is to keep the refugees busy. The municipalities are required to make sure that all refugees are 'activated', which means that in addition to language classes, they have to participate in employment-directed activities. As a rule, there can be no more than a six-week break between activation periods. Because it can be difficult to find relevant internships for all refugees, the internships often seem to primarily fulfil an activation goal. This is also how Lise recounts the municipal perspective: "many municipalities ... have had the attitude that they should be activated more than the (.) fifteen hours they spend at the language school (.) because they may as well get used to (.) being ready for a job". Here the internships are seen as a means to ensure that the refugees are ready for a full-time workload.

Within this logic, the internships are not work, hence the refugees are not paid for their labour. Rather, the internships are part of the obligations the refugees have while they receive integration benefits. This means that the fit between intern and placement is not a primary concern. This disregard of previous educational and work experience is a key complaint in the refugee interviews. The well-educated refugees in particular question the choice of internships for them and report having asked for placements that match their experience and education. In one case, Marwa, who was a doctor in Syria, was offered an internship in a hospital kitchen. When she questioned the relevance of this, she was told by her case worker that "you have to do an internship". The case worker also emphasised that this was a "rule" and that if she did not do the internship, there would be "no money". While the refugees are also considered cultural Others in this logic, the lack of attention to individual experience and background is evidenced in the fact, reported by the managers, that people with very different backgrounds, often unrelated to service work, are assigned to supermarket internships, ranging from an experienced engineer to a 48-year-old woman with no work experience whatsoever.

The activation logic that is built into Danish integration policy also entails a lack of progression for the refugees. Michael, who as warehouse manager had experience working with interns, reported having interns who were doing their third internship. Not only did they not seem to have learned anything in their previous internships (often in different supermarket chains), he says, but since they had at this point given up hope that the internship would result in paid employment, they were also not very motivated for doing the internship. Signe also concludes that those interns who are doing their first internship are clearly more motivated than those further into the integration programme.

The framing of the internships as primarily 'activation', in which the work is compensation for the cost brought on society thus contrasts both with the diversity logic of the supermarket chain, and with the refugees' interpretation of the internships as the means to gaining paid employment (see below). Constructing the refugees primarily as unemployable clients who need to follow the rules and fulfil their obligation to 'the system' also contrasts with the refugees' view of themselves as people with relevant experience and strong motivation to find work (as discussed in more detail in Lønsmann, 2020).

The Internships as the Road to Becoming Self-Supporting

For the refugee participants, the central operating logic is that the internships are, or should be, a long- or short-term means to becoming self-supporting. Several of the refugee participants stress that their main priority is to leave the integration system. When I asked Fawzi and Yasmin about their plans for the next five years, they first talk about their dream of opening a food truck, and then Fawzi adds: "the most important one that we (.) go out from the system (.) yes (.) and we be (.) on our feet (1.0) standing by ourselves (.) doing (.) what we would like to do". With the exception of one woman with six children who had been a homemaker in her home country, all my participants say that they want to get a job in Denmark.

This underlying logic clearly influences how they experience the internships. This can be seen both in the positive and negative experiences the participants relate. From a structural perspective, several are very critical of internships that do not lead to a job, for instance Farnaz who says that she is "trying to find a new internship for getting job". Since her current internship is in a municipal project for job seekers, that is, with no chance of permanent employment, she is looking for another internship that may lead to paid employment. Others criticise the iterative nature of the integration programme where they have to participate in a seemingly endless and pointless cycle of internships. Fawzi argues that if the tables were turned, and I had arrived as a refugee in Syria, I would not accept "three four times they send you (.) three months in each time (.) and (.) nothing happens". As mentioned above, especially the well-educated refugees argue that the internships should reflect their existing experience and education or – in the case of young participants – their wishes for a future job. Yara who is one of the youngest participants says her current internship in a daycare is "okay", but she does not "love daycare". She would love being a hairdresser or working in a clothes store, hence she would like to do an internship in a hair salon or a clothes store. When the refugees repeatedly criticise the lack of job opportunities, and the lack of fit between their profile and the internships they have to do, it is based on an underlying logic that the internships should be a way for them to get a job (and not places to be activated or socialised into Danish workplace culture). Interestingly, none of the refugee participants mention culture as an issue. Where the positioning of them as cultural Others features heavily in the diversity and activation logics, it is completely absent from their own accounts.

In the 'Danish at work' classroom, it was made clear to the participants that the internships were intended primarily as 'language internships'. This emphasis had been added after it became clear to the teachers and case workers that the refugees were very focused on transitioning from unpaid internships into paid work, and that the internships in no cases led to paid employment (partly because half of the participants were placed in a municipal project because no other placements could be found). The teachers actively tried to redirect focus to language learning, framing this as a first step on the way to employment. Perhaps because of this framing, the participants frequently evaluated their internships in terms of opportunities for interaction and language learning. Significantly, those participants who claimed to be happy with their internships were all placed in daycare centres which yielded the best opportunities for interaction. Yara says for instance that "in the daycare I learn a lot of Danish", clarifying that even though her colleagues are busy, the children are always happy to talk to her and teach her new words. In contrast, all the other participants were critical of the lack of interaction that the internships offered. They report speaking only very little, mainly due to the isolated nature of the work, and because their colleagues are too busy. Issam explains that even though his colleagues asked him some questions about himself, there was no collaboration involved in the work he did in the supermarket. Fawzi reports a similar experience: "when I go to [the supermarket] I didn't speak to anybody and nobody speak to me just when they need something to give me". The participants are very motivated for learning Danish since they perceive this as the key to the labour market (as discussed in more detail in Kirilova and Lønsmann, 2020). In those cases where the internships do not provide opportunities for language learning, the interns perceive the time spent there as a waste of time, and say that they would prefer to be in school instead since this is where they learn Danish.

DISCUSSION AND CONCLUSION

Where previous research into language internships and language learning at work has focused on the interactional aspects of the internships (e.g. Sandwall, 2010), this study highlights how the often contradictory logics surrounding the language internships impact stakeholders' expectations and motivation. The language and political economy perspective taken here shows the advantages of considering the structural embedding of the language internships into different logics.

The key problem arising from the clash of these logics is the mismatched expectations regarding employment opportunities. The retailer works primarily within a diversity logic in which the internships are about helping people by socialising them into Danish workplace culture, and not about hiring large numbers of new employees. In contrast, the interns themselves see the internships primarily as opportunities for obtaining paid employment. For the manager, the internship is a success if the intern gets some experience from a Danish workplace and is socialised into Danish workplace culture. For the refugee, the internship is a success if it either results in paid employment here and now or in improved Danish competences which will aid them in obtaining that goal eventually. This mismatch of expectations based in the different underlying logics leads to one of the biggest problems from the perspective of the Super managers: the interns' lack of motivation for the internships. Drawing on neoliberal discourses, the Super managers talk about the importance of "motivation", "the right attitude" and "interest", but they also recognise that in many cases motivation decreases when it becomes clear that the intern cannot expect permanent paid employment after the end of the internship. When we consider that from the refugee perspective the internships are seen as the road to paid employment, it is quite easy to see how an internship programme designed through an activation logic and executed from within a diversity logic fails to motivate the interns.

The transient and iterative nature of the internships also links up with the question of motivation. Within the activation logic, the refugees are supposed to spend their time in temporary 'activation' as part of the company's efforts to help people and be responsible, and as part of the municipalities' efforts to make sure that those who receive benefits work for that money. With the lack of tangible benefits (economic, linguistically or otherwise), and with no real opportunity to be included in the workplace long-term, it is hard for the interns to stay motivated. Instead the repeated internships become a vicious cycle of meaningless projects which the refugees are obliged to take part in.

A second key issue is the positioning within the diversity logic of the refugees as an undifferentiated group of cultural Others whose main barrier to the Danish labour market is their lack of knowledge of Danish workplace culture and Danish language skills. This is in stark contrast to the self-supporting logic that the refugees themselves operate from. Here the refugees construct themselves as resourceful individuals with education, experience, dreams and plans, but also personal challenges, including health and family issues. One consequence of the construction of the refugees as a group of cultural Others is that the workplaces in this study receive interns who lack the motivation and training to do the work required of them, and who therefore fail to get any of the intended benefits from the internship. This is also problematic for employers who are left with the impossible task of training people with no relevant background in a very short period of time. Another consequence is the stereotyping of refugees as a group that is currently unemployable due to cultural and linguistic barriers, which in turn leads to further marginalisation of individuals who are already at the margins of society.

The logics discussed above play into the discourse of employability. Whether the internships are regarded as a CSR measure or as a step on the way to becoming self-supporting, the underlying discourse is that of employability, and the idea is that an internship will help the interns become more employable. Even the activation logic in which the primary aim is to keep welfare clients busy has the long-term goal of turning clients into self-supporting contributors to society, and the internships are nominally one way of increasing employability and hence their chances of becoming self-supporting. Unpaid internships or voluntary work undertaken with the long-term goal of finding paid employment have previously been discussed in terms of 'hope labour'. Hope labour is work "premised on the logic of investment. Hope labour promises that exposure and experience will possibly lead to employment" (Allan, 2019, 67). While this form of labour may benefit the workers as a way of keeping busy, the workers in Allan's study were quickly disillusioned of its value as a way to get paid employment. In this study, we have also seen how unpaid internships from the refugee perspective function as hope labour. From the public and private perspectives, however, it is not even that. Seeing as how hiring a large number of the interns was never part of the plan, it would seem that the internships are closer to no-hope labour.

ACKNOWLEDGEMENTS

The work on this chapter has been supported by Independent Research Fund Denmark | Humanities grant number 6107-00351, "Transient Multilingual Communities and the Formation of Social and Linguistic Norms". I would like to thank Spencer Hazel, Katherine Kappa, Kamilla Kraft and Janus Mortensen for their input to this work during discussions within the TMC project team, and Sirin Eissa, Ida Moth Kej and Solvej Helleshøj Sørensen for invaluable assistance with transcriptions and translations.

NOTES

1. Transcription conventions: ellipsis is marked with …, pauses shorter than 0.5 seconds with (.), and longer pauses denote the length of the pause. Where the original excerpt was in Danish, it has been translated by the author.
2. While in this study I only have the managers' and refugees' interpretation of this, a study of case worker perspectives that is part of the same project (Lønsmann, 2020) corroborates these results.

REFERENCES

Allan, K. (2019), 'Volunteering as hope labour: The potential value of unpaid work experience for the un-and under-employed', *Culture, Theory and Critique* **60** (1), 66–83.

Allan, K. and McElhinny, B. (2017), 'Neoliberalism, language and migration', in Suresh Canagarajah (ed.), *The Routledge handbook of migration and language*, London: Routledge, pp. 79–101.

Angouri, J. and Piekkari, R. (2018), 'Organising multilingually: Setting an agenda for studying language at work', *European Journal of International Management* **12** (1/2), 8–27.

Betts, A. and Buith, J. (2017), *Talent displaced: The economic lives of Syrian refugees in Europe. Survey by Deloitte and Refugees Studies Center*. Deloitte. https://www2 .deloitte.com/global/en/pages/about-deloitte/articles/talent-displaced.html, accessed 25 March 2022.

Buch, D. (2017), Tusindvis af flygtninge sendes i praktik – Ligner misbrug af ulønnet arbejdskraft. *TV2*. https://nyheder.tv2.dk/samfund/2017-04-26-tusindvis-af -flygtninge-sendes-i-praktik-ligner-misbrug-af-uloennet-arbejdskraft, accessed 25 March 2022.

Confederation of Danish Employers (2019), Flygtninge kommer hurtigere i job. https:// www.da.dk/politik-og-analyser/integration/2019/flygtninge-kommer-hurtigere-i -job/, accessed 25 March 2022.

Creese, G. and Kambere, E.N. (2003), 'What colour is your English?', *Canadian Review of Sociology/Revue canadienne de sociologie* **40** (5), 565–573.

Del Percio, A., Flubacher, M-C. and Duchêne, A. (2018), 'Language and political economy', in Ofelia García, Nelson Flores and Massimiliano Spotti (eds), *The Oxford handbook of language and society*, Oxford, UK: Oxford University Press, pp. 55–75.

Duchêne, A. and Heller, M. (2012), *Language in late capitalism: Pride and profit*, New York: Routledge.

Flubacher, M-C., Duchêne, A. and Coray, R. (2017), *Language investment and employability: The uneven distribution of resources in the public employment service*, Basingstoke: Palgrave Macmillan.

Goethals, S., Bardwell, J., Bhacker, M. and Ezzelarab, B. (2017), 'Business human rights responsibility for refugees and migrant workers: Turning policies into practice in the Middle East', *Business and Human Rights Journal* **2** (2), 335–342.

Henry, A. (2016), 'Swedish or English? Migrants' experiences of the exchangeability of language resources', *International Journal of Bilingual Education and Bilingualism* **19** (4), 442–463.

Kamil, C. (2016), Ikea har haft 76 flygtninge i praktik: "Det er urealistisk, at vi skulle ansætte mange flere." *Berlingske.* https://www.berlingske.dk/samfund/ikea-har-haft -76-flygtninge-i-praktik-det-er-urealistisk-at-vi-skulle-ansaette-ma, accessed 25 March 2022.

Karhunen, P., Kankaanranta, A., Louhiala-Salminen, L. and Piekkari, R. (2018), 'Let's talk about language: A review of language-sensitive research in international management', *Journal of Management Studies* **55** (6), 980–1013.

Kirilova, M. and Lønsmann, D. (2020), 'Dansk – nøglen til arbejde? Ideologier om sprogbrug og sproglæring i to arbejdskontekster i Danmark', *NordAnd – Nordisk tidsskrift for andresspråksforskning* **15** (1), 37–57.

Lecomte, P., Tenzer, H. and Zhang, L.E. (2018), 'Thematic issue: Working across language boundaries: New perspectives on language-sensitive international management research', *European Journal of International Management* **12** (1/2).

Lønsmann, D. (2020), 'Language, employability and positioning in a Danish integration programme', *The International Journal of the Sociology of Language* **264**, 49–71.

OECD and UNHCR (2016), Hiring refugees: What are the opportunities and challenges for employers? Migration Policy Debates, 10. https://www.oecd.org/els/mig/ migration-policy-debates-10.pdf, accessed 25 March 2022.

Rosén, J.K. and Bagga-Gupta, S. (2013), 'Shifting identity positions in the development of language education for immigrants: An analysis of discourses associated with "Swedish for immigrants"', *Language, Culture and Curriculum* **26** (1), 68–88.

Salling Group (2017), HK løber fra sit ansvar med kritik af supermarkedskæder. *Ritzau.* https://via.ritzau.dk/pressemeddelelse/hk-lober-fra-sit-ansvar-med-kritik -af-supermarkedskaeder?publisherId=3307957&releaseId=9518819, accessed 25 March 2022.

Sandwall, K. (2010), 'I learn more at school: A critical perspective on workplace-related second language learning in and out of school', *Tesol Quarterly* **44** (3), 542–574.

Strauss, A. and Corbin, J. (2003), *Basics of qualitative research: Techniques and procedures for developing Grounded Theory. Second Edition.* Thousand Oaks, CA: Sage.

Svansø, V-L. (2016), 14.000 flygtninge skal have job i år. *Berlingske.* https://www .berlingske.dk/karriere/14.000-flygtninge-skal-have-job-i-aar, accessed 25 March 2022.

TV2 (2017), Er det sådan man bliver dansk? https://omtv2.tv2.dk/nyheder/2017/04/er-det-saadan-man-bliver-dansk/, accessed 25 March 2022.

Urciuoli, B. (2008), 'Skills and selves in the new workplace', *American Ethnologist* **35** (2), 211–228.

Wang, Y. and Chaudhri, V. (2019), 'Business support for refugee integration in Europe: Conceptualising the link with organizational identification', *Media and Communication* **7** (2), 289–299.

4. Agency and multilingualism in public health care: how practitioners draw on local experiences and encounters

Yaron Matras, Rebecca Tipton and Leonie Gaiser

INTRODUCTION

In this contribution we show how practitioners in the health care sector draw on experiences and encounters with local multilingualism. The health care sector is particularly intriguing, as here language 'needs' can have far-reaching consequences if they are not identified or responded to appropriately. Despite being a sector in which effective accommodation of language needs has long been identified as vital for ensuring accessibility and quality of treatment (cf. Phillimore, 2015; Zeeb et al., 2015), it is one in which practitioners can often be under immense pressure to produce ad hoc solutions and take decisions as they go along, based on their experience and knowledge.

Our contribution focuses on the role of individual agency in understanding the complexities and dynamics of responding to perceived language 'needs'. We show that there are many opportunities for a range of participants to assume agency roles in the process and to co-manage or shape the organisation of individual encounters. We discuss how they enact practical solutions that have the potential to transform into habitual practice through iteration, and how they forge what Liddicoat and Taylor-Leech (2020) define as 'projectivity' or future-oriented policy. We show how practitioners' ability to make decisions relies on their personal experiences and encounters with population groups gained in the local multilingual urban setting. Actors' experience of the multilingual city thus constitutes a resource that informs and empowers them in institutional contexts.

The discussion is set against developments in interlingual and intercultural communication research in public services in what has been termed 'super-diverse' settings (cf. Vertovec, 2007). Various interpreting modes, including on-site face-to-face (bilateral) interpreting, telephone interpreting, video interpreting, and translation of signs (Tipton and Furmanek, 2016) are seen not just as a way of ensuring equal access (and social justice in general, cf. Piller, 2016, 134ff.) but also as a way of managing risk (Schenker et al., 2011) and avoiding unnecessary reliance on emergency services (Ngai et al., 2016). The health care sector in England and Wales requires the use of professional language services rather than relying on staff language skills (NHS, 2018). Nevertheless, staff attitudes towards, and awareness of their multilingual environment have been shown to play a role in the delivery of professional services (Cadier and Mar-Molinero, 2012).

Research on health care interpreting has tended to focus on the nature of provisions and their relevance to the quality of care (Flores, 2005; Bischoff and Hudelson, 2010; Schuster et al., 2016) as well as the collaborative dimension of interpreter-mediated events (Angelelli, 2003; Bührig et al., 2012) with some consideration given to the health care sector in the wider context of responses to urban language diversity (e.g. Matras and Robertson, 2015; Gaiser and Matras, 2016). This contribution explores the interpreting encounter in the wider context, embedded in and shaped by the diverse setting, its actors (defined as those whose behaviour is rule-governed) and their forms of agency and skills and knowledge. In this sense we move away from traditional understandings of policy development and enactment, and show the relevance of local decision-making processes and practices in the field of Interpreting and Translation. In so doing, we foreground the micro-level dynamics and practicalities around meeting language 'needs', building on other research that has shown how, in activating their own multilingual resources, practitioners assume agency, which contributes in effect to policy enactment within the institution (cf. Johnson and Johnson, 2015; Hornberger et al., 2018; Gaibrois, 2019; Keshet and Popper-Giveon, 2019).

AGENCY AND PRACTICE-BASED POLICY ENACTMENT

Research into language policy increasingly emphasises the role of local practice as opposed to the study of policy documents (cf. Bonacina-Pugh, 2012, 2020; Pennycook, 2013). More attention is also being given to the concept of agency as the enactment of policy through discourse and individual initiative. Liddicoat and Taylor-Leech (2020) define agency in language policy as a process of social engagement that is impacted by iteration (drawing on past experience), projectivity (future-oriented action) and practical evaluation. Iteration refers to the continuation of established practice routines. Liddicoat and Taylor-Leech argue that agency is not found only in the reproduction of past experiences, but also involves a creative reconstruction of the world that gives shape and direction to it. They regard projectivity as a future-oriented component of agency that involves a process of imagining possible future trajectories of action that are relevant to the actor's hopes, fears, and desires for the future (Liddicoat and Taylor-Leech, 2020, 5–6).

This understanding of agency draws on the notion that agency entails the capacity of individuals to influence a pre-existing state of affairs or course of events and that such capacity may be enacted as part of an exercise of choice or as an act of resistance, variously constrained by context and circumstance (cf. McNamara, 2019, 16–20). Agency is often understood as the capacity to introduce variation on repetitive processes thereby subverting them and the identities that they produce (Butler, 1990 [1999], 198–199) and as breaking away from a given frame of action in order to transform it (Lipponen and Kumpulainen, 2011, 816). It is thus also a temporally embedded social process, one that incorporates past practices as well as undertaking future-oriented actions (Emirbayer and Mische, 1998). Ahearn (2001, 112ff.) therefore views agency as a "socio-culturally-mediated capacity to act": While an 'actor' might be somebody whose action is rule-governed, the "agent" according to Ahearn (2001) exercises their own power in the sense of an ability to bring about effects. The process of claiming agency involves conscious reflection and deliberation as well as having motivation, skills and ability (in terms of social positioning) to act. In order to capture the fluidity of the process we maintain our reference to the health care practitioners whom we interviewed as 'actors' rather than try to introduce what would risk being a somewhat random distinction between 'actors' and 'agents'. Instead, we assess how actors may at times assume a greater sense of agency: Common to these various positions is an understanding of agency as deviation from script or non-conformity; it does not follow an expected routine as prescribed by an institution but takes on some form of autonomy, though often with the pragmatic goal of achieving an end result in a way that is simpler and more practical rather than with the explicit goal of resisting power.

If the above description of agency is accepted, policy can be seen as something that is constantly re-practised and hence contested. However, the outcomes are nevertheless bound up in various power asymmetries that are manifest in the institutional encounter. This explains the level of variability in practised policies of language: An institutional service provider with mul-tilingual competence may be more open than a colleague who speaks only the majority language to a service user's desire for autonomy over the trans-lation process; however, as our examples later show, the multilingual service provider may over-estimate their own and others' capacities and repertoires, leading to questions about whether institutional imperatives of risk manage-ment and patient choice are always effectively addressed.

Investigation of individual agency in institutions has relied on participant observation as well as analysis of discourse practices and testimonials.

Hornberger et al. (2018) introduce an ethnographic approach that relies on observation and long-term immersion to derive insights into actors' patterns of behaviour and engagement in policies and practices. Special attention is given to tension between ideologically driven formulations of policy or ideological spaces that are monoglossic and implementation spaces that support the sustainability of actual heteroglossic (multilingual) practices. Investigating school programmes in the US state of Washington, Johnson and Johnson (2015) show how nominally identical models harbour different practices. They conclude that local actors have power over decision-making processes, which they describe as processes of appropriating policy to local contexts. They take a multi-site approach to examine how local power constellations affect policy appropriation and implementation in multiple centres. Wodak and Savski (2018) present a critical ethnographic approach to examining the inner workings of organisations and their role in policy implementation arguing that an examination of discursive practices, interactions and contextual knowledge should allow researchers to go beyond observation and explicitly evoke a normative stance. Gaibrois (2019) also adopts a discursive approach to practice suggesting that speaking about multilingual practices in the work environment can affect relations within an organisation. Basing her analysis on interviews she examines where and how employees feel empowered to seize opportunities, take responsibility and decisions and create new possibilities. She interprets such instances of empowerment as the creation of agency through resistance towards established practice, requests for adaptation, offers of support and legitimising practice diversity ('bricolage').

METHODS AND SETTING

We position our analysis in the context of these studies. We focus on interviews with actors who represent different roles in the health care sector in the same city. We show how testimonials provide insights into the knowledge that actors rely on when navigating the institutional setting. We are interested in particular in elements of knowledge that equip actors to take decisions and enact a course of action to structure the encounter between service user and professional practitioner. We show how personal experience in the multilingual city is an important resource from which actors derive empowerment and agency.

Our research draws on nearly a decade of observations on language practices in the local health care sector with a focus on Central Manchester Universities Hospitals NHS Foundation Trust (CMFT) and surrounding General Practitioner (GP) practices. This included semi-structured interviews and focus group conversations with health care professionals and with interpreters and translators.

In the present contribution we focus on testimonials extracted from interviews with altogether seven health care professionals: four GPs, a dentist, a pharmacist, and a GP practice manager. We consider as 'testimonials' statements that are embedded into narration or conversation that contain evaluations of provisions, and descriptions through which participants reconstruct their own actions and the considerations that led them to take these actions.

TESTIMONIALS AND FINDINGS

Engagement with Scripted Practice

The first two testimonials show how participants understand, accept and engage in institutionally scripted practice routines around the provision of interpreting services:

Example 1: GP 1

> By and large, they always have the language we need. I think we're delivering here a world-class service, we can deal with anybody from the world now, irrespective of their language skills. And I think, having telephone translators specifically is a good option, because it's versatile. It doesn't disrupt the consultation. It provides intimacy for the patients.

Example 1 is from a GP based at a practice in South Manchester and concerns interpreter services that the practice has access to through an external interpreting agency. The comments show pride in the service and awareness of its importance to the health care system. They also show an implicit level of trust in the provisions and an assumption that they generally resolve communication barriers. Drawing on his past experience to assess available language provisions, the GP highlights the advantages of telephone interpreting both from the viewpoint of the practitioner (non-disruptive) and the patient (provides intimacy). This shows an awareness of the way different interpreting modes that are among his "repertoire of routine actions" (Liddicoat and Taylor-Leech, 2020, 5) can be used strategically. It is noteworthy, however, that the potential disruption deriving from telephone-based provisions (due to the logistics of handling a phone, lack of a clear connection, and fragmented narratives) is underplayed, suggesting an uneven understanding of the risk of different modes of interpreting in this setting.

Example 2: Dentist

> It was a case of she had come to her first appointment and didn't understand a word so it was picked up that she needed an interpreter so then we arranged another appointment and we had an interpreter brought out for that visit.

Example 2 shows practitioners as decision-makers in the use of language pro-visions, a role accepted by the patient. It also suggests that ensuring effective communication is perceived as a priority, as practitioner and patient accept a delay of the treatment so that an interpreter can be present. The example indicates an absence of pre-registration of interpreter needs. The practitioner, in what should have been the central encounter in the action chain, had to mitigate an issue that should have been addressed at an earlier point. The lack of specificity in regard to identifying the patient's needs ("it was picked up") suggests that the chain of communication extends beyond the practice team; the emphasis on the collective "we" suggests a service-level response and cross-team knowledge of appropriate provisions that are not reflected across the wider action chain.

Actors' Personal Initiative and Decision-Making

In the next example, a general practitioner based at a hospital comments on a personal strategy that appears to be driven by convenience, as the personal choice of provision from outside the system is not foreseen by regulations and guidelines:
Example 3: GP 2

And the best option, which works for me, and which sounds really silly, is Google Translate. I just type it in, and it works great, yeah. Really easy.

The statement (especially the meta-comment "sounds really silly") expresses the perception that this ad hoc solution may not be recognised officially or more widely as a way of facilitating communication during consultation. However, based on his own experience of using this strategy successfully he deems it as a legitimate practice for the everyday encounter with patients. The GP's evaluation of the strategy to use Google Translate as "best option" is in itself a dimension of agency (Emirbayer and Mische, 1998) as it responds to emerging needs. The comment shows the efficiency of the software tool but highlights a compromise in the principle of patient-centred care: Reliance on phrases of limited length to construct a medical encounter is risky and is likely to mean that much of the patient-centred phraseology used by practitioners (medical scripts) is likely to be dropped, calling into question the principle of equal access.

The next three examples show the relevance of individual decision-making in shaping practice. Individual actors take the initiative to deal with commu-nication difficulties in a way that they perceive as effective. They make use of a multiplicity of multi-modal support tools, sometimes in an improvised manner and otherwise as a matter of routine. Decisions on the choice of tools and modes are often based on prior experience and driven by actor initiative rather than institutional regulations or recommendations. Actors assume agency when they identify gaps in scripted language provisions, which is a way of negotiating power relations and implicitly contesting decisions and recommendations that are pre-formulated by institutional arbiters (cf. Hornberger et al., 2018). This may result in an imbalance in power, where macro-level actors and their policy decisions are overridden by micro-level actors, who can assume power positions in practice.

Example 4: GP 3

> On one occasion, when a patient needed to speak to staff and the staff were unable to identify which language they spoke (to get the appropriate interpreter) … The only thing we could do was to use their mobile phones to their friend [*sic*], which was really uncomfortable.

The GP in example 4 works in a practice in a small town around 20 miles from Manchester, where two thirds of patients were asylum seekers or refugees. The decision to use a patient's mobile phone and talk to their friend to overcome communication difficulties is an ad hoc response to an unusual situation, one that is not directly anchored either in scripted or in past practices. The unease at the involvement of an unknown third party reflects awareness of risks and ethical implications. These reflections had led the interviewee to create several support resources: printed leaflets in various languages, and a YouTube video with voice overs in ten different languages with information about the health care system, registration, and appointments, which discouraged patients from using family members and friends as informal interpreters. Deviation from the scripted routine thus led to projectivity in the form of the design of pre-emptive or educating measures.

Example 5: Pharmacist

> We had a family, actually an entire family, had TB, Tuberculosis. They had very poor English. So as opposed to getting it all translated, their reading and writing wasn't great either, so we did a pictorial step-by-step with the nurses.

Example 5 shows another example of ad hoc decision-making and improvised solutions by a team of practitioners during an interaction with service users. In the team's perception, conventional provisions were insufficient to resolve practical communication difficulties and this required a bespoke initiative, which the team felt able and empowered to take. The description is an example of how institutional policy may fail to effectively respond to patients' needs in a particular situation; staff make choices to override default procedures and develop strategies to overcome such challenges. It also shows awareness of the multi-modality of language use and the limitations, in some cases, of modes that rely on literacy, testifying to practitioners' active reflection on service users' language repertoires.

Example 6: GP 4

> that was a patient, again in my old practice, who refused a translator but then when it actually came to the consultation struggled with some of the medical terms. And that's awkward. Because they feel they don't need an interpreter, you feel they do, but you don't want to be insulting to their English.

The GP based at a suburban South Manchester clinic comments on the way that power relations are negotiated and the extent to which language skills evaluation can be projected onto power and self-esteem. The comment testifies to an awareness of the need to share power and agency with the patient while still making optimal use of the institutional provision and managing risk in that way. The GP's comment that he did not want to "insult" the patient's English suggests that the use of interpreting services may be interpreted as disempowering service users, or at least emphasising a disadvantage. The patient's decision to go without an interpreter reflects their desire for autonomy and self-determination. The GP's reflections indicate an awareness of the complex factors that may affect an individual's decision regarding the use of interpreting services.

Local Knowledge and Personal Experience

The next three examples demonstrate how local knowledge and personal experience is presented in the testimonials as a legitimate reference point to justify and explain actors' decision-making processes. Personal experience can empower actors to override a course of action that is set by scripted procedure:

Example 7: GP 1

> We did a little survey not that long ago and what we found was that there is a certain group of patients, particularly ladies, actually preferred the telephone translators. Because then they could divulge details of say domestic abuse, domestic violence, or sensitive topics, which they found, if there was another person present, they may be less open. And also, they could talk more about intimate symptoms that they have, whereas having a translator physically set there was a little bit prohibited.

The group of patients described in this example show a perceived preference for disembodied interpreter mediation as a means to address culturally sensitive topics (while the technical challenges presented by telephone interpreting appear to be overlooked). The statement testifies again to an established routine of using certain strategies to address particular situations and circumstances, thus opting between available modes of encounter management – face-to-face and telephone interpreting.

Example 8: GP 2

> When it comes to Asian communities, again, I can cover all ground. When it comes to African, I cover the ground there, and parts of India, I can cover. [...] I can have someone there from the interpreting service, saying they speak one language. And when they're actually speaking [it is] either very very slang, so it's not even formal. Or, it's a completely different language they claim is the language they're speaking. And in such situations I just say "Look, you may as well stop, because I speak the language myself".

This example shows the intertwining of professional with personal experience. What is at stake is the issue of epistemic authority, or which actor's knowledge about language has currency or is most trusted: The GP highlights perceived gaps in the professional interpreter's ability to offer a particular language combination while potentially over-estimating their own capacity to acquire and deploy language knowledge in the workplace. The GP is resistant to appropriating the dominant discourse of professional interpreter provisions. As someone with a degree of proficiency in several languages and a social back-ground that suggests exposure to situations in which 'getting by' with partial communicative ability has worked, this GP intervenes with the interpreter's management of the event, departing from scripted procedure including the dominant NHS discourse of safeguarding and risk management.

Example 9: GP Practice Manager

> We overcome that [language barriers] by a lot of our doctors speak the languages spoken in our area, except for Bengali, 'cause we haven't got a Bengali speaking doctor, we have to get our own interpreter. Or usually they do manage to bring their families, they do manage to communicate that way. And if there isn't anybody that they can bring, we have to book someone. It's a huge cost to the NHS. In the mornings it becomes a huge problem because they're ringing to make an appointment at eight o'clock I'm struggling sometimes if a member of staff has not turned up who speaks the language it becomes a huge problem but then I don't speak Bengali but then the Bengali-speaking people will understand a little bit of Urdu so I can sort of/ I speak a few words of Bengali so, so I usually manage.

The Practice Manager, an Urdu speaker, notes a range of ad hoc solutions and overlapping language resources for distinct communicative functions: The experience of Bengali-speaking people understanding "a little bit of Urdu" licenses the booking of appointments through receptive multilingualism (communication across similar languages; cf. ten Thije and Zeevaert, 2007). The description of staff language skills illustrates the practice's embedding in the local area and its language composition. It also conveys the belief that health care professionals support the NHS when using informal interpreters where possible, as this saves money. There is thus a subjective balancing of NHS interpreting guidelines against a more tacit commitment to contribute to economic efficiency, one that derives from the everyday experience in the work environment rather than scripted policy.

Narratives about Language

Our final pair of examples shows how practitioners explain and justify taking initiative by constructing narratives on language:
Example 10: GP 2

> And again, it depends what part of Romania they are from, Roma travellers speak slightly different. It's all slang, it's language bits from everywhere, bits of language from India, bits from there. But they're officially from Romania, and your language is slightly different there, as well.

Example 11: GP 1

> So, to give you an example, there is three Kurdish languages. There is Kurmanji, Sorani, and Badini. There is two Farsi languages, Afghani and Persian. There is two types of Chinese, Mandarin and Cantonese. Both, which are provided. Actually, there is no point of giving a Badini Kurdish translation for a Kurmanji, because they don't understand each other.

The construction of language narratives appears to draw on an accumulation of everyday experiences with a diverse population of service users in the multilingual city. It is then presented as part of the actors' portfolio of specialised knowledge as professionals working in this setting and in that way as knowledge that qualifies them to manage decision-making nodes when it comes to encounters with service users. We thus witness once again the intertwining of professional authority with everyday personal experience (for the context for these two testimonials see Examples 3, 8 and 1, 7 respectively).

DISCUSSION

Several themes emerge from the testimonials considered above. First we note actors' awareness of and, by and large, confidence in the institutional provisions to manage communication and overcome language barriers. At the same time they report on their own initiative in taking decisions, either by compartmentalising settings and types of encounter and selecting among different options to manage them, or by enriching provisions at their own initiative and sometimes by overriding scripted procedures at their own discretion.

Reported strategies include the use of receptive multilingualism (capitalising on similarities between languages), using family members as a resource and drawing on technological tools. In their testimonials actors indicate that their decisions are informed by established practice routines. They are also shaped by a comprehensive assessment of the multilingual environment and experience of cross-language communication as well as by specific knowledge about languages acquired through such experience. These are justifications and qualifications which actors provide in their testimonials to explain and assert their own sense of agency in negotiating decision-making nodes in encounters between practitioners and service users. Recall that, as we explain above, we identify the fluidity of reclaiming agency in this sense; for that reason, we choose not to introduce a hierarchical distinction between 'actors' and 'agents'. Instead, we view 'actors' as participants whose performance and practice routines are generally governed by rules, but who may in a particular context assume agency by taking their own decisions.

Contextualised testimonials thus serve as a way of reconstructing actors' own sense of agency and of mapping elements of knowledge on which actors rely at pivotal decision-making nodes. They allow us to access the level of policy enactment and implementation at a local level and assess how individuals contribute to shaping policy through practice. The testimonials reveal that encounters between service users and practitioners in the institutional setting of the health care sector are sites in which language policy is appropriated, enacted, and implemented by a range of actors in different roles. Power relations are derived not just from institutional roles; rather, in an environment that is highly de-regulated and where there are often different options to manage encounters, actors rely to a considerable degree on accumulated knowledge. This includes local knowledge, gained passively by virtue of being immersed in the everyday locale, as well as first-hand experience gained from accumulated interactions in the work environment of public service in a diverse city. The multilingual urban setting is thus a key source of knowledge about language practices, provisions, options for support in heteroglossic encounters and about language itself.

Experience in the linguistically diverse city allows actors to gauge their knowledge and course of action against their own and others' expectations and aspirations and empowers them to take the initiative and to narrate explanations and justifications for their own initiatives. In this respect the material illuminates a different perspective to those discussed by Cadier and Mar-Molinero (2012), who focus on practitioners' language skills, and by Keshet and Popper-Giveon (2019), who address the language skills of practitioners and patients and the social values attached to them. We present a case where decisions, actions and initiatives draw on the kind of urban, super-diverse repertoire described by Busch (2012) and by Blommaert and Backus (2013).

This approach problematises the notion of 'language' as a pre-defined set of structures and replaces it with the view that language and communication experience constitute a dynamic pattern of practices, potentially detached from pre-defined groups or speech communities and placed instead within emerging and evolving networks of practice. Crucially, it views language repertoires not just as language skills in the conventional sense of fluency and lexical and grammatical competence but also as the sum of impressions and experiences gained through a variety of encounters within such networks of practice.

In the context of language support provisions in the hospital, Liddicoat and Taylor-Leech's (2020) assertion that policy development is an essentially dialogic process merits particular attention. This is because users of health care services are seldom likely to have been involved in the formation of policies that govern the commissioning, delivery and quality management of language support provisions (cf. Tipton, 2017). Inevitably they 'receive' policy as it has been interpreted institutionally, for example provision of a professional interpreter who will expect to participate in accordance with an established framework. Broadly speaking, this also applies to practitioners, who are "actors" as described by Ahearn (2001). However, our observations show that policy is not just passively absorbed and accepted but rather frequently undergoes processes of negotiation, as interactants adjust their interpretations of policy (whether formal scripted policy or personal micro policies shaped by language repertoires) to the situation at hand.

In part, this may be due to a very practical reason that actors (service providers) within the health care system may not be fully aware that there exists an institutional set of guidance on working with service users with low English proficiency. The policy basis on which encounters are anchored may therefore vary considerably, operating along a spectrum between ad hoc micro-level policy innovations based on a speculative and intuitive understanding of what constitutes effective communication with service users, and service interventions that are framed by the overarching structures of the institutional policy document on commissioning translation and interpreting services (NHS, 2018). Following Ahearn (2001), we may be interested in investigating practices that reproduce or transform the very structures that require such policies to exist in the first place. However, in our case what we understand by 'structure' is multi-layered and unstable (both at the institutional level of policy-as-structure, and at the interactional level of participation framework-as-structure). The structures, mutually constituted by language practices in the interpreter-mediated encounter, are characterised by their temporality; traces of structure may be re-enacted in other settings by both parties but they cannot serve as clear predictors of outcomes in each case. We embrace Emirbayer and Mische's (1998, 971) view of projectivity as "the imaginative generation by actors of possible future trajectories of action". They argue that social actors negotiate paths towards the future and that they receive their driving impetus to do so from the conflicts and challenges of social life. Agency arises, they suggest, "as actors attempt to reconfigure received schemas by generating alternative possible responses to the problematic situations they confront in their lives" (1998, 984).

Some of our testimonials suggest that individuals make conscious choices not to involve professional interpreters even though they are entitled to request support. Such decisions are indicative of projectivity, as defined above: future-oriented actions in which the individual actor construes the self as capable of employing even limited language resources to facilitate autonomy and determine a course of action without having to draw on an available script or established routine. However, as stated above, these decisions are not without risk and come up against the practical evaluation strategies of institutional representatives who may take several courses of action as the lead agent with overall accountability for risk management and mitigation: override the decision and request an interpreter to attend, tolerate the decision and muddle through, tolerate the decision and proactively support the interaction by pooling personal resources (e.g. employing own language knowledge and repertoires, collaborating by using technology-based solutions such as Google Translate).

Similar to the observations discussed by Hornberger et al. (2018) from educational settings, we identify in health care settings implementational spaces that are 'carved out' from the bottom up and can resist the pressure of top-down policies. Such 'carving out' of implementational spaces rests in our study on a broad range of accumulated knowledge, site-specific and conjectural contingencies, that is, unanticipated events that arise as a consequence of external factors that are specific to a particular time period. This shows what Gaibrois (2019) identifies as the 'productive power' of multilingualism in these settings. New spaces are opened up by the various actors in the action chain when scripted institutional provisions are renegotiated in various ways, resisted and even rejected. But the testimonials also point to a trend towards expediency as the driver of decision-making as opposed to institutional values of patient safety and patient dignity. From a policy perspective, this pragmatism and flexibility afforded by the de-regulated Public Service Interpreting and Translation environment may therefore require further critical attention to ensure that the chosen intervention strategies do not compromise patient choice and patient experience.

REFERENCES

Ahearn, L.M. (2001), 'Language and agency', *Annual Review of Anthropology*, **30** (1), 109–137.

Angelelli, C-V. (2003), 'The visible co-participant: The interpreter's role in doctor–patient encounters', in Melanie Metzger, Steven Collins, Valerie Dively and Risa Shaw (eds), *From topic boundaries to omission*, Washington DC: Gallaudet University Press, pp. 3–26.

Bischoff, A. and Hudelson, P. (2010), 'Access to healthcare interpreter services: Where are we and where do we need to go?', *International Journal of Environmental Research and Public Health*, **7** (7), 2838–2844.

Blommaert, J. and Backus, A. (2013), 'Superdiverse repertoires and the individual', in Ingrid de Saint-Georges and Jean-Jacques Weber (eds), *Multilingualism and multimodality: The future of education research*, Rotterdam: Sense Publishers, pp. 11–32.

Bonacina-Pugh, F. (2012), 'Researching "practiced language policies": Insights from conversation analysis', *Language Policy*, **11** (3), 213–234.

Bonacina-Pugh, F. (2020), 'Legitimizing multilingual practices in the classroom: The role of the "practiced language policy"', *International Journal of Bilingual Education and Bilingualism*, **23** (4), 434–448.

Bührig, K., Kliche, O., Meyer, B. and Pawlack, B. (2012), 'Explaining the interpreter's unease: Conflicts and contradictions in bilingual communication in clinical settings', in Kurt Braunmüller and Christoph Gabriel (eds), *Multilingual individuals and multilingual societies*, Amsterdam: Benjamins, pp. 407–418.

Busch, B. (2012), 'The linguistic repertoire revisited', *Applied Linguistics*, **33** (5), 503–523.

Butler, J. (1990 [1999]), *Gender trouble: Feminism and the subversion of identity*, London: Routledge.

Cadier, L. and Mar-Molinero, C. (2012), 'Language policies and linguistic super-diversity in contemporary urban societies: The case of the city of Southampton, UK', *Current Issues in Language Planning*, **13** (3), 149–165.

Emirbayer, M. and Mische, A. (1998), 'What is agency?', *American Journal of Sociology*, **103** (4), 962–1023.

Flores, G. (2005), 'The impact of medical interpreter services on the quality of health care: A systematic review', *Medical Care Research and Review*, **62** (3), 255–299.

Gaibrois, C. (2019), 'From resistance to "bricolage": Forms of power to get active and create possibilities in multilingual organizations', *Revista Internacional de Organizaciones*, **23**, 125–147.

Gaiser, L. and Matras, Y. (2016), 'Language provisions in access to primary and hospital care in central Manchester', Multilingual Manchester, The University of Manchester, accessed 23 September 2019 at mlm.humanities.manchester.ac.uk/wp-content/uploads/2016/09/Language-provisions-in-access-to-primary-and-hospital-care-Sept-2016.pdf.

Hornberger, N.H., Tapia, A.A., Hanks, D.H., Dueñas, F.K. and Lee, S. (2018), 'Ethnography of language planning and policy', *Language Teaching*, **51** (2), 152–186.

Johnson, D.C. and Johnson, E.J. (2015), 'Power and agency in language policy appropriation', *Language Policy*, **14** (3), 221–243.

Keshet, Y. and Popper-Giveon, A. (2019), 'Language practice and policy in Israeli hospitals: The case of the Hebrew and Arabic languages', *Israel Journal of Health Policy Research*, **8** (1), 1–11.

Liddicoat, A.J. and Taylor-Leech, K. (2020), 'Agency in language planning and policy', *Current Issues in Language Planning*, 1–18.

Lipponen, L. and Kumpulainen, K. (2011), 'Acting as accountable authors: Creating interactional spaces for agency work in teacher education', *Teaching and Teacher Education*, **27**, 812–819.

Matras, Y. and Robertson, A. (2015), 'Multilingualism in a post-industrial city: Policy and practice in Manchester', *Current Issues in Language Planning*, **16** (3), 296–314.

McNamara, T. (2019), *Language and subjectivity*, Cambridge: Cambridge University Press.

Ngai, K.M., Grudzen, C.R., Lee, R., Tong, V.Y., Richardson, L.D. and Fernandez, A. (2016), 'The association between limited English proficiency and unplanned emergency department revisit within 72 hours', *Annals of Emergency Medicine*, **68** (2), 213–221.

NHS. (2018), 'Guidance for commissioners: Interpreting and translation services in primary care', accessed 11 February 2021 at www.england.nhs.uk/publication/guidance-for-commissioners-interpreting-and-translation-services-in-primary-care/.

Pennycook, A. (2013), 'Language policies, language ideologies and local language practices', in Lionel Wee, Robbie B.H. Goh and Lisa Lim (eds), *The politics of English: South Asia, Southeast Asia and the Asia Pacific*, Amsterdam: John Benjamins, pp. 1–18.

Phillimore, J. (2015), 'Delivering maternity services in an age of superdiversity: The challenges of novelty and newness', *Ethnic and Racial Studies*, **38** (4), 568–582.

Piller, I. (2016), *Linguistic diversity and social justice: An introduction to applied sociolinguistics*, Oxford, UK: Oxford University Press.

Schenker, Y., Pérez-Stable, E.J., Nickleach, D. and Karliner, L.S. (2011), 'Patterns of interpreter use for hospitalized patients with limited English proficiency', *Journal of General Internal Medicine*, **26** (7), 712–717.

Schuster, M., Elroy, I. and Elmakais, I. (2016), 'We are lost: Measuring the accessibility of signage in public general hospitals', *Language Policy*, **1** (16), 23–38.

ten Thije, J. D. and Zeevaert, L. (eds) (2007), *Receptive multilingualism: Linguistic analyses, language policies and didactic concepts* (Vol. 6), Amsterdam: John Benjamins.

Tipton, R. (2017), 'Contracts and capabilities: Public service interpreting and third sector domestic violence services', *Special Issue on Translation, Ethics and Social Responsibility of The Translator*, **23** (2), 237–254.

Tipton, R. and Furmanek, O. (2016), *Dialogue interpreting. A guide to interpreting in public services and the community*, London: Routledge.

Vertovec, S. (2007), 'Super-diversity and its implications', *Ethnic and Racial Studies*, **30** (6), 1024–1054.

Wodak, R. and Savski, K. (2018), 'Critical discourse-ethnographic approaches to language policy', in James W. Tollefson and Miguel Pérez-Milans (eds), *The Oxford handbook of language policy and planning*, Oxford, UK: Oxford University Press, pp. 93–112.

Zeeb, H., Makarova, N., Brand, T. and Knecht, M. (2015), 'Superdiversity – a new concept for migrant health?', *Public Health Forum*, **23** (2), 124–125.

PART II

Language practices in multilingual workplaces
and implications for human resource
management

5. Introduction to *Language practices in multilingual workplaces and implications for human resource management*

Mary Vigier

Despite the growing body of literature on language in multilingual workplaces for nearly three decades (Horn et al., 2020), greater attention has been devoted to multilingual skills in oral workplace interaction (e.g. Bilbow, 1998, 2002; Poncini, 2002, 2003, 2013), while fewer studies have focused on multilingualism in written workplace communication. Kankaanranta (2006) explored internal corporate email communication and its genres in *lingua franca* English in a multinational company following the merger of a Swedish and Finnish company. Machili (2014, 2015) investigated the official and unofficial written use of global and local languages in email chains in multinational companies based in Greece. Yet, owing to the paucity of attention given to written workplace discourse, 'further research is still needed to address the multilingual and multimodal reality of workplace written interaction' (Machili and Angouri, 2016, 6).

Methodologically speaking, the most promising approach to language-based research in multilingual work contexts is to view language as a social practice (Karhunen et al., 2018). This view basically holds that meaning is created through actions, and that research analysis needs to focus on the effects of language on the facilitation or restriction of these actions in multilingual contexts (Tietze, 2020). It has also been shown that meaning emerges during data analysis processes (Outila et al., 2020). Another approach (Xian, 2020) states that researchers' reflexivity relates to their respective roles in multilingual research and to researchers' potential impact on results as they recreate meaning while making sense of the data. In fact, through reflexivity researchers develop a greater awareness of their own involvement in the process, their own interpretation of the data, and their engagement with the research context (Horn et al., 2020).

Overall, it is widely recognised that increased globalisation has led to more multilingualism at work. Several studies focus on the negative effects of multilingualism and consider it as a barrier (Feely and Harzing, 2003; Madera et al., 2014), an impediment (Marschan-Piekkari et al., 1999) or a disruptive element (Tenzer et al., 2014). Consequently, the reality of today's multilingual workplace landscape raises human resource management (HRM) implications for training professionals to effectively meet the multifaceted requirements of linguistically diverse organisations. Researchers, educators, and professional trainers have a role to play to ensure that employees are better prepared to adjust to the linguistic complexity of globalised workplace communities (Hagen, 1999; Feely and Harzing, 2003; Machili and Angouri, 2016) and to acquire the linguistic and sociolinguistic skills to manage interactional dynamics in contemporary workplace settings (Hazel and Svennevig, 2018).

The three chapters in this section will address and build on these topics to move the field forward. Acknowledging that very few studies have examined authentic written discourse and genre use by business professionals, **Tiina Räisänen** and **Anne Kankaanranta** take an ethnographic approach in **Chapter 6** to study a business professional's dynamic engagements with written workplace genres in a multilingual context. The authors differentiate between frontstage 'official English' used in corporate communication and the backstage 'working language' used among colleagues and close business partners. Frontstage English observes the norms of Standard English, and is typically used in one-way written, external communication reflecting the corporate image. The backstage language, conceptualised as English as a Business Lingua Franca (BELF), emerges in everyday interactions in both spoken and written language. The authors apply the conceptualisation of frontstage and backstage to analyse authentic data. In the mid-position, genres drawing on and combining features of both stages were identified as 'mixed genres'. The authors' findings reveal how the manager engages with multiple genres simultaneously and demonstrate what it means to view language as a social practice in the multilingual reality of an MNC, where both the manager and the subordinates bring discourse practices from their various lingua-cultural backgrounds into genre use. The authors' dynamic view of genres enables them to illustrate how a professional's voice shifts in relation to the genre in question and the work tasks carried out. Through the ethnographic focus, this chapter shows how language viewed as a social practice emphasises the role of individuals and their interactions in the everyday processes of multilingual organisations.

Chapter 7 by **Kristina Humonen** and **Jo Angouri** focuses on the concept of reflexivity in analysing language data. The authors' reflexive accounts from two different research sites seek to illustrate how ethnographic reflexivity can enable researchers to capture multiple readings of the data and to demonstrate the influence of field relations on the research process. The authors suggest that the appeal of the constructionist paradigm for language-sensitive scholars and workplace sociolinguistics is not surprising as language provides a way to see the world, multiple selves, and different concepts. In their first example, the authors provide three different readings of the same interaction and show the potential of ethnographic research for a multilevel analysis of the language data. They demonstrate that a single encounter can be read in multiple ways depending on the researchers' interests, framing, and positioning, requiring close reflexive examination of the field-world. In their second example, their reflexive account draws on the data collected from one context whereby they capture the fieldworker's voice by drawing on fieldnotes, audio-recorded data, and on an email exchange between the authors about the researcher's lived experiences. The authors reflect on multiple datasets to address how a researcher's subjectivities can impact the reading of the data and enhance their awareness of the co-existence of multiple truths and interpretations. Rather than taking data at face value, the authors claim that reflexive practice requires researchers to recognise individual and social complexities to question assumptions and interpretations.

In **Chapter 8, John Fiset** uses a critical incident paradigm to explore employee motives underlying the engagement in speaking a non-mutually understood language in the workplace. Fiset's study reveals three non-surreptitious motives to explain participants' desire to use a non-mutually understood language. These include: (1) process loss avoidance by switching to a language in which the speaker is more proficient; (2) solidarity and a shared sense of identity; and (3) making a positive impression. Although the intent behind these three motives is primarily constructive from the speaker's perspective, Fiset suggests that switching to a non-mutually understandable language at work can have negative effects on those who feel excluded from the interaction and can contribute to ambiguous outcomes. Fiset reports that two surreptitious motives for speaking a non-mutually understandable language relate to (1) concealing information that tends to be relevant to the organisation or that involves workgroup members; and (2) the desire to increase personal privacy. Drawing on the findings he recommends four procedures that HRM professionals can enact to reduce linguistic ostracism perceptions and to foster harmonious workplace interactions in a linguistically diverse workplace: (1) selection and hiring processes; (2) employee training; (3) leadership development; and (4) transmission of safety-related information in multiple languages to ensure that employees work in a secure environment. Overall, Fiset argues that HRM practitioners should be sensitive to the unanticipated consequences that language use has on employees in a multilingual environment and to the important role that motives may play in how HRM professionals adapt practices to a precise organisational context.

REFERENCES

Bilbow, G. T. (1998), 'Look who's talking: An analysis of "chair-talk" in business meetings', *Journal of Business and Technical Communication*, **12**, 157–197.

Bilbow, G. T. (2002), 'Commissive speech act use in intercultural business meetings', *International Review of Applied Linguistics in Language Teaching*, **40**, 287–303.

Feely, A. and A.-W. Harzing (2003), 'Language management in multinational companies', *Cross-Cultural Management: An International Journal*, **10** (2), 37–52.

Hagen, S. (1999), *Business communication across borders: A study of language use and practice in European companies*, Languages National Training Organisation.

Hazel, S. and J. Svennevig (2018), 'Multilingual workplaces: Interactional dynamics of the contemporary international workforce', *Journal of Pragmatics*, **126**, 1–9.

Horn, Sierk, Philippe Lecomte and Susanne Tietze (eds) (2020), *Managing multilingual workplaces: Methodological, empirical and pedagogic perspectives*, New York: Routledge.

Kankaanranta, A. (2006), '"Hej Seppo, could you pls comment on this!" Internal email communication in lingua franca English in a multinational company', *Business Communication Quarterly*, **69**, 216–225.

Karhunen, P., A. Kankaanranta, L. Louhiala-Salminen and R. Piekkari (2018), 'Let's talk about language: A review of language-sensitive research in international management', *Journal of Management Studies*, **55** (6), 980–1013.

Machili, I. (2014), '"It's pretty simple and in Greek…": Global and local languages in the Greek corporate setting', *Multilingua*, **33** (1–2), 117–146.

Machili, I. (2015), '"*It's not written on parchment but it's the way to survive*": Official and unofficial use of languages in MNCs', *Language in Focus Journal*, **1** (2), 54–84.

Machili, I. and J. Angouri (2016), 'Language awareness and multilingual workplace', in J. Cenoz, D. Gorter and S. May (eds), *Language awareness and multilingualism* (3rd edn), Springer, pp. 1–10.

Madera, J. M., M. Dawson and J. A. Neal (2014), 'Managing language barriers in the workplace: The roles of job demands and resources on turnover intentions', *International Journal of Hospitality Management*, **42**, 117–125.

Marschan-Piekkari, R., D. Welch and L. Welch (1999), 'Adopting a common corporate language: IHRM implications', *The International Journal of Human Resource Management*, **10** (3), 377–390.

Outila, V., R. Piekkari and I. Mihailova (2020), 'How to research empowerment in Russia: Absence, equivalence and method', in Sierk Horn, Philippe Lecomte and Susanne Tietze (eds), *Managing multilingual workplaces: Methodological, empirical and pedagogic perspectives*, New York: Routledge, pp. 29–44.

Poncini, G. (2002), 'Investigating discourse at business meetings with multicultural participation', *International Review of Applied Linguistics in Language Teaching*, **40**, 345–373.

Poncini, G. (2003), 'Multicultural business meetings and the role of languages other than English', *Journal of Intercultural Studies*, **24** (1), 17–32.

Poncini, G. (2013), 'Investigating communication and professional communities at international events', *Ibérica*, **26**, 131–150.

Tenzer, H., M. Pudelko and A. W. Harzing (2014), 'The impact of language barriers on trust formation in multinational teams', *Journal of International Business Studies*, **45**, 508–535.

Tietze, S. (2020), 'Methods and methodologies in multilingual research', in Sierk Horn, Philippe Lecomte and Susanne Tietze (eds), *Managing multilingual workplaces: Methodological, empirical and pedagogic perspectives*, New York: Routledge, pp. 3–8.

Xian, H. (2020), 'Translating Western research methodology into Chinese: A contextualised approach in practice', in Sierk Horn, Philippe Lecomte and Susanne Tietze (eds), *Managing multilingual workplaces: Methodological, empirical and pedagogic perspectives*, New York: Routledge, pp. 45–59.

6. Ethnographic study of a manager's engagements with written 'English' workplace genres in MNCs

Tiina Räisänen and Anne Kankaanranta

INTRODUCTION

Language-sensitive management research has recently begun to utilise linguistic approaches, particularly from applied and sociolinguistics, to advance the field and gain a better understanding of the dynamics involved in language use in managerial and professional contexts. Various researchers (e.g., Janssens and Steyaert, 2014; Angouri and Piekkari, 2018; Gaibrois, 2018; Karhunen et al., 2018; Lecomte et al., 2018; Tietze and Piekkari, 2020) have called for adopting qualitative methodologies including ethnographic approaches such as observation and recordings of authentic interactional professional practices at the workplace. These approaches would not be possible without conceptualising 'language' as a social practice emerging in interactions. For instance, the notion of English as corporate language should not simply be seen as an object to be managed in a multinational corporation but instead as a set of dynamic practices that manifest in different ways depending on the situation and context (see Kankaanranta et al., 2018). Concurrently, as Tietze (2018) argues, traditional standards of language use are changing and her argument about the powerful gatekeepers of standard written English seems to imply another type of 'English', which would not conform to such norms and standards and for which sociolinguistic research uses the label of English as Business Lingua Franca (BELF in short; Louhiala-Salminen et al., 2005).

Although some ethnographic and ethnographically informed studies (Angouri, 2014; Lauring and Klitmøller, 2015; Räisänen and Kankaanranta, 2020) and those focusing on linguistic experts such as translators (see Tietze, 2018; Koskinen, 2020) already exist in the field, very few studies have investigated authentic written discourse by business professionals. Still, with ethnography it is possible to understand professionals' meaning-making and everyday practices in the analysis as it combines both the participants' (emic) and researcher's (etic) perspectives (Blommaert and Dong, 2020).

Integrating the concept of English as corporate language (ECL) with (socio) linguistic genre theory (Bhatia, 1993, 2008), this chapter takes an ethnographic approach to study an individual business professional's dynamic engagement with written workplace genres (text types). We analyse data from the professional's management work over a period of four years, including audio- and video-recordings of work practices, email communication, interviews and ethnographic fieldnotes. We aim to find out the dynamics of different written genres when the professional handles his daily management jobs in the multilingual organisational context. We show how the manager functions as a legitimate user of English and as a gatekeeper (see also Angouri, 2014; Logemann and Piekkari, 2015; Tietze, 2018) of written genres in the organisation. Taking the individual professional's management work as our starting point, we bring a new approach to looking at writing in the ECL (Kankaanranta et al., 2018).

We contribute to language-sensitive international management research by showing how an ethnographic approach and focus on written 'English' workplace genres can reveal the dynamics of the professional's language practices and management tasks. Simultaneously, we illustrate how organisational practices are manifested in actual genre use and how they are linked with other genres used in the corporation and with wider structures such as professional roles and responsibilities and organisational hierarchies. In essence, ethnographic and situated approaches enable capturing the relationship between global demands and local affordances.

ENGLISH AS CORPORATE LANGUAGE

The conceptualisation of English as corporate language (ECL) in MNCs entails two views. First, it has been seen as a tool, a language that is a bounded entity which can be put to use and managed (e.g., Fredriksson et al., 2006; Luo and Shenkar, 2006; Piekkari et al., 2014). In this view, corporate language is seen at the top of the corporate language hierarchy and those with competence in the corporate language gain access to power (e.g., Neeley, 2013; Hinds et al., 2014). Second, ECL can be conceptualised as a social practice that manifests in actual contextualised language use when people work (e.g., Kassis-Henderson, 2005; Gaibrois, 2018; Langinier and Ehrhart, 2020). From the sociolinguistic language-as-practice view, language only emerges in social action and is always embedded in various layers of context, including the participants, the situation, and the organisational and societal context. Moreover, even if a person has linguistic and grammatical proficiency, it does not automatically mean that they are able to communicate effectively in a specific corporate situation (see Andersen and Rasmussen, 2004).

To maintain conceptual clarity (Suddaby, 2010), Kankaanranta et al. (2018) addressed this dual conceptualisation of ECL by applying Goffman's (1959) dramaturgical metaphor of social life. Their framework illustrates how the two different views to ECL may show at the two ends of a continuum: the front-stage 'official English' used in corporate communication (see Cornelissen, 2017) and the backstage 'working language' used among colleagues and close business partners. Although the framework does not address written and spoken language separately, implicitly the frontstage ECL seems to refer to written language and backstage ECL to both. Accordingly, the frontstage ECL would typically be used in one-way external communication reflecting corporate image and voice (see e.g., Hatch and Schultz, 1997) and would manifest as Standard English (SE), typically found in genres such as annual reports and media releases. It is different from the backstage ECL because it should make sense to a global, multilingual audience on its own, which calls for observing the norms and conventions of Standard English.

The backstage working language, conceptualised as English as a Business Lingua Franca (BELF, see Louhiala-Salminen et al., 2005), emerges in everyday – typically two-way – interactions such as emails and meetings between colleagues and business partners with diverse first languages. This sociolinguistic BELF resource emerges as a dynamic hybrid and its manifestation depends on the users' linguacultural backgrounds. It does not exist a priori with a certain identifiable structure that can be described in grammar books and dictionaries, which is the case with Standard English. In other words, BELF neither has native speakers nor does it exist as a language. Indeed, because of the speakers' multiple first languages, the resource can be conceptualised as inherently multilingual and multicultural (Janssens and Steyaert, 2014; Jenkins, 2015; Cogo, 2016; Ehrenreich 2016; Komori-Glatz, 2018; Räisänen, 2018). Since BELF emerges in two-way interactions, meaning-making is automatically negotiable: both in spoken and written interactions there is an opportunity to signal (non)comprehension, paraphrase and ask for and give clarifications. Although email is 'written' in the sense that it provides a permanent record, it is shown to consist of inherently two-way interactions comparable to dialogue with features of spoken language (e.g., Kankaanranta, 2005; AlAfnan, 2017; Roshid et al., 2018). BELF hence emerges in emails just as it emerges in other two-way interactions, and as the 'B' in the label advocates, the domain of its use is business, meaning that its users need to have knowledge and skills about working in business (Kankaanranta and Louhiala-Salminen, 2018).

By applying the conceptualisation of front and backstage ECL to authentic data, Räisänen and Kankaanranta (2020) identified a third, in-between stage on the ECL continuum where the language in spoken and written genres draws on and combines features of the two extremes. The mixed genre does not manifest in pure frontstage SE or as backstage BELF, meaning it is neither shared among the public-at-large, nor only with colleagues. Rather, it could, for example, be an agreement template in SE, which is adjusted in BELF interactions with the customer to fit the particular situation. The process of producing such mixed genres can involve various stakeholders both from within and outside the company.

Finally, although both international management research and sociolinguistics use the concept of 'lingua franca', the first one views it as language-as-tool, often close to SE (Harzing et al., 2011; Karhunen et al., 2018; for an overview, see Komori-Glatz, 2018) and the other one as language-as-practice, BELF (e.g., Kankaanranta, 2005; Pullin, 2013; Cogo, 2016; Ehrenreich, 2016; Millot, 2017; Roshid et al., 2018). Depending on the users and situations, BELF can emerge as closely resembling SE or as far removed from it. As Louhiala-Salminen et al. (2005; see also Kankaanranta and Louhiala-Salminen, 2018) argue, business is primary in BELF interactions, not grammatical correctness.

THE DYNAMIC NOTION OF GENRE

The concept of genre has been used as an analytical tool in various fields, such as organisation theory (e.g., Yates and Orlikowski, 1992), applied linguistics and sociolinguistics, to account for workplace practices in business (e.g., Louhiala-Salminen, 1997; Angouri and Marra, 2010; Flowerdew and Wan, 2010; Lehtinen and Pälli, 2011). Instead of the structural characteristics of the genre, recently more emphasis has been devoted to the social practices, and knowledge production and dissemination through genres (Bhatia, 2008). In line with social constructivism, genres respond to and construct recurring situations in the workplace, and participants engage in the situation through genre. In a particular community of users, genres represent typified social actions: the users recognise the genres, what they mean in a particular situation, how to produce them, and how to react and respond to them (Miller, 1984). The users also identify the communicative purpose, content and form (including structure, language, vocabulary) of the particular genre (Swales, 1990; Bhatia, 1993). Genres thus disclose the corporate context and the specific situation with its participants and their relationships and should thus be seen in their context (see e.g., Yates and Orlikowski, 1992; Kankaanranta, 2005; Angouri and Marra, 2010; Lehtinen and Pälli, 2011).

In other words, business manifests in genres in both public arenas outside the company – in official documentation, annual reports, media releases, social media spaces – and in private ones inside the organisation – in meetings, emails and chats. Some genres are more conventionalised than others (face-to-face vs. Zoom meetings) although most researchers adopting the social constructionist perspective seemingly agree on the dynamic nature of genres: they develop and change with the changing affordances and circumstances.

Emails developed from business letters and memos (Yates and Orlikowski, 1992) are an illustrative example of an established, predominantly written genre that employees in the workplace engage with (e.g., Louhiala-Salminen, 1999; Nickerson, 2000; Park et al., 2021). For example, Kankaanranta (2005) showed how email genres in an MNC were used to further corporate activities and maintain relationships; more specifically, they exchanged information, for-warded other messages and made announcements. Thus, the genres responded to the various situations arising in the corporate context and operationalised the MNC's mission and strategy into everyday activities of its employees. To appropriately use a genre, the professional must have knowledge of the corpo-rate and social context (Kankaanranta, 2005).

When looking at genres from the individual professional's viewpoint, which is our aim in this chapter, the picture becomes more complex. The individual carries out their work as part of the organisational practices, strat-egy and mission. The work is embedded in the trajectories of the business realised in various genres, with which professionals engage with, receiving, producing and disseminating essential knowledge. Typically, business pro-fessionals engage with multiple genres at work, often simultaneously: while participating in a meeting, a professional may read emails on the computer and respond to them, or comment on a document in an email message (e.g., Louhiala-Salminen, 2002). Such an approach to genre discloses not only the product but also the process and the business practices associated with genres.

Our chapter combines the ECL framework with genre theory by investigat-ing how the ECL comes into being as different written genres and as embed-ded in their production processes in the individual's everyday management work. While doing that it also reflects the daily linguistic reality of the MNC, where employees engage with genres at various points on the ECL continuum depending on their roles, responsibilities and hierarchical positions. Our sociolinguistic and ethnographic approach views genres from the individual professional's language-in-use perspective and investigates the genre produc-tion process through looking at what he does at work, with whom and through what medium.

ETHNOGRAPHIC APPROACH TO WRITTEN GENRES BY A MANAGER

This chapter is based on a multi-site ethnographic research project with the first author following a professional's life in 2003–2020, from his student days in mechanical engineering through career advancement towards management positions in small and medium-sized (SMEs) and multinational companies (MNCs). The data include both the professional's reported practices (i.e., talk about his work in audio-recorded interviews and informal discussions recorded with notes) and actual practices (i.e., recordings and fieldnotes of the professional's work activities at work with the researcher present) and written texts collected at various times and at different fieldwork sites (see also Räisänen, 2018). The professional is referred to as a 'participant' as he was active in distributing research materials for the researcher (e.g., self-recordings and written texts) due to personal and professional interests (e.g., established confidential relationship with the researcher and interest in professional development). The first author has maintained regular contact with the participant throughout the years and has kept track of his work practices.

The participant (pseudonym Oskari) has worked in several management positions, first as a Project Manager and later as Operations (OM) and Key Account Manager (KAM), being based both in Finland and in China. He studied English as a foreign language for over ten years (including during his three-year professional education), progressing towards advanced proficiency level (C2). He has also completed an English-language MBA degree. Throughout his management career, Oskari has used both English and Finnish, his first language. Although he worked in China for several years and encountered and learned some Chinese, he never studied it systematically.

The focus of this chapter is on the four years (2016–2020) Oskari spent at Service MNC as Operations Manager (OM, in 2014–2018) in China and Key Account Manager (KAM, in 2019–2020) in Finland. To exemplify the types of written genres and Oskari's engagement with them, we will use extracts from his jobs in Service MNC because the number of different written genres is the highest there of his career. Service MNC employs almost 4000 people and provides customers with services and solutions. Its headquarters are in Finland, and it has offices in nearly a dozen countries on three continents; English is Service MNC's corporate language. The OM position entailed managing the operations in one of the Chinese offices, including team management in their communication and collaboration with the customers, starting from quotations, compilation of mutual non-disclosure agreements all the way to ending collaboration. As KAM, Oskari handled contract management for a customer with related documentation, such as non-disclosure and frame agreements. During his time in the company, Oskari had become an expert of contract-related language use (clauses specifically) and while working as a KAM he was frequently asked for advice by his colleagues.

Oskari was interviewed twice in 2016 and 2018 and once in 2020 in Finnish, later translated into English by the first author (total 4.5 hours of interview data). His work practices were collected and recorded in 2016–2018 with the first author present in various face-to-face interactions between Oskari and his colleagues, superiors, subordinates and customers, and observing his work practices at the office. The data comprise fieldwork with observation during 13 working days, 15.5 hours of video and audio recordings, 137 pages of fieldnotes and 341 photos focusing on face-to-face interactions, meetings, emails, messenger chat, business presentations, surveys and non-disclosure documents. Oskari has submitted research material in textual form (e.g., emails, messenger chat, survey for distributors, technical documentation, presentation slides).

Although the second author did not participate in data collection and fieldwork, she contributed to thorough discussions of the entire dataset in the context of other projects, and actively analysed the data for the purposes of this project. We acknowledge that tacit knowledge involved in the situations may still not be available for her despite the thorough discussions. However, this limitation has been alleviated with an aim for triangulation by means of additional, clarifying questions posed to the participant, who has explained the practices of the industry, companies and their activities, and verified authors' interpretations. These ethnographic research practices have enabled gaining an overall understanding of the context and situations.

DATA ANALYSIS

In the analysis, the researchers first immersed themselves in the whole dataset and identified types of work situations (face-to-face, online) involving written discourse. Second, they identified emerging genres in written discourse, such as emails, chat messages, project log documents, non-disclosure documents and websites. To contextualise situated language use, including the manifestation of different genres, the analysis of selected instances of genres applied genre analysis (Bhatia, 1993, 2008). First, textual genre study was applied to investigate genre features (lexico-grammar, pragmatic features, discourse organisation) after which contextual features of genre use (Bhatia, 2008) were analysed including the writer and the audience, the function and role of the genre in itself and in relation to other genres in the manager's work in particular and as part of the organisational practices in general.

After these analytical steps and drawing on an earlier investigation in the participant's genre repertoire (Räisänen and Kankaanranta, 2020), we identified frontstage SE and backstage BELF genres, and those mixing the two appearing in between the two stages. We classified the participant's engagement with the written genres into:

- writing (also editing and participating in drafting);
- reading (reviewing, confirming and accepting e.g., an official document);
- sharing, referring to and forwarding (an email);
- using (one document when writing another, e.g., a company PowerPoint presentation in a customer meeting); and
- commenting.

For example, when Oskari's job included writing an email to a Chinese colleague, the genre would be classified as appearing in the backstage, the corporate language would be BELF by definition (i.e., interacting with a Chinese speaker), and Oskari's engagement 'writing'.

FINDINGS: WRITTEN GENRES IN THE MANAGER'S WORK

In both of his positions in Service MNC, Oskari was in charge of ensuring that contracts with customers abide by the company principles and enable legally binding collaboration with them. All our examples illustrate these manager responsibilities via genre use, showing that genre work is about getting the job done and ultimately, about advancing the business of the company. This point is highlighted by Oskari in Example 1 when he elaborates on his managerial position (interview in 2020) where writing and language use are inherently involved.

Example 1:

> Yes, the big picture shows in practice, or if it doesn't, I'm not doing my job correctly. They are not two separate things. My job is the big picture, both in customer relationship and sales work.

As Oskari says, one cannot separate the specific job tasks from the company's mission. For example, when a colleague was trying to advance their own specific viewpoint, Oskari would explicitly say that they must consider their company point of view and their business in the organisation (the global company or the cost centre). Hence, the company strategy and management communication were inseparable.

Oskari exercises his role as OM by assigning tasks for his team, simultaneously considering the wider organisational and legal points of view. Example 2 is an email message sent by Oskari to his two subordinates with an attached non-disclosure agreement (NDA). Before writing the email, Oskari had received an email from a customer (entitled 'Non-disclosure agreement') with the NDA document attached, which he then forwards to his subordinates and refers to in the beginning of the email. Oskari engages in writing a backstage email using BELF and referring to a document manifesting in the in-between stage and having SE features.

Example 2:

> From: Oskari Lastname
> To: Tim Lastname, John Lastname
> Subject: FW: Non-disclosure agreement
> Attachment: nondisclosureagreement.xlsx

Hi,

FYI, I shortly discussed about this with John. This file must be handled with **utmost care**, it **must not** be distributed to anybody who is not directly working with the case or who has not signed a labor contract or the NDA with [our company].

Tim, could we have a meeting regarding this case tomorrow?

Best Regards,
Oskari Lastname

Oskari manages his team via colloquial, everyday language: salutation *Hi*, the abbreviation *FYI*, and addressing subordinates by their first name (John, Tim). These practices were common among the colleagues at the workplace. However, one example of more formal style is using the signature with first and last name. Here the signature appears automatically, which can be seen in the video recording of Oskari writing this email. He leaves it as it is, probably for the sake of efficiency.

Example 2 shows two genres at play: first, the email genre visible here illustrating ECL use at the backstage, BELF by definition, emerging between colleagues in their everyday work interaction. Oskari actively engages with the email genre by producing the message. Second, Oskari refers to the NDA document attached, which is a document between the company and a customer and where the language and the content has to be carefully written, checked, agreed upon and confirmed by the parties involved before project collaboration can begin (due to the confidential nature of the document it cannot be disclosed here). In the email, Oskari does not comment on the actual contents of the agreement, but only refers to it and explains how it should be treated and by whom. The level of attention is signalled by bold font to highlight that the file must be handled with utmost care. Compared to Oskari's email message to colleagues, the NDA document between business partners has more at stake. The engagement with the NDA genre requires participants' comprehensive understanding of agreements and overall business knowledge. Hence, we argue that the NDA genre falls in the category of the in-between stage and represents a mixed genre, because at some point the key content pertaining to agreements has been checked by the company and customers to adhere to specific SE legal terminology and discourse, although some sections will be revised by Oskari to fit the situation at hand.

In Example 3 Oskari explicitly comments on the contents and the language of an attachment, not only referring to it as in Example 2. The email message belongs to a trajectory of a business practice, manifested in different genres: starting from customer contact via email, leading to a customer meeting where Oskari introduced the company, using the PowerPoint presentation genre, which then led to compilation of the quotation by his subordinates and, subsequently, the email message. Example 3 provides information about producing a mixed genre, a quotation, which is attached to a backstage email. The quotation typically observing a predetermined format was first compiled by a local team of Oskari's subordinates (Tim, Department Manager, L1 Chinese; John, Team Leader, L1 Chinese; Leena, Quality Manager, L1 Finnish), then emailed to Oskari who read it and then replied with requests for revision and editing. The task behind the use of the two genres involves serving the customer and ultimately – from the business point of view – closing a new deal. The tasks are accomplished in parallel in different genres – spoken, written, digital – and sometimes simultaneously through professionals' engagements.

Example 3:

From: Oskari Lastname
To: Tim Lastname, Leena Lastname, John Lastname
Subject: RE: Review of Quotation for [customer] – Urgent!
Attachment: Quotation

Hi,

Some basic comments for the Detail Engineering quotation:
• Fix the headline, this is not onsite

3. Scope
• Add also here that work is conducted at [our company] office.
• add a clause to state that actual amount of work is defined and agreed mutually

4. Schedule and resources
• [customer] will not select resources, the work is managed by [our company]

5. Project Execution and documentation
• [our company] will arrange people work in [customer] office for communication if needed.
• Site visits must be excluded, unless they are quoted with adequate price and times are specified. We can't create a situation that we need to go there e.g., twice a week and nobody pays a dime. For onsite work [hours] is too little.

I think we need to take some time to prepare the quotation properly. I would like that also Leena has time to give comments as well.

John, if customer wants to know our opinion on price, you can tell that via phone, but quotation can't be send before noon, that is clear.

Best Regards,
Oskari Lastname

The genre here is a BELF email depicting interaction between colleagues in the backstage. The other genre is the Detail Engineering quotation to be ultimately sent to a customer. In the email, characterised as urgent, Oskari provides his 'basic comments' on the quotation document with requested edits listed in a numerical order under each corresponding point. By doing so, Oskari enacts his expertise and professional role as superior with the three recipients as his subordinates. Thus, Oskari's requests, although direct imperatives (*Fix the headline* and *Add also here that work is conducted at [our company] office*) can be viewed as illustrating the routine nature of the situation for both parties. Oskari's job is team management by making requests, while his team's job is to draft the quotation, revise it according to Oskari's requests, and in the pressing situation to do it quickly. Still, Oskari's first language and culture being Finnish may also contribute to his directness (e.g., Kankaanranta, 2005; Stopniece, 2019). The quotation, a high-stake document, reflects corporate image and calls for a comprehensive understanding of contracts, knowledge of legal and contract terminology and overall business knowledge. The quotation genre is not pure backstage BELF used among colleagues, nor is it meant for the frontstage public-at-large. Rather, as quotations are format-bound, critical for business and customer relations, which Oskari's email highlights, we classified the genre as mixed.

Although Oskari was in charge of the content and the language of various written genres as exemplified above, the company communications policy had established guidelines for communications in Service MNC which defined responsibilities in external communication and speaking to the media. Example 4, an interview extract, showcases the use of the company presentation genre (see also Räisänen and Kankaanranta, 2020). The PowerPoint presentation was compiled by the Head Office's Communications Department which is responsible for producing frontstage genres, that is, official texts and documentation, including media releases and annual reports for various stakeholders including the general public, as well as company templates for various documentation purposes. Oskari explains the company guidelines below (interview in 2018).

Example 4:

> We have company guidelines for communications, which defines templates, and even fonts that we should use.

The company PowerPoint presentation was one of the templates produced by the Communications Department and applicable for employees in their individual presentations. In the three customer meetings observed during fieldwork, Oskari used the presentation template with basic information about the company but in each of the meetings the content of the spoken presentation and thus use of the PowerPoint varied. Each presentation was tailored for the specific customer to account for their business involvement and interests regarding Service MNC. As observed by the first author, and later verified by Oskari, his engagement with the presentation genre was that of using it as the basis in accordance with communications policy, but depending on the business at hand, its application in customer meetings was always a strategic decision by Oskari.

DISCUSSION AND CONCLUSION

This chapter showcased an individual manager's engagement with written workplace genres in a multilingual organisation with English as corporate language (ECL) by using an ethnographic approach and data. Applying genre analysis and drawing on the notion of ECL, we identified some written genres in the ECL continuum with which the professional engaged with to do his management work in the organisational context.

The findings show how ECL and the genres used tend to correlate: BELF emerges in email genres in the backstage and as mixed genres in quotation and non-disclosure documents in the in-between stage, in which an SE template is modified and revised according to the situation. Moreover, the findings reveal how the manager engages with multiple genres simultaneously: in writing the email (backstage) the manager comments on a document to be sent to a customer (in-between stage) and manages his subordinates in their work. These findings thus concretely show what it means to view language as a social practice in the inherently multilingual reality of an MNC. Interestingly, some of the textual data could be characterised as SE when only the textual product and its linguistic form were investigated. However, as soon as we dive deep into the inherently multilingual backstage situation in its organisational context, in which the product is embedded and produced, do we see that actually the emerging language is backstage BELF. As the 'B' in BELF suggests, business is primary and grammar secondary in such interactions (see e.g., Louhiala-Salminen et al., 2005), but it does not prevent BELF from manifesting as grammatically flawless.

Our dynamic view of genre allows us to identify how a professional's voice shifts in accordance with the genre in question and the work practices involved in doing so. The manager engages with genres to do his work from a specific professional role, juggling between different genres and ECLs and acting as a mediator – even a gatekeeper (see e.g., Angouri, 2014) – between subordinates and customers. The Operations Manager's professional tasks, including assistance and guidance of his subordinates and securing a deal following organisational practices, become visible in his multifaceted engagement with a specific genre; simultaneously, he manages his team, conforms to legal obligations and advances the business of the company. Hence, the manager must develop generic competences: recognising, understanding and using specific genres appropriately to complete specific tasks.

Our ethnographic focus on everyday practices enabled us to make visible both the individual professional's tasks and the organisational, management and business practices that emerge in the individual's tasks. Indeed, the participant's reflections and understanding of his role as observing 'the big picture' can be seen in the authentic texts in which he comments on his subordinates' work and thus leads them towards company goals. This is how our ethnographic and situated approach allowed us to capture the relationship between local and global dynamics as called for by, for example, Angouri and Piekkari (2018), Gaibrois (2018), and Lecomte et al. (2018). To put it in linguistic terms: to capture the complexity of professional discourse and the engagement of professionals with genres, methodologies such as ethnography are needed for an integration of text-internal and text-external factors such as professional roles and responsibilities and organisational hierarchies (Bhatia, 2008, 171).

This research has various practical implications. First, for individual professionals, active self-reflection on one's work practices involving language and genre use would make life-long learning more concrete and meaningful (e.g., Manuti et al., 2015). Individual employees would benefit from training in situation-specific language and genre use. For instance, as we have argued previously, engagement with mixed genres may require participants' comprehensive understanding of legal agreements and overall business knowledge to identify what is relevant and what is not (see Räisänen, 2018). Implications could also involve gaining insight about how business is carried out in different genres, how genres are embedded in business trajectories and how they change. With our dynamic view of genre in the ECL continuum we can identify practices involved in writing in multilingual contexts with recipients of different linguacultural backgrounds.

Second, implications for business education could involve incorporating individual perspectives and holistic approaches to business practices, for example, by being introduced to and working with authentic business genres while solving a business case. Students should learn how to engage with genres in different roles (e.g., as manager, customer, superior, team member), and what it means that genres do things such as managing interpersonal relationships and transmitting organisational strategies.

Third, our findings have implications for international management research in revealing how organisations are written into being in English as corporate language. Language and language use in multilingual organisations should be studied holistically as closely intertwined and situated within its context and as socially co-constructed by all its users, not only as corporate or management-level decisions, practices and processes. As Karhunen et al. (2018) argue, viewing language as a social practice emphasises the role of individuals and their interactions in the everyday process of forming an MNC. Such a dynamic social constellation should be investigated on the grassroots level, employing ethnographic approaches, which this study on a manager's written genre use demonstrates. Avenues for further research could therefore include ethnographic projects that study the whole organisation and with focus groups from different departments. Studies could follow trajectories of business practices and how they are manifested as different genres engaged by individuals, teams, departments and the entire organisation.

REFERENCES

AlAfnan, M. A. (2017), 'Critical perspective to genre analysis: Intertextuality and interdiscursivity in electronic mail communication', *Advances in Journalism and Communication*, **5** (1), 23–49.

Andersen, H. and E. S. Rasmussen (2004), 'The role of language skills in corporate communication', *Corporate Communications: An International Journal*, **17**, 255–271.

Angouri, J. (2014), 'Multilingualism in the workplace: Language practices in multilingual contexts', *Multilingua*, **33** (1–2), 1–9.

Angouri, J. and M. Marra (2010), 'Corporate meetings as genre: A study of the role of the chair in corporate meeting talk', *Text & Talk*, **30** (6), 615–636.

Angouri, J. and R. Piekkari (2018), 'Organising multilingually: Setting an agenda for studying language at work', *European Journal of International Management*, **12** (1–2), 8–27.

Bhatia, V. K. (1993), *Analyzing Genre: Language Use in Professional Settings*, London: Longman.

Bhatia, V. K. (2008), 'Genre analysis, ESP and professional practice', *English for Specific Purposes*, **27** (2), 161–174.

Blommaert, J. and J. Dong (2020), *Ethnographic Fieldwork*, 2nd edition, Bristol: Multilingual Matters.

Cogo, A. (2016), '"They all take the risk and make the effort": Intercultural accommodation and multilingualism in a BELF community of practice', in Lopriore, L. and Grazzi, E. (eds), *Intercultural Communication: New Perspectives from ELF*, Rome: Roma Tre Press, pp. 364–383.

Cornelissen, J. (2017), *Corporate Communication: A Guide to Theory and Practice*, 5th edition, London: Sage.

Ehrenreich, S. (2016), 'English as a lingua franca (ELF) in international business contexts: Key issues and future perspectives', in Murata, K. (ed.), *Exploring ELF in Japanese Academic and Business Contexts: Conceptualization, Research and Pedagogic Implications*, London and New York: Routledge, pp. 135–155.

Flowerdew, J. and A. Wan (2010), 'The linguistic and the contextual in applied genre analysis: The case of the company audit report', *English for Specific Purposes*, **29** (2), 78–93.

Fredriksson, R., W. Barner-Rasmussen and R. Piekkari (2006), 'The multinational corporation as a multilingual organization: The notion of a common corporate language', *Corporate Communications: An International Journal*, **11** (4), 406–423.

Gaibrois, C. (2018), '"It crosses all the boundaries": Hybrid language use as empowering resource', *European Journal of International Management*, **12** (1/2), 82–110.

Goffman, E. (1959), *The Presentation of Self in Everyday Life*, New York: Doubleday.

Harzing, A.-W., K. Köster and U. Magner (2011), 'Babel in business: The language barrier and its solutions in the HQ–subsidiary relationship', *Journal of World Business*, **46** (3), 279–287.

Hatch, M. J. and M. Schultz (1997), 'Relations between organizational culture, identity and image', *European Journal of Marketing*, **31** (5/6), 356–365.

Hinds, P. J., T. B. Neeley and C. D. Cramton (2014), 'Language as a lightning rod: Power contests, emotion regulation, and subgroup dynamics in global teams', *Journal of International Business Studies*, **45** (5), 536–561.

Janssens, M. and C. Steyaert (2014), 'Re-considering language within a cosmopolitan understanding: Toward a multilingual franca approach in international business studies', *Journal of International Business Studies*, **45** (5), 623–639.

Jenkins, J. (2015), 'Repositioning English and multilingualism in English as a Lingua Franca', *Englishes in Practice*, **2** (3), 49–85.

Kankaanranta, A. (2005), '"*Hej Seppo, could you pls comment on this!*": Internal email communication in lingua franca English in a multinational company', University of Jyväskylä, Centre for Applied Language Studies. http://urn.fi/URN:ISBN:951-39 -2320-7

Kankaanranta, A. and L. Louhiala-Salminen (2018), 'ELF in the domain of business -BELF: What does the B stand for?', in Jenkins, J., Baker, W. and Dewey, M. (eds), *The Routledge Handbook of English as a Lingua Franca*, Abingdon: Routledge, pp. 309–320.

Kankaanranta, A., P. Karhunen and L. Louhiala-Salminen (2018), '"English as corpo-rate language" in the multilingual reality of multinational companies', *Multilingua*, **37** (4), 331–351.

Karhunen, P., A. Kankaanranta, L. Louhiala-Salminen and R. Piekkari (2018), 'Let's talk about language: A review of language-sensitive research in international man-agement', *Journal of Management Studies*, **55** (6), 980–1013.

Kassis-Henderson, J. (2005), 'Language diversity in international management teams', *International Studies of Management and Organization*, **35** (1), 66–82.

Komori-Glatz, M. (2018), 'Conceptualising English as a business lingua franca', *European Journal of International Management*, **12** (1/2), 46–61.

Koskinen, K. (2020), 'Translatorial linguistic ethnography in organizations', in Horn, S., Lecomte, P. and Tietze, S. (eds), *Managing Multilingual Workplaces: Methodological, Empirical and Pedagogic Perspectives*, New York: Routledge, pp. 60–78.

Langinier, H. and S. Ehrhart (2020), 'When local meets global: How introducing English destabilizes translanguaging practices in a cross-border organization', *Management International / International Management / Gestiòn Internacional*, **24** (2), 79–92. https://doi.org/10.7202/1072643ar

Lauring, J. and A. Klitmøller (2015), 'Corporate language-based communication avoidance in MNCs: A multi-sited ethnography approach', *Journal of World Business*, **50** (1), 46–55.

Lecomte, P., H. Tenzer and L. E. Zhang (2018), 'Introduction of thematic issue: Working across language boundaries: New perspectives on language-sensitive inter-national management research', *European Journal of International Management*, **12** (1/2), 1–7.

Lehtinen, E. and P. Pälli (2011), 'Conversational use of genres in managerial meetings', *Scandinavian Journal of Management*, **27** (3), 287–296.

Logemann, M. and R. Piekkari (2015), 'Localize or local lies? The power of lan-guage and translation in the multinational corporation', *Critical Perspectives on International Business*, **11** (1), 30–53.

Louhiala-Salminen, L. (1997), 'Investigating the genre of a business fax: A Finnish case study', *The Journal of Business Communication*, **34** (3), 316–333.

Louhiala-Salminen, L. (1999), '"Was there life before them?": Fax and e-mail in business communication', *Journal of Language for International Business*, **10** (1), 24–42.

Louhiala-Salminen, L. (2002), 'The fly's perspective: Discourse in the daily routine of a business manager', *English for Specific Purposes*, **21** (3), 211–231.

Louhiala-Salminen, L., M. Charles and A. Kankaanranta (2005), 'English as a lingua franca in Nordic corporate mergers: Two case companies', *English for Specific Purposes*, **24** (4), 401–421.

Luo, Y. and O. Shenkar (2006), 'The multinational corporation as a multilingual community: Language and organization in a global context', *Journal of International Business Studies*, **37**, 321–339.

Manuti, A., S. Pastore, A. F. Scardigno, M. L. Giancaspro and D. Morciano (2015), 'Formal and informal learning in the workplace: A research review', *International Journal of Training and Development*, **19** (1), 1–17.

Miller, C. R. (1984), 'Genre as social action', *Quarterly Journal of Speech*, **70** (2), 151–167.

Millot, P. (2017), 'Inclusivity and exclusivity in English as a Business Lingua Franca: The expression of a professional voice in email communication', *English for Specific Purposes*, **46**, 59–71.

Neeley, T. B. (2013), 'Language matters: Status loss and achieved status distinctions in global organizations', *Organization Science*, **24** (2), 476–497.

Nickerson, C. (2000), *Playing the Corporate Language Game: An Investigation of the Genres and Discourse Strategies in English used by Dutch Writers Working in Multinational Corporations*, Utrecht studies in language and communication. Amsterdam: Rodopi.

Park, S., J. Jeon and E. Shim (2021), 'Exploring request emails in English for business purposes: A move analysis', *English for Specific Purposes*, **63**, 137–150.

Piekkari, R., D. Welch and L. S. Welch (2014), *Language in International Business: The Multilingual Reality of Global Business Expansion*, Cheltenham, UK and Northampton, MA, USA: Edward Elgar Publishing.

Pullin, P. (2013), 'Achieving "comity": The role of linguistic stance in business English as a lingua franca (BELF) meeting', *Journal of English as a Lingua Franca*, **2** (1), 1–23.

Räisänen, T. (2018), 'Translingual practices in global business: A longitudinal study of a professional communicative repertoire', in Mazzaferro, G. (ed.), *Translanguaging as Everyday Practice*, Cham: Springer, pp. 149–174.

Räisänen, T. and A. Kankaanranta (2020), 'The use of English as corporate language in global knowledge work over a 15-year business career', *European Journal of International Management*, https://doi.org/10.1504/EJIM.2020.10028833.

Roshid, M. M., S. Webb and R. Chowdhury (2018), 'English as a business lingua franca: A discursive analysis of business e-mails', *International Journal of Business Communication*, https://doi.org/10.1177%2F2329488418808040

Stopniece, S. (2019), 'Language as a site of search for common ground and power positioning in Chinese–Finnish negotiation', *Journal of Intercultural Communication*, **49**, https://www.immi.se/intercultural/nr49/stopniece.html

Suddaby, R. (ed.) (2010), 'Editor's comments: Construct clarity in theories of management and organization', *Academy of Management Review*, **35**, 346–357.

Swales, J. M. (1990), *Genre Analysis: English for Academic and Research Settings*, Cambridge: Cambridge University Press.

Tietze, S. (2018), 'Multilingual research, monolingual publications: Management scholarship in English only?', *European Journal of International Management*, **12**, (1/2), 28–45.

Tietze, S. and R. Piekkari (2020), 'Languages and cross-cultural management', in Szkudlarek, B., Romani, L., Osland, J. and Caprar, D. (eds), *The Sage Handbook of Contemporary Cross-Cultural Management*, London: Sage, pp. 181–195.

Yates, J. and W. J. Orlikowski (1992), 'Genres of organizational communication: A structurational approach to studying communication and media', *Academy of Management Review*, **17** (2), 299–326.

7. Revisiting ethnography and reflexivity for language-sensitive workplace research

Kristina Humonen and Jo Angouri

INTRODUCTION

Research focusing on language issues has been burgeoning in the past two decades in the fields of international business (IB) and organisation studies (Tenzer et al., 2017; Karhunen et al., 2018). The recent evolvement of language-sensitive management research (Lecomte et al., 2018) can be seen in the introduction of new methodological approaches such as translatorial linguistic ethnography (Koskinen, 2020) and experimental research (Fan and Harzing, 2020). Despite an increasing number of studies adapting the linguistic lens, current scholarship acknowledges the opportunity for closer connections with cognate fields and disciplines, particularly workplace sociolinguistics (Angouri and Piekkari, 2018) where this chapter is situated.

We focus on the concept of reflexivity in analysing language data and suggest that engagement with the notion can be more holistic and consequential in language-sensitive studies. Reflexivity often takes the form of a short acknowledgement of a researcher's biographical information (such as gender, age, ethnicity, language profile, etc.); however, the exact *implications* of the researcher's positionality for the analysis of data typically remains untold (see also Piekkari and Tietze, 2016). We suggest that (epistemic) reflexivity could make a positive contribution to language-sensitive research by making explicit the relationship between knowledge claims and acquired positions in academic fields. Thus, this chapter forwards the ideas that (1) reflexivity is not merely limited to methodology and should be treated as part of epistemological considerations throughout the research process, (2) reflexivity can enhance the criticality of a researcher's knowledge claims and disciplinary assumptions, and (3) that a reflexive approach provides access to multiple possible readings of data, particularly in the area of language, and language use in workplace settings.

There is an expansive body of literature in the philosophy of science focusing on the notions of knowledge and truth (Audi, 2011). However, addressing the myriad of existing philosophical debates goes beyond the scope of this chapter. Instead, our interests lie in reflecting on the multiple ways in which language data are interpreted and presented. As will be demonstrated through our own reflexive account, language data are inherently connected to meaning systems and social structures that are available to both participants and researchers. A critical examination of *multiple realities* can potentially lead to a more in-depth and multi-layered analysis. As well-noted by Alvesson and Sköldberg (2018), good research is 'pluralistic and democratic', and receptive to diverse viewpoints. In this respect, workplace sociolinguists, in particular, have argued that different datasets and methodologies provide access to different layers of meaning in professional contexts. This is the position we adopt (see also Angouri, 2018).

Studies drawing on the ethnographic tradition are still relatively rare in language-sensitive research (Karhunen et al., 2018). Our multi-sited ethnographic study contributes to the limited body of existing work. Focusing on a Finnish multinational food services corporation it examines multiple organisational levels. However, noting the heavy scholarly focus on senior-level employees (Westney and Van Maanen, 2011), in this chapter we draw specifically on the voices of floor-level staff; namely, a duty manager and a restaurant manager. Our accounts from two different contexts seek to illustrate how reflexivity can enable the researcher to: (1) capture multiple readings of the data, and (2) unpack the influence of field relations on the research process. These positions are not new in research methodology discussions. We believe, however, that deeper engagement can provide an opportunity for theoretical advancement and interdisciplinary research in this line of enquiry.

The remaining chapter is organised in five sections. Next, we will briefly describe how we understand ethnographic inquiry in organisational settings. We then turn to philosophical considerations by exploring the relationship between reflexive practice and the production of knowledge. Following this, we illustrate the arguments put forward by revisiting two datasets. Finally, we conclude the chapter with a critical discussion and directions for further research.

ETHNOGRAPHY: FROM A METHOD TO EPISTEMOLOGY

There is a widespread perception of ethnography as a method for collecting certain types of data. This view is narrow and can lead to inaccurate interpretations. We follow a holistic conceptualisation of ethnography, as suggested by Bate (1997), encompassing: a method (a way of 'doing' fieldwork), a way of writing, and a paradigm (intellectual thinking and contextual awareness). In considering what counts as 'real' ethnography, Agar (2006) extends the discussion by conceptualising ethnography as an epistemological approach in its own right. He summarises ethnographic logic and its connection to the theory of knowledge as follows:

> It is first of all abductive logic, taking surprises seriously and creating new explanations for them. It is also iterative, something that is applied over and over again in the course of a piece of work. And it is recursive, calling on itself to solve a problem that comes up even as it is solving a problem. (Agar, 2006, 14)

While traditional *deductive logic* derives conclusions from old premises and *inductive logic* centres on fitting material to existing concepts, Agar's *abductive* logic entails new understanding of the data and learning from our experiences, as opposed to researchers being 'creatures of habit and seekers of certainty' (Agar, 2006, 11). Ethnographic logic, then, can be characterised as being procedural and pointing to a way of coming to know about meanings. From this perspective, ethnographic analysis is always influenced by the ethnographer's *own point of view* as 'we keep looking for evidence that what we think is going on in fact is not' (Agar, 2006, 17), thus we cannot draw any definite conclusions of a single possible reading.

Yet, developing 'objective' knowledge is often positioned as the aim of organisational ethnography (Fine and Shulman, 2009). This is in line with ideals of 'good' research which are still influenced by positivism and ensuing expectations of generalisability, validation and replication (e.g., Bonache, 2020). Such an approach to ethnographic inquiry is not without problems. As Fine and Shulman (2009) note, the idealised expectations of the ethnographer may result in 'lies from the field' and 'partial truths' (Fine, 1993). Also, Piekkari and Tietze (2016) make the critical remark that even though positivist criteria are inappropriate for context-sensitive inquiries, such idealised markers of 'quality' dominate management research.

Ethnographic work in linguistics, on the other hand, has traditionally acknowledged that researchers' subjectivities play a crucial role throughout the research process and urges fieldworkers to be open to complexities, contradictions and reinterpretations (Patiño-Santos, 2020). In applied and sociolinguistic research, ethnography has led to theoretical and methodological developments which have influenced general thinking in the field (e.g., linguistic ethnography – Rampton, 2007; Copland and Creese, 2015; Tusting, 2020; critical ethnography of language – Heller, 2011). More relevant to the approach we are taking is the Interactional Sociolinguistics (IS) tradition which draws on the work by John Gumperz. An IS approach allows for an analysis that combines situated interactions with the wider sociocultural context. Language is viewed as being constitutive of and constituting sociocultural practices. IS's explanatory value is based on looking at how un/conscious (sociocultural) expectations and discourses create meanings in workplace interaction (e.g., Holmes and Stubbe, 2015; Angouri, 2018; Canagarajah, 2020). The relevance with ethnography and the ideal of accessing 'the insider's views' is evident here.

More specifically, ethnographic research often promotes the ideal of reaching an emic status. Dwyer and Buckle (2009, 60), however, argue against the traditional dichotomy between insider and outsider status because 'it is restrictive to lock into a notion that emphasizes either/or, one or the other, you are in or you are out'. Instead, a dialectical approach that 'allows the preservation of the complexity of similarities and differences' (Dwyer and Buckle, 2009, 60) is a more appropriate way of addressing the researcher's position in the field. In a similar vein, Cunliffe and Karunanayake (2013) propose using the notion of hyphen-spaces that emphasises the fluidity of ethnographic research and agentic nature of relationships during the fieldwork. The authors suggest four hyphen-spaces to describe overlapping boundaries: insiderness–outsiderness, sameness–difference, engagement–distance, and political activism–active neutrality. The mapping of these hyphen spaces is illustrated in Figure 7.1.

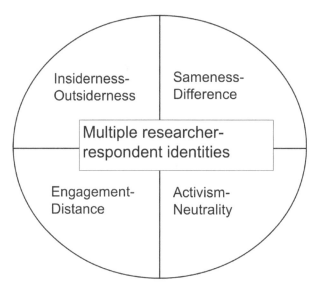

Figure 7.1   Multiple researcher–respondent identities

We agree with researchers arguing that the presupposed linearity in terminology (in/outsider or emic/etic) reduces the complexity of the fieldwork experience and the multi-level relationship between the researcher and the participants (see Sarangi, 2007, for research paradoxes in workplace discourse studies; Angouri, 2018, for a review on workplace; and Litosseliti, 2018, for a broader methodological discussion in linguistics). We will illustrate in our examples that the boundaries between those are porous and influence the inferences available to the researcher.

REFLEXIVITY: AN INDIVIDUAL AND COLLECTIVE CONSTRUCTION OF KNOWLEDGE

The 'reflexive turn' in social sciences (Mauthner and Doucet, 2003) forwards the demystification of knowledge construction processes. Alvesson and Sköldberg (2018, 11) define reflexive research simply as having 'two basic characteristics: careful interpretation and reflection'. In order to understand the important relationship between 'knowledge' and 'the ways of doing knowledge' means attending to:

> The way different kinds of linguistic, social, political and theoretical elements are woven together in the process of knowledge development, during which empirical material is constructed, interpreted and written. (Alvesson and Sköldberg, 2018, 10–11)

Most existing publications in management studies appear to place emphasis on what Johnson and Duberley (2000) term, *methodological reflexivity*. Such reflexivity addresses the researcher's (various) role(s) in the data collection process. Another popular and interrelated form is *autobiographical reflection* (Coffey, 2002) in which a researcher provides a (critical) self-narrative with the intent that the audience will get an idea of 'where you're coming from' (see Maton, 2003, for a review of different forms of reflexivity). As autobiographical approaches may shift the attention away from the researched subject, some scholars have criticised it for resulting in 'reflexive narcissism' (Bourdieu and Wacquant, 1992) and 'hermeneutic narcissism' (Maton, 2003). Bourdieu (1988; 1990), for example, sees no need for private revelations, and, instead, proposes the distinctive conception of *epistemic reflexivity*.

In epistemic reflexivity the analysis focuses on a researcher's social dispositions within existing structures. Bourdieu (1990; Bourdieu and Wacquant, 1992) suggests three main components for more rigorous reflexive analysis by identifying: (1) a researcher's trajectory in the social field(s); (2) a researcher's positioning in the 'academic field'; and finally, (3) 'intellectual biases' that are shaped by the 'sense of the (academic) game'. For example, the specific disciplinary vocabulary and mindset as well as competition for material resources (including financing of the research practice itself) influence the whole research process. Critical awareness of this, according to Bourdieu, helps to 'avoid being the toy of social forces in your practice' (Bourdieu and Wacquant, 1992, 183). In other words, Bourdieu's primary focus is not on the individual analyst, rather, the 'collective enterprise' (Bourdieu and Wacquant, 1992, 36).

While Bourdieu provides an appealing approach for reflexive analysis, it is worth noting that no epistemological stance is without its limitations. Bourdieu's conceptualisation leans towards critical realist claims in suggesting that a researcher can objectify their own biases, that is, the 'knower' having the ability to 'know' how structures and agency are connected. We refrain from making assumptions of objectivity or discussing the nebulous concept of truth here. Instead, we follow the social constructionist paradigm and understand the notion of 'reality' as being subjectively constructed (Berger and Luckmann, 1966). The appeal of the constructionist paradigm for language-sensitive scholars and workplace sociolinguists is not surprising as language provides a way to see the world, multiple selves, and different concepts.

Following the preceding discussion, we adopt the stance that there is no one way of doing ethnography or reflexivity. We see social-structural forces and individual agency as inseparable, and therefore propose that a more holistic approach to reflexivity is needed to address multifactorial issues affecting the reading of data, and, subsequently, the production of knowledge. We next illustrate our attempt to operationalise reflexivity and show how we associate it with multiple possible readings available to the researcher.

FIELD SITE

The dataset we are drawing on is from the first author's (KH) ethnographic PhD research concentrating on a Nordic multinational food and catering corporation, pseudonymised as D&C Services. The researcher's journey in the field and formed relationships with different participants have a significant impact on the reading of the data, as will be discussed below. First, we will focus briefly on the content of the data in order to elaborate on our critical reflections.

Example 1: Language Policies and the 'Naturalness' of Data

We focus on one D&C Services employee, 'Kevin', who is the Duty Manager for dozens of restaurants and cafes. The analysis of our data indicates a complex linguistic profile for Kevin. Specifically, he considers himself to have two 'first'[1] languages; his indigenous language and English. His superiors, in line with D&Cs language guidelines, have requested that he only uses Finnish at work. This language requirement and the linguistic market, however, do not match; namely, English is a necessity in Kevin's role because it is the official language of many of D&C Services' corporate clients and suppliers. Furthermore, many lower-level kitchen positions are filled with English-speaking migrant staff. For these reasons, Kevin uses both English and Finnish on a daily basis.

The overall data from this site consists of ethnographic observations (45 hours and 20 minutes), interviews and audio-recorded workplace interactions. The excerpt below is collected by employing the shadowing technique (McDonald, 2005) in which the researcher carried the recording device.

In what follows, we will provide three different readings of the same interaction. The first one focuses on the relationship between (in)formal language use and (alleged flattened) organisational hierarchies. The second interpretation takes a social justice approach and addresses linguistic Othering[2] processes. Finally, we will place the interaction within its wider context and discuss the performative aspects of the participant's professional role enactment. With this we show how our reading of the data changes depending on different positions in the field, our own interest, time and access to multiple data sources.

Excerpt 1: Multiple Readings and Co-construction of Data

Context: On his way to the office Kevin stops by one of the coffee shops to speak to a new employee 'Elli' and more experienced 'Minttu'. As Kevin enters the cafe and walks towards the till, where the two Finnish employees are standing, Minttu starts the interaction with:

Excerpt 1:

		Spoken data	English translation of Finnish utterances
1	Min:	oi! good to see you ma:n	
2	Kev:	kaikki hyvin?	*everything's good?*
3	Min:	everything's perfect gotta love	
4		this girl <laughs>	
5		I know she knows (.) I can trust her	
6	Kev:	joo alright okay	*yeah*
		((in lines 7–15 Kevin starts speaking to Elli in Finnish until Minttu's interruption:))	
16	Min:	can I (.) can I ask one thing?	
17	Kev:	joo absolutely	*yeah*
18	Min:	this morning this machine has given	
19		wrong amount of water so it's it's	
20		kinda okay I can measure it but um	
21	Kev:	is it hot water?	
		((Kevin's phone rings and he answers it))	
		((In lines 22–35 the researcher introduces herself to Minttu and Elli, and asks:))	
36	RES:	mietin et miksi sä puhut hänelle	*I was wondering why do you [=Elli] speak to*
37		suomeksi ja sä taas englanniksi?	*him in Finnish and you [=Minttu] in English?*
38	Min:	sen takii et raha ja *machine* asiat	*because money and machine things*
39		um ku niis ollaa puhuttu englantii	*um with those we've used English*
		((Kevin finishes the phone call and joins the conversation))	
40		hän kysyy että miksi puhumme	*she is asking why we are speaking in*
41		englantia? kun täällä vaan puhutaan	*English? because we just do [use English] in here*
42	Kev:	<u>sun</u> kanssa joo	*with <u>you</u> yes*
43	Min:	[ja raportit ne on <u>tosi</u>	*and the reports they're <u>very</u>*
44		tärkeät	*important*
44	Kev:	joo niissä pitää saada viesti	*yes with those you need to*
45		eteenpäin	*get the message across*
		((all three continue speaking in Finnish to fix the problem with the coffee machine))	

First reading (in/formal language use and power distance): At the surface level Minttu's informal greeting style suggests familiarity with Kevin. Expressions like '*oi*' and '*man*' (line 1), and relaxed pronunciations '*gotta*' and '*kinda*' (lines 3 and 20) are markedly informal. Traditionally such language use in sociolinguistics could be considered as a sign of flattened power hierarchies in the workplace (e.g., Holmes and Stubbe, 2015). In contrast to the speech style in English, Minttu and Elli are using more formal language in Finnish. For example, in lines 38 and 39 Minttu speaks in a colloquial manner to the researcher but as Kevin joins the conversation in line 40, she accommodates her speech style by slowing down the pace and starts using more formal language. Specifically, if we look at Minttu's conjunctions in lines 38 and 39, she is using shorter forms; 'et' rather than 'että' (= that) and 'ku' instead of 'kun' (=when/as) whereas with Kevin (lines 40–41) she spells the full words. From an analytical point of view, the more formal use of Finnish need not be viewed as a manifestation of increased manager–subordinate power distance but rather that perhaps Minttu's (and other employees') use of formal English is limited. Namely, in our overall dataset it was not uncommon for younger Finnish employees to draw on popular English expressions like '*what's up?*', '*cool*', and '*see ya*'. As such, making connections between in/formal language use and employees' relationships require time and immersion in the field to understand various meanings behind language use.

Second reading (linguistic Othering): Minttu keeps addressing Kevin in English and ignores his attempts at using Finnish, despite him responding in the local language (line 2) and continuing using the same language with Elli. By doing so, Minttu appears to assume that Kevin cannot comprehend the Finnish language well enough, which is indexed in the ways she labels 'money', 'machines' and 'reports' as '*very*' important facets (lines 38 and 43), implying that English is the more appropriate medium in such matters. Furthermore, overlaps and interruptions are normally seen to signify power imbalance between the speakers. On this point, Minttu interrupts Kevin (lines 16 and 43) and does not allow him to answer the researcher's question which she instead answers herself (line 41). In addition, her over-emphasised slow pace in Finnish can be regarded as (in)directly categorising Kevin as being different to the other colleagues on the grounds of his *perceived* language proficiency and/or country of origin. So, language practice in this context can be understood as contributing to the processes of Othering, particularly if comparing Minttu's interactions with other (Finnish) managers in which she appears to be more deferential. Whereas this reading may provide one 'truth' from a social justice lens, a closer examination of relational and contextual factors is critical for discovering more 'hidden' readings, as will be unpacked below.

Third reading (role performance): the final analytical layer became available to us when Minttu elaborated in a follow-up interview of being slightly surprised with Kevin's language choice because according to her 'they', that is, staff, always spoke to him in English. We knew that Kevin's role comes with a requirement set by his superiors of him addressing subordinates in Finnish. If we focus our analysis on Kevin's (inter)actions and role enactment, it could be that Minttu's informality and assertiveness was perceived by Kevin as face-threatening in the presence of the researcher. In order to portray his understanding of the 'correct' performance of a duty manager, in line with his superior's expectations, he states that he uses English only with Minttu (line 42). However, our total dataset from this context does not support this claim; specifically, the observations and later recordings suggest that Kevin tends to use Finnish with older Finnish employees and equal colleagues, whereas with younger staff and migrant workers he prefers English.

To close this short discussion, we have shown that a single encounter can be read in multiple ways depending on the researcher's (subjective) interests, framing and positioning. The discussion is, evidently, an oversimplification as any good piece of research would involve iterative readings. However, it is also common to focus on one reading and get in 'tunnel vision' mode. Although this is necessary for in-depth analysis and for moving from description to abstraction, it risks missing the multiple layers of meaning.

We next turn to a different example that addresses the relationship between a researcher's emotional disposition in the field and the possible implications this may have on the analysis.

Example 2: A Researcher's Emotions in Knowledge Construction

When undertaking fieldwork, researchers always carry certain dispositions based on their personal experiences and acquired (academic) knowledge. Discrepancies between a researcher's belief systems and observed practices can pose serious challenges to the 'idealised' researcher identity and raise value conflicts. Tensions and emotional work, thus, are inherent during ethnographic fieldwork (Kleinman and Copp, 1993) and sometimes ethnographers' relations with participants are only 'provisionally friendly' (Fine and Shulman, 2009). Despite the potential impact of the research process on the analysis, there is relatively little discussion covering these areas (Fine and Shulman, 2009; Cunliffe and Karunanayake, 2013).

The following account draws on the data collected from one restaurant, 'Tasty Plate', in which KH spent six working days. We attempt to capture the fieldworker's voice and draw on fieldnotes (translated from Finnish to English), an email exchange between the authors and audio-recorded data. This section has two primary goals: first, it discusses the significance of a researcher's positioning in the field site and shows what a 'less flattering but more realistic' (Fine and Shulman, 2009) account may entail; second, we will address how single datasets are confined by participant viewpoints. We align with the view that a deeper exploration of sensitive areas of research and analysis can be acquired only through multiple datasets and reflexive practice.

The researcher's lived experiences

> (Name) knew I was going next to ('Tasty Plate') ... apparently (she) quit her job at ('Tasty Plate') because of the manager: reputation more important than employees' wellbeing. (Name) said I can make my own judgement whilst there. (KH's field-notes, January 2018)

The excerpt above illustrates information that was made available prior to KH entering a new research site, Tasty Plate. Unavoidably, this comment raises particular readings relevant to the behaviour of the 'manager' which will have an impact on the researcher's engagement with the field. These impressions can be further accentuated or changed depending on the interpersonal relationships between the fieldworker and research participants. Being cautious of the 'warning', KH called Tasty Plate's manager 'Maria' prior to the fieldwork to confirm whether the agreed time for the data collection was still convenient for her and Tasty Plate's team. The manager agreed and expressed a welcoming attitude towards the researcher. During the phone call she also emphasised the importance of a 'relaxed and open work culture' (fieldnotes), which reconstructed the researcher's frame of refence about the manager. Admittedly, this helped KH to enter the field with a more 'relieved' mindset.

The field observations, however, started presenting a more complex picture; specifically, tensions and power hierarchies between the employees became quickly noticeable, as exemplified in the email exchange below between the two authors.

> Hi Jo,
>
> Hope all is good!
>
> I'm facing the most awkward kitchen environment. Don't think I'll get any interactional data but will start interviewing people tomorrow – unless the employees are not too terrified of their managers.
>
> To put it mildly, they have rather interesting ways of managing the restaurants. Today one of them [=managers] made a joke how [NAME of a political leader often used as a metonym to autocratic practices] controlled people with fear and violence: 'that's what it takes to manage these people'.
>
> (Email exchange between the authors, January 2018)

The email above summarises a brief conversation that followed an interaction with one of the Duty Managers. KH's feeling of being in an 'awkward' environment points to both the visible critical incident, which is significant in ethnographic research, and a mismatch between a researcher's understanding of a supportive work community and observed workplace practices. The need to discuss with the thesis supervisor (second author) shows an ongoing conflict and multiple levels of 'self' in the field. For example, the assertation that employees must be controlled with 'fear and violence', and reference to a political leader associated with authoritarian practices, goes against the researcher's understanding of 'good' management practice.

Ensuing experience in the field site and ongoing interviews reinforced the perception of tense management–subordinate relationships. For example, the restaurant manager did not let the employees participate in the interviews during working hours and positioned the interviews as a trade-off between KH's participant observer role and full-time employees' taking time to talk to the researcher.[3] This was evident from the first interview (three days after entering the field) which was interrupted by Maria addressing the interviewee:

Excerpt 2:

Maria:	you're getting paid to do real work ((walks off))
Res:	okay (.) um
Interviewee:	((whispers to the researcher:)) this is the fucking shit we have to deal with(.) I'm
	sorry to disappoint you but I better go. (Recorded interview data)

Considering that the interview took place during the employee's own lunch time, the manager's interference was interpreted by the researcher as a threat which challenged her perceptions of mutual respect that had been, up to that point, assumed to be in place. Following this incident, other employees had heard about the interrupted interview and apologised for the manager's behaviour and offered to help with the research. Although this was read as a display of support and could be indicative of 'normalised' behaviour in that context, it was not the kind of attention researchers aim to get. Specifically, one of the core ideals of ethnographic practice, 'unobstructedness', was fundamentally challenged here.

Preserving a dual identity of the 'idealised researcher' and the 'inner self' while managing the social boundaries in the field is not an easy task. After seeing how some of the employees were treated, KH thought it was necessary to discuss the continuation of the research with Maria. KH went to the manager's office and re-clarified that the primary reason for the researcher being present was the fieldwork and not to carry a full workload in lieu of interview time. In this conversion, reference was made to the support of senior management and to the report that was to be submitted at the end of the research process. The concluding part of this encounter involved asking Maria if she still wished KH to carry on with the study, while also being given the opportunity to withdraw from the research anonymously if she felt the researcher's presence was distracting her team's work.

Analysis of the encounter, and personal assessment of the lived experience, indicate that this was an occasion when the (idealised) 'neutral' researcher role was lost temporarily and feelings of resentment towards the manager took over. It was also the only time when reference to links with the senior figures of the corporation was used to stabilise an emotionally difficult situation. In spite of this encounter, Maria approved the continuation of the research and interactions in the following days indicated that the researcher–participant relationship was at least partially repaired. For instance, we received an invitation to return to Tasty Plate for more data. We are aware that this could have been because of the corporation's interest in the research and Maria's attempt to pre-empt any negative reporting. Evidently, this would have been inappropriate practice and was never KH's intention. With that said, it did provide a useful critical point where the researcher's own feelings took over in a professional situation. It also had a didactic character as it made the researcher acutely aware of the power asymmetries and the implications it may have on the fieldwork relations.

When it comes to the analysis of data, despite the ideal of 'open-mindedness' (Angouri, 2018), lived experiences and subjective understandings of reality are part of any research project and play a profound role in the interpretation of the data. In particular, when KH scheduled a post-fieldwork follow-up interview with Maria, she found herself to be highly sceptical towards Maria's narrative due to the earlier experiences and observations. Had we had the interview *before* the fieldwork, the perceptions would have been significantly different; especially since Maria's interview provided a positive description of an inclusive and collaborative work community. Against this depiction, our analysis of multiple datasets presented a more complex picture. More specifically, we argued in another work that the Finnish language was used as a management control tool for sustaining relations of inequality between Finnish employees and migrant employees, with the latter group being systematically excluded and marginalised. This illustrates well how a single dataset (i.e., interview) could have resulted in an entirely different account. At the same time, in retrospect, it is difficult to say how much of our inferencing is influenced by our own subjective experiences.

Whereas reflexive practice may attempt to make analysis more transparent and raise awareness of one's own subjectivity, accessing deeply hidden motivations and biases seems to be impossible. It is also easy to fall into the 'process of endless reflexive loops' (Johnson and Duberley, 2000, 182) that can create self-doubt of one's own knowledge claims. It would be impossible to disentangle in our case here the exact boundaries between deep power struggles on site and the researcher's perceptions and orientation towards equality. We address this further in the next and final section of the chapter.

DISCUSSION AND FINAL REMARKS

Doing ethnography is like tightrope walking: maintaining the right balance between knowledge production and reflexivity presents a significant challenge. We reflected on multiple datasets from two different research sites and sought to address how a researcher's subjectivities can impact the reading of the data. Reflexive practice, as we see it, is useful for facilitating engagement with critical self-awareness and conscientiousness. It can enhance one's awareness of the co-existence of multiple realities. Also, rather than accepting data at face value and presenting the illusion of 'truth', reflexive practice that acknowledges both individual and social complexities force the researcher to question 'common sense' assumptions and interpretations.

However, reflexive practice also poses a paradox: namely, while reflexivity is praised as a salient tool for rigour and trustworthiness, its contribution to rigour and knowledge raises uncertainty (Probst, 2015). For example, how can we evaluate or teach reflexivity? The actual practicalities and methods of doing reflexivity remain ambiguous (Mauthner and Doucet, 2003). It also raises philosophical questions regarding epistemological and ontological subjectivities in terms of our ability to approach scientific knowledge construction reflexively. Even after engaging with reflexive practice, what is meant by 'knowledge'? And how many 'realities' can we capture and report if our understanding of the social world is constantly co-constructed? Latour (1988), for example, criticises reflexive practice as exhibiting arrogance. He suggests that meta-reflexivity provides layers of text to researchers' supposedly naive readers:

> The reflexivists spend an enormous amount of energy on the side of the knowing, and almost none on the side of the known. They think that any attempt to get at the things themselves is proof of naive empiricism. (Latour, 1988, 173)

As far as naive empiricism is concerned, we do not see reflexivity as providing 'proof' or validating qualitative data. What reflexive practice can illustrate is the co-existence of multiple truths and interpretations that are open to both the researcher and the participants. The researcher, however, has the power to represent the participants' realities and in this respect the stakes are high.

To make research more transparent, accounts that include fieldwork experiences can provide useful frames within which the inferences are drawn. Reporting these experiences acknowledges the researcher's role as an active agent and knowledge producer. Furthermore, considering that academic writing reveals strong epistemological positions, surprisingly little attention has been placed on the power of writing in methodological and epistemological debates. This could provide a fruitful ground for future research: for example, a closer inspection of word choices and literary devices could provide interesting insights into researchers' (disciplinary) writing dispositions and the ways epistemic status is present.

We believe there is a need to develop further the notion of being vs. doing reflexivity and engage in interdisciplinary research with cognate fields, notably between Management Studies and Workplace Sociolinguistics, which engage with complementary questions regarding language-sensitive workplace research from their own angle. As Bourdieu (1988) notes, analysts are biased products of their academic training who (re)produce accounts that are in line with their distinct disciplinary expectations. These constraints are both unavoidable and part of the interpretive process of any research. Academic thinking is part of a 'chain' and most research is a 'product' of its time. Allowing more time, however, for discussing these conflicts is useful and significant for the quality of our accounts.

We hope our chapter contributes to a methodological discussion and we invite language-sensitive scholars and workplace sociolinguists to share the experience of good practice in their fields.

ACKNOWLEDGEMENTS

Kristina Humonen gratefully acknowledges the support of the Economic and Social Research Council (UK). Grant: ES/V011413/1.

NOTES

1.   We use the term to refer to the dominant variety of the participant and to avoid ideological claims in relation to nativeness.
2.   We understand Othering as the process of exclusion and marginalization of people based on perceived differences. Language-wise it follows local and non-local positioning against the dominant (language) ideologies.
3.   As participant observer, KH was working side-by-side with the research participants and took part in Tasty Plate's work activities. This approach was chosen to provide a first-hand experience of the participants' daily work practices.

REFERENCES

Agar, M. (2006), 'An ethnography by any other name...', *Forum Qualitative Sozialforschung/ Forum: Qualitative Social Research*, **7** (4), art 36. Retrieved from: http://www.qualitative research.net/index.php/fqs/article/viewFile/177/ 396

Alvesson, M. and Sköldberg, K. (2018), *Reflexive Methodology: New Vistas for Qualitative Research* (3rd ed.), London, UK: Sage Publications.

Angouri, J. (2018), *Culture, Discourse, and the Workplace*, Abingdon, UK: Routledge.

Angouri, J. and Piekkari, R. (2018), 'Organising multilingually: Setting an agenda for studying language at work', *European Journal of International Management*, **12** (1–2), 8–27.

Audi, R. (2011), *Epistemology: A Contemporary Introduction to the Theory of Knowledge* (3rd ed.), London, UK: Routledge.

Bate, S. P. (1997), 'Whatever happened to organizational anthropology? A review of the field of organizational ethnography and anthropological studies', *Human Relations*, **50** (9), 1147–1175.

Berger, P. and Luckmann, T. (1966), *The Social Construction of Reality: A Treatise in the Sociology of Knowledge*, New York, US: Anchor Books.

Bonache, J. (2020), 'The challenges of using "non-positivist" paradigm and getting through the peer-review process', *Human Resource Management Journal*, **31**, 37–48.

Bourdieu, P. (1988), *Homo Academicus*, Cambridge, UK: Polity Press.

Bourdieu, P. (1990), *The Logic of Practice*, Cambridge, UK: Polity Press.

Bourdieu, P. and Wacquant, L. (1992), *An Invitation to Reflexive Sociology*, Cambridge, UK: Polity Press.

Canagarajah, S. (2020), 'Transnational work, translingual practices, and interactional sociolinguistics', *Journal of Sociolinguistics*, **24**, 555–573.

Coffey, A. (2002), 'Ethnography and self: Reflections and representations', in Tim May (ed.), *Qualitative Research in Action*, London, UK: Sage Publications, pp. 312–331.

Copland, F. and Creese, A. (2015), *Linguistic Ethnography: Collecting, Analysing and Presenting Data*, London, UK: Sage Publications.

Cunliffe, A. L. and Karunanayake, G. (2013), 'Working within hyphen-spaces in ethnographic research: Implications for research identities and practice', *Organizational Research Methods*, **16** (3), 364–392.

Dwyer, S. C. and Buckle, J. L. (2009), 'The space between: On being an insider-outsider in qualitative research', *International Journal of Qualitative Methods*, **8** (1), 54–63.

Fan, S. and Harzing, A.-W. (2020), 'Moving beyond the baseline: Exploring the potential of experiments in language research', in Sierk Horn, Philippe Lecomte and Susanne Tietze (eds), *Managing Multilingual Workplaces: Methodological, Empirical and Pedagogic Perspectives*, New York, US: Routledge, pp. 9–28.

Fine, G. A. (1993), 'Ten lies of ethnography: Moral dilemmas of field research', *Journal of Contemporary Ethnography*, **22** (3), 267–294.

Fine, G. A. and Shulman, D. (2009), 'Lies from the field: Ethical issues in organizational ethnography', in Sierk Ybema, Dvora Yanow, Harry Wels and Frans Kemsteeg (eds), *Organizational Ethnography: Studying Complexities of Everyday Life*, London, UK: Sage Publications, pp. 177–195.

Heller, M. (2011), *Paths to Post-nationalism: A Critical Ethnography of Language and Identity*, Oxford, UK: Oxford University Press.

Holmes, J. and Stubbe, M. (2015), *Power and Politeness in the Workplace: A Sociolinguistic Analysis of Talk at Work* (2nd ed.), Abingdon, UK: Routledge.

Johnson, P. and Duberley, J. (2000), *Understanding Management Research: An Introduction to Epistemology*, London, UK: Sage Publications.

Karhunen, P., Kankaanranta, A., Louhiala-Salminen, L. and Piekkari, R. (2018), 'Let's talk about language: A review of language-sensitive research in international management', *Journal of Management Studies*, **55** (6), 980–1013.

Kleinman, S. and Copp, M. (1993), *Emotions and Fieldwork* (Qualitative research methods series 28), London, UK: Sage Publications.

Koskinen, K. (2020), 'Translatorial linguistic ethnography in organizations', in Sierk Horn, Philippe Lecomte and Susanne Tietze (eds), *Managing Multilingual Workplaces: Methodological, Empirical and Pedagogic Perspectives*, New York, US: Routledge, pp. 60–78.

Latour, B. (1988), 'The politics of explanation: An alternative', in Steve Woolgar (ed.), *Knowledge and Reflexivity: New Frontiers in the Sociology of Knowledge*, London, UK: Sage, pp. 155–177.

Lecomte, P., Tenzer, H. and Zhang, L. E. (2018), 'Working across language boundaries: New perspectives on language-sensitive international management research', *European Journal of International Management*, **12** (1/2), 1–7. Retrieved from https://www.inderscience.com/info/inarticletoc.php?jcode =ejim&year=2018&vol=12&issue=1/2

Litosseliti, L. (2018), *Research Methods in Linguistics* (2nd ed.), London, UK: Bloomsbury Academic.

Maton, K. (2003), 'Reflexivity, relationism, & research: Pierre Bourdieu and the epistemic conditions of social scientific knowledge', *Space and Culture*, **6** (1), 52–65.

Mauthner, N. S. and Doucet, A. (2003), 'Reflexive accounts and accounts of reflexivity in qualitative data analysis', *Sociology*, **37** (3), 413–431.

McDonald, S. (2005), 'Studying actions in context: A qualitative shadowing method for organizational research', *Qualitative Research*, **5** (4), 455–473.

Patiño-Santos, A. (2020), 'Reflexivity', in Karin Tusting (ed.), *The Routledge Handbook of Linguistic Ethnography*, Abingdon, UK: Routledge, pp. 213–228.

Piekkari, R. and Tietze, S. (2016), 'Doing research on power and politics in multinational corporations (MNCs): A methodological perspective', in Florian Becker-Ritterspach, Susanne Blazejewsju, Christoph Dörrenbächer and Mike Geppert (eds), *Micropolitics in the Multinational Corporation: Foundations, Applications and New Directions*, Cambridge, UK: Cambridge University Press, pp. 208–240.

Probst, B. (2015), 'The eye regards itself: Benefits and challenges of reflexivity in qualitative social work research', *Social Work Research*, **39** (1), 37–48.

Rampton, B. (2007), 'Neo-hymnesian linguistic ethnography in the United Kingdom', *Journal of Sociolinguistics*, **11** (5), 584–607.

Sarangi, S. (2007), 'The anatomy of interpretation: Coming to terms with the analyst's paradox in professional discourse studies', *Text & Talk*, **27** (5–6), 567–584.

Tenzer, H., Terjesen, S. and Harzing, A.-W. (2017), 'Language in international business: A review and agenda for future research', *Management International Review*, **57**, 815–854.

Tusting, K. (ed.) (2020), *The Routledge Handbook of Linguistic Ethnography*, Abingdon, UK: Routledge.

Westney, D. E. and Van Maanen, J. (2011), 'The casual ethnography of the executive suite', *Journal of International Business Studies*, **42** (5), 602–607.

8. Multilingual organisations: employee motives and human resource management adaptive strategies

John Fiset

INTRODUCTION

The importance of language in an international business context cannot be overstated (e.g., Harzing and Pudelko, 2013). Linguistic diversity in many ways serves as a boon for organisations as it increases the talent pool of available candidates (Kulkarni, 2015). Language can also serve as a competitive advantage as it enables organisations to reach a broader and increasingly multilingual customer base (e.g., Duchêne, 2009; Harzing and Pudelko, 2013). Nevertheless, firms that operate in a multinational or linguistically diverse context generally face challenges associated with language and communication barriers (e.g., Piekkari et al., 2014).

Despite the consequential nature of workplace communication, many organisations struggle to address knowledge sharing concerns resulting from changing workplace demographics. Extant international business research has identified how evident and hidden language barriers (Tenzer et al., 2021) arising from language diversity contribute to trust and group cohesion decrements (Tenzer et al., 2014; Klitmøller et al., 2015) which lead to increased employee perceptions of uncertainty and negativity (e.g., Neeley et al., 2012). In addition, heterogeneous language use at work contributes to perceptions of linguistic ostracism, defined as 'instances where focal employees perceive that others at work have rejected and/or excluded them by using a language that they do not comprehend' (Fiset and Bhave, 2021, 431). Thus, effective management of multilingual organisations continues to be an increasingly important challenge for leaders (Tenzer and Pudelko, 2015).

Many organisations have responded to these challenges through the enactment of explicit strategies and policies that serve to limit overt language diversity and ensure mutual understanding (e.g., Harzing and Feely, 2008). The most popular policy in this domain is the adoption of a *lingua franca* or common language across organisation units (Marschan-Piekkari et al., 1999). On one hand, the adoption of a *lingua franca* policy, which generally involves the universal use of English, often contributes to improved inter-organisational communication (Neeley and Kaplan, 2014). However, these same policies also lead to a number of aversive effects on employees including increased group polarisation, status loss, and poor performance among language outgroup members (e.g., Neeley and Kaplan, 2014; Neeley and Dumas, 2016). Thus, the enactment of these policies creates the potential to isolate and exclude those with different language backgrounds. In response to the proliferation of such management strategies, a number of groups have actively spoken out against the ethical implications of these policies, including the American Psychological Association (Padilla et al., 1991). As such, organisations who wish to implement these policies require a well-thought-out implementation strategy that takes all stakeholders into consideration (e.g., Neeley and Kaplan, 2014).

In response to the aforementioned concerns, a growing number of scholars have advocated for alternative approaches that attempt to manage apprehensions around multilingual workplaces. Recently, scholars have directed their attention to developing a greater understanding of micro-level processes that undergird multilingual workplace communication (Lecomte et al., 2018). Specifically, work in this domain has explored how and why language diversity at work can serve as a 'lightning rod' (Hinds et al., 2014, 537) for interpersonal conflict and social categorisation (e.g., Harzing and Feely, 2008; Peltokorpi, 2010). This chapter outlines issues around the management of the multilingual workplace by examining it through the lens of language barriers. Specifically, using a critical incident paradigm (Flanagan, 1954), employee motives underlying the desire to engage in speaking a non-mutually understood language at work are examined. Drawing on these findings, a number of policies and procedures are presented that Human Resource Management (HRM) professionals can enact to foster harmonious workplace interactions in a linguistically diverse workplace.

Motives Underlying the Desire to Speak a Non-Mutually Understood Language at Work

Much in the same way that language can facilitate the exchange of ideas and bring others together, it can also act as a means of excluding others from workgroup interactions (e.g., Kulkarni, 2015). The experience of perceiving others speaking in a language that one does not understand is associated with a number of negative outcomes including anger, suspicion, and fear (Kulkarni, 2015; Hitlan et al., 2016) and lower workgroup commitment, creativity, and citizenship behaviour (Hitlan et al., 2006; Dotan-Eliaz et al., 2009; Fiset and

Bhave, 2021). On the other hand, employees can be motivated to use multiple languages at work out of a desire to include others or to facilitate knowledge sharing (e.g., Ahmad and Barner-Rasmussen, 2019). Recognising these divergent and often ambiguous effects, I conducted a critical incident study (Flanagan, 1954) in which participants disclosed their rationale for speaking a non-mutually understandable language at work. In addition, participants also describe their beliefs about how these interactions affected workgroup members who could not understand.

METHOD

Sample

One hundred and fifty multilingual employees took part in a critical incident study on language use at work via Amazon Mechanical Turk, a crowdsourcing platform allowing individuals to complete tasks in exchange for compensation. This method of data collection is an effective means of recruiting representative samples of workers of comparable quality to research labs, or marketing research companies (e.g., Kees et al., 2017) when steps are taken to improve the quality of the data. With this in mind, only respondents who achieved an approval rating 90% or higher on previous tasks were selected and the IP addresses of respondents were examined to ensure that participants did not complete the survey more than once (Peer et al., 2014). Out of the original sample, 122 respondents (50% female) reported speaking more than one language at work over the past six months and were retained for the final sample. Participants had a mean organisational tenure of 4.84 years (SD = 4.69) and spoke an average of 2.80 languages (SD = 1.02). Sectors most prominently represented in my sample were from Healthcare (19%) and Education (15%).

Procedure

After completing a short demographic questionnaire, participants recalled a specific incident over the past six months in which they spoke in a non-mutually understandable language at work. This is consistent with previous work that has taken a problem-centred approach to data collection that focusses on language-centred critical incidents (e.g., Tenzer and Pudelko, 2015). Specifically, participants described a particular workplace incident and provided a rationale for why they spoke in a language that others in their workgroup did not understand. Next, participants evaluated the perceived severity of their behaviour in relation to their workgroup members using Wenzel et al.'s (2010) three-item measure (e.g., 'I believe that in this instance, my behaviour pained my workgroup members who could not understand me'), on a five-point scale (1 = strongly disagree to 5 = strongly agree; α = .81). In addition, participants identified five different interlocutor groups (client/customers, coworkers, family/friend, patients, and students) in the critical incident conversation.

Upon completion of the data collection, participants' motives were analysed using open-coding and constant comparisons, where each participant response was coded based on any information that they provided regarding their underlying rationale for speaking a non-mutually understood language at work. As this study was exploratory in nature, emergent codes were based only on the data provided by respondents and were not initially informed by the literature. This yielded nine fragmented codes and a number of vivid participant descriptions (Glaser, 1998). In the next step, I merged nine initial fragmented codes together to create five first-order codes. For example, initial codes of 'efficiency' and 'good customer service' were merged together to form the first-order code 'process-loss avoidance'. After several iterations, I collapsed the five first-order codes into two emergent higher-order categories based on the furtive or covert nature of participants' non-mutual language use at work. This process of working with the original data, first-order codes, and higher-order categories continued throughout the data analysis process until data saturation had been achieved (Locke, 2001).

RESULTS

Based on the analysis and through constant comparison of the critical incident motives associated with speaking a non-mutually understandable language at work, the data yielded five first-order codes and two higher-order categories, detailed below. I labelled the first of these higher-order categories 'Non-surreptitious motives' and involved instances where language either improved workplace relationships or enabled organisational performance. The second category 'Surreptitious motives' involved using language to actively hide the contents of the message and inhibit organisational functioning.

Non-surreptitious Motives for Speaking a Non-Mutually Understandable Language

An overwhelming majority of critical incidents described by participants reflected situations where employees engaged in speaking a non-mutually understandable language at work for non-surreptitious reasons (81%). This suggests that employees were not necessarily attempting to hide information, but rather to achieve a number of objectives including: reduce communication process loss, develop solidarity with similar others, and influence how others see and think of them at work. Each of these first-order motive codes are described in detail below.

In a significant number of cases (59%), participants indicated their desire to use language as a means of *Process-Loss Avoidance*. This is in response to what scholars call thin communication (e.g., Marschan-Piekkari et al., 1999) whereby non-fluent speakers of a particular language are limited by the number of words at their disposal, which can contribute to lower-quality exchange and process loss (Salas et al., 2004). Thus, as a means of reducing the proficiency disparity where one speaker must converse in a language that they were not comfortable with, many participants described how they voluntarily switched to speaking a second language in order to improve the level of communication quality with their conversation partner. In the following case, a retail employee discussed how they switched languages to help a customer:

> I elected to speak Chinese with the customer because he was having trouble express-ing himself in English. Since I am bilingual, I switched to Chinese to make him feel comfortable. He really appreciated it. (45, Female, Retail)

As demonstrated in the quote, the customer felt more comfortable during the interaction as they were more readily able to express their needs during the interaction, thus contributing to a reduction in process loss and an improved overall customer service experience (Harzing and Pudelko, 2013; Madera, 2013). These responses, however, extended beyond improving customer service and often involved helping colleagues by switching languages to improve the overall communication quality of the interaction as demonstrated by the following quote.

> We have a multicultural staff because we work with different business in different countries. I speak Spanish a lot when talking to employees that work in Latin American countries so it makes it easier to communicate in their native language. (35, Male, Professional Services)

In many ways, this mirrors the work of Harzing et al. (2011), where multilin-gual employees are perceived to act as boundary spanners between members of linguistic groups (e.g., Barner-Rasmussen et al., 2014). This in turn contributes to easing communication barriers for the person being helped (e.g., Harzing et al., 2011), but may contribute to confusion for others who do not understand what is being said.

The second non-surreptitious motive revolved around *Solidarity* (14%) with workgroup members with similar language backgrounds. In these cases, par-ticipants described the enjoyment and comfort that they experienced speaking their mother tongue at work. They also described how it contributed to forging a shared identity with their communication partner:

> They speak Spanish and so do I, so why not? I guess it's like a form of solidarity because Spanish-speakers/Hispanics are definitely underrepresented at our work. My center has about 10 people, I'm the only Chicana...the person I spoke with is from another center in the same building/research institute...she is the only other Hispanic I know of in the building of 50+ people. (Female, 26, Educational Services)

It is obvious from the above quote of the importance of communicating in one's mother tongue. This is consistent with self-categorisation theory (Tajfel and Turner, 1979) as language plays an important role in the categorisation of workgroup members and the distinctions between linguistic ingroups and out-groups (e.g., Neeley et al., 2012). Similarly, the third code entitled *Impression Management* (8%) denotes a desire to use language as a way to make a positive impression and to improve work relationships with their communication partner.

> I decided to speak in Urdu to impress and flirt with a cute girl at work. I think it worked. She was very attractive. This also allowed me to say things that wouldn't exactly be work appropriate. This made her laugh and smile. (Male, 24, Utilities)

While *Solidarity* and *Impression Management* codes share much in common, they are distinguished by the level of strategic intent. *Solidarity* lacks a specific intent beyond improving relationships and improving one's sense of identity, whereas *Impression Management* revolves around the development of a targeted relationship with a particular workgroup member or members and uses one's shared language as a leveraging tool for personal gain. For all three non-surreptitious motives, the intent behind these actions is inherently constructive from the perspective of the perpetrator. However, a growing body of research asserts that switching to a non-mutually understandable language at work, regardless of intent, can contribute to aversive outcomes for those who are left out of the conversation (e.g., Tenzer et al., 2014).

Surreptitious Motives for Speaking a Non-Mutually Understandable Language

The next category of surreptitious motives (19%) involved speaking a non-mutually understandable language to hide part or all of their conversation. In this case, participants were motivated to speak another language at work for two distinct reasons. The first rationale involved *Information Hiding* (11%), whereby participants elected to communicate in a surreptitious manner to ensure that their conversations about the organisation or other workgroup members would not be overheard.

> We spoke in Spanish because that was the most comfortable language among my coworkers. Even thou [sic] I speak fluent in English, the majority of the coworkers preferred to speak in Spanish because they knew that Management only spoke English and would be unaware of what they were talking about. (Male, 30, Information Technology)
>
> We were talking about how some of the other workers were being lazy and not doing their jobs... [me] and the other coworker did not want them to know what we were talking about especially since they were the subject. (Female, 37, Manufacturing)

This rationale is consistent with work on linguistic ostracism (e.g., Fiset and Bhave, 2021) and knowledge hiding (Connelly et al., 2012), suggesting that language can act as a means of impeding and withholding information (Klitmøller and Lauring, 2013), which in turn has significant effects on workgroup outcomes including trust formation (Tenzer et al., 2014).

Second, participants indicated that they spoke another language at work out of a desire for *Personal Privacy* (8%). This was particularly relevant when participants held discussions with friends or close family members while at work:

> There are other members at work who would understand Mandarin Chinese, and for privacy reasons, I used another language. (Male, 36, Education)
>
> I spoke on the phone to a family member in Ukrainian, as it is our native language. No one in my office speaks Ukrainian, so they [coworkers] could not understand our conversation. (Female, 20, Information Technology)

The idea that language use can act as a means of increasing the level of privacy experienced at work is a relatively novel finding. While both motives are covert in nature and involve a general reluctance to engage in communication that all workgroup members can understand (e.g., Lauring and Klitmøller, 2015), the distinction between the two motives lies in the content and type of the information being concealed. Those engaging in *Information Hiding* will likely transmit information that is either organisationally relevant, or gossip that pertains to workgroup members who cannot understand the content of the message. Those who specified a *Personal Privacy* motive, however, wanted to transmit personal information that likely did not concern their workgroup members or their organisation.

Effects of Motives and Communication Partner on Perceived Severity

An independent samples t-test was conducted to compare the perceived severity of speaking a non-mutually understood language on both higher-order categories that emerged from the data. There was a significant difference in perceived severity scores for surreptitious (M = 2.54, SD = 1.29) and non-surreptitious (M = 1.78, SD = .97) motives; $t(120)$ = 3.16, p < .01. This suggests that participants are aware of the potential negative ramifications of engaging in speaking a non-mutually understood language for surreptitious reasons. The perceived severity of the five first-order motive codes to speak a non-mutually understandable language at work were also assessed using a one-way between-subjects analysis of variance (ANOVA). There was a significant effect of motive on perceived severity ($F(4, 117)$ = 4.17, p < .01). Post-hoc comparisons using the Tukey HSD test indicated that participants who engaged in speaking another language for the purpose of *Information Hiding* (M = 2.82, SD = 1.22) reported the experience as more severe than those who reported a *Process-Loss Avoidance* (M = 1.68, SD = .87) motive. No significant differences were observed for the *Solidarity* (M = 2.36, SD = 1.20), *Personal Privacy* (M = 2.17, SD = 1.34), or *Impression Management* (M = 1.90, SD = 1.14) motives.

In addition to exploring motives to communicate using a non-mutually understandable language, participants also disclosed their communication partner during the focal critical incident. In total, participants revealed five different communication partners. The largest group was coworkers (52%), followed by clients/customers (27%), family/friends (10%), patients (7%), and students (5%).

To assess the perceived severity of speaking with a specific communication partner on workgroup members, a one-way between-subjects ANOVA was conducted. There was a significant effect of communication partner on perceived severity ($F(4, 117)$ = 6.06, p < .001). Participants who spoke in another language with coworkers (M = 2.33, SD = 1.16) reported the experience as more severe than those who reported their communication partner as patients (M = 1.20, SD = .46) or students (M = 1.22, SD = .27). No differences were observed when the communication partner was a client/customer (M = 1.59, SD = .65) or family/friend (M = 1.42, SD = 1.14).

DISCUSSION

This chapter contributes to the literature by examining employee motives to speak a non-mutually understandable language at work. Previous work in this domain has examined these questions from the target's perspective (e.g., Kulkarni, 2015); however, this work specifically examines how perpetrators interpret their own actions. The results uncover two core rationales: using a non-mutually understandable language for surreptitious or non-surreptitious purposes. By identifying these motives, multilingual employees create an important narrative around their behaviours that have implications on how the speaker and workgroup members interpret these actions. Specifically, surreptitious motives to engage in speaking a non-mutually understood language at work are higher in perceived severity than non-surreptitious motives. In addition, participants rated the perceived severity of their actions highest when they engaged in *Information Hiding* and their communication partners were coworkers.

One limitation to the current study is that although we observed differences in severity depending on the participant's focal motive to speak a non-mutually understandable language at work, this may not be consistent or even contradict the experiences of linguistic outgroup members. This assertion is supported by research on code-switching whereby employees who switch languages at work – even with the best of intentions – can contribute to ambiguous and often conflicting outcomes (e.g., Neeley et al., 2012; Ahmad and Barner-Rasmussen, 2019).

Thus, the question remains what HRM professionals can do to improve communication practices in multilingual organisations? Based on a review of the literature of strategies that organisations can enact to reduce language barriers (e.g., Feely and Harzing, 2003; Harzing et al., 2011), it is evident that HRM professionals play an important role in reducing workplace language barriers. In particular, HRM professionals have significant influence over selection, retention, and training practices and are generally a key point of contact for employees who wish to raise concerns about their work environment.

Recent work supports this claim as supportive HRM practices contribute to the development of a congenial workplace environment in multilingual settings (e.g., Yamao and Sekiguchi, 2015). Below, several tools, policies, and procedures that HRM departments and organisations have at their disposal to ease linguistic tensions at work and foster a harmonious work environment are reviewed and are organised into four aspects of supportive HRM practices: selection and hiring practices, employee training, leadership development, and occupational health and safety. In each case, I examine how HRM professionals can implement these practices and their impacts on employee motives to engage in speaking a non-mutually understood language.

Selection and Hiring Practices

The hiring and selection process provides HRM professionals with an opportunity to select candidates that they believe would provide the greatest contribution to the organisation. In a linguistically diverse work context, it may be prudent to consider a number of employee characteristics and personality factors when selecting candidates. In particular, hiring professionals should take language proficiency or multilingual ability into consideration, especially when selecting candidates for foreign assignment. Being able to speak more than one language enables employees to act as boundary spanners, and facilitates cultural adjustment and knowledge transfer, particularly in expatriate employees (Peltokorpi and Vaara, 2012; Peltokorpi, 2017).

Although language-sensitive selection and recruitment can play an important role in developing a shared workplace language (e.g., Peltokorpi and Vaara, 2014), these practices do not fully remove the potential for others to engage in speaking a language that not all colleagues understand (Kulkarni, 2015). To cope with this eventuality, HRM practitioners can work to select candidates based on intercultural competence as a greater understanding of how language transmits culture may assuage some of the stress of working in a multilingual environment (Bordia and Bordia, 2015). For example, candidate assessments could integrate the Multicultural Personality Questionnaire to inform hiring decisions and help select candidates that would be best suited to work in multilingual environments (e.g., Van der Zee and Van Oudenhoven, 2000). This questionnaire is easy to use, reliable, and related to a number of important outcomes including employee sociocultural adjustment and multicultural activity (Van Oudenhoven et al., 2003).

Finally, HRM professionals can also probe for additional employee competencies to ensure that new candidates are better able to handle the complexities associated with a multilingual workplace environment. For instance, cultural intelligence, cosmopolitanism, and social self-efficacy are associated with improved functioning in a multilingual environment (Ang et al., 2007; Dotan-Eliaz et al., 2009; Fiset and Bhave, 2021). Thus, in addition to being able to speak multiple languages, HRM practitioners should seek candidates with a high level of tolerance for linguistic and cultural diversity.

Employee Training

Scholars have proposed a number of training initiatives that serve to enhance overall communication efficacy and develop employees' capacity to work in a linguistically diverse environment. As this is a relatively nascent field, Neeley and Dumas (2016) suggest organisations hire third-party facilitators to help coach and model desired behaviour, while ensuring that the company-specific language is adopted as part of the training (Reeves and Wright, 1996). Others have suggested training employees to use translation software or the integration of interpreters to reduce language barriers (Harzing et al., 2011). Regardless of how these training programmes are conducted, it is important that employees be provided with adequate tools to navigate linguistic complexities at work.

Easily the most discussed training aspect in the field of language-sensitive management research are HRM practices that promote employee cultural and communication proficiency (e.g., Tenzer and Pudelko, 2015). In this regard, organisations can encourage these proficiencies in any number of ways. The most comprehensive means of managing workplace linguistic tensions involves initiatives that facilitate the acquisition of additional language skills (e.g., Harzing et al., 2011) via classroom, one-on-one, or online learning and are often well appreciated by employees, particularly when the language is necessary for work and proficiency levels are low (e.g., Yamao and Sekiguchi, 2015).

Organisations should also be aware that language fluency without cultural understanding might also cause significant conflict and misunderstanding. Thus, cultural sensitivity training, which helps trainees to appreciate their own language and cultural beliefs and respect these differences in others (e.g., Dicker, 1998) are best served embedded within existing language training programmes (Neeley and Kaplan, 2014). Empirical tests of these training programmes generally demonstrate positive results; however, future research is required to test the cross-industry efficacy of these initiatives.

Depending on the organisation, these training programmes can take place on company time, or using external resources where employees are reimbursed upon successful completion (Harzing et al., 2011). In both cases, these approaches appear to provide an important means of improving organisational communication. Programmes that successfully integrate such training content can help reduce linguistic conflict in multilingual workplaces and improve the ability for employees to make connections with one another, thus reducing the need to speak in a non-mutually understandable language for non-surreptitious reasons. The costs, associated with holistic language and cultural training programmes, however, can be substantial, and the returns on these investments are likely to take significant time to yield results (Piekkari et al., 2014).

Leadership Development

Organisational leaders have an important role to play in fostering an inclusive work environment. However, not all leaders are equipped to manage multilingual work environments. This tension presents an important leadership challenge for many organisations. Below, a number of areas which leadership development and mentorship initiatives can focus on to reduce communication barriers and improve employee communication are discussed.

In a recent study by Tenzer and Pudelko (2015), the authors explored leadership capabilities that serve to manage the challenges inherent in a multilingual workplace context. Their work revealed that the process of engaging in metacommunication and conveying appreciation for the contributions of all workgroup members acted as two key methods to help mitigate negative emotions associated with language barriers.

The first strategy of metacommunication, or conducting discussions pertaining to the overall communication process (Roberts, 2010), deals with leaders' attempts to reduce follower anxiety and tension via open communication and dialogue around how information is exchanged within the group. The effective use of metacommunication strategies is likely to increase employee perspective taking and serves to reduce negative emotions in a multilingual environment (Hinds et al., 2014). Training programmes can ensure that leaders are comfortable engaging followers in discussions about the potentially disruptive effects of language barriers, while remaining sensitive to the linguistic backgrounds of colleagues. This, in turn, contributes to increased psychological safety among workgroup members (Volk et al., 2014).

Second, leader training can incorporate being more appreciative of the contributions made by workgroup members, regardless of language proficiency (Tenzer and Pudelko, 2015). By encouraging leaders to place themselves in the shoes of their followers, they are better able to help low language proficiency employees by highlighting their knowledge, skills, and abilities. This process of highlighting the work of those who may not be as effective in conveying their own contributions is likely to reduce surreptitious information hiding motives as followers feel more acknowledged and valued. These actions are also likely to spur a number of positive team outcomes including an enhanced diversity climate, which may mitigate negative language-related emotions and linguistic ostracism perceptions (e.g., Kulkarni and Sommer, 2015).

Finally, in order to address broader issues of workplace inclusion, training can also integrate intervention strategies where leaders can intervene when they perceive that their followers are left out of conversations. Recent work by Fiset and Boies (2018) found that leaders who demonstrated proactivity, an interest in developing harmony within their workgroup, social awareness of the relationships between workgroup members, and maintaining a positive social environment contributed to reductions in perceived ostracism among followers.

Occupational Health and Safety

The primary intention for many organisations is to ensure that employees are able to work in a safe and secure environment. The ambiguous intent behind speaking a non-mutually understood language, regardless of its motive, may cause targets to attribute these actions as aversive (Fiset and Bhave, 2021), particularly if safety-related information is not being transmitted efficiently (e.g., Lindhout et al., 2019). One way in which organisations can ensure a safe and healthy working environment is to ensure that followers treat each other in a courteous and inclusive manner. As such, the more that language acts as a means of reducing process loss and creating relationships at work, the better the effect will be on follower health outcomes. Thus, HRM professionals can act to build redundancy in how safety-related communication is transmitted to employees, both in terms of translating information into multiple languages and using various media (i.e., pictograms, videos) to ensure that core safety information is disseminated widely and universally understood (Harzing et al., 2011).

CONCLUSION

The successful integration of a linguistically diverse workforce has become a key and pressing aspect of contemporary management practice. Based on a sample of 122 employees, a number of personal motives to engage in speaking a non-mutually understandable language at work were observed. The resulting analysis uncovered two higher-order categories (surreptitious and non-surreptitious) and five first-order codes (*Process-Loss Avoidance, Solidarity, Impression Management, Information Hiding*, and *Personal Privacy*). The results outline both desirable and undesirable consequences of working in a multilingual environment that arise regardless of whether organisations implement policies that mandate the use of a particular language during work hours (e.g., Neeley et al., 2012). The results of the current study also suggest that HRM practitioners should be sensitive to the unanticipated effects that language use has on employees and the important role that motives may play in how HRM professionals tailor practices to a particular organisational context. The findings also echo the sentiments outlined by Harzing and colleagues (2011) in that there is no perfect solution to issues around linguistic barriers, but that organisational initiatives must simultaneously act to balance individual and collective rights.

Thus, we build on previous work exploring language barrier solutions (e.g., Feely and Harzing, 2003; Harzing et al., 2011) and encourage organisations to take a more holistic approach to linguistic diversity issues at work that takes into account both structural (e.g., language training) and informal (e.g., meta-communication) solutions. Similar to this work, we advocate for organisations to adopt a combination of policies and practices 'into a blend that is right for the company context' (Feely and Harzing, 2003, 50). This chapter also discusses the importance of a highly considered set of HRM policies to select, hire, and train employees, to alleviate linguistic barriers in the workplace. It is through a greater understanding of the process by which employees experience linguistic ostracism that organisations can better predict and manage the barriers that may develop in a linguistically diverse workplace.

REFERENCES

Ahmad, F. and W. Barner-Rasmussen (2019), 'False foe? When and how code switching practices can support knowledge sharing in multinational corporations', *Journal of International Management*, **25** (3), 100671.

Ang, S., L. Van Dyne, C. Koh, K. Y. Ng, K. J. Templer, C. Tay and N. A. Chandrasekar (2007), 'Cultural intelligence: Its measurement and effects on cultural judgment and decision making, cultural adaptation and task performance', *Management and Organization Review*, **3**, 335–371.

Barner-Rasmussen, W., M. Ehrnrooth, A. Koveshnikov and K. Mäkelä (2014), 'Cultural and language skills as resources for boundary spanning within the MNC', *Journal of International Business Studies*, **45** (7), 886–905.

Bordia, S. and P. Bordia (2015), 'Employees' willingness to adopt a foreign functional language in multilingual organisations: The role of linguistic identity', *Journal of International Business Studies*, **46**, 415–428.

Connelly, C. E., D. Zweig, J. Webster and J. P. Trougakos (2012), 'Knowledge hiding in organisations', *Journal of Organizational Behavior*, **33** (1), 64–88.

Dicker, S. J. (1998), 'Adaptation and assimilation: US business responses to linguistic diversity in the workplace', *Journal of Multilingual and Multicultural Development*, **19** (4), 282–302.

Dotan-Eliaz, O., K. L. Sommer and Y. S. Rubin (2009), 'Multilingual groups: Effects of linguistic ostracism on felt rejection and anger, coworker attraction, perceived team potency, and creative performance', *Basic and Applied Social Psychology*, **31** (4), 363–375.

Duchêne, A. (2009), 'Marketing, management and performance: Multilingualism as commodity in a tourism call centre', *Language Policy*, **8** (1), 27–50.

Feely, A. J. and A.-W. Harzing (2003), 'Language management in multinational companies', *Cross Cultural Management: An International Journal*, **10** (2), 37–52.

Fiset, J. and D. P. Bhave (2021), 'Mind your language: The effects of linguistic ostracism on interpersonal work behaviors', *Journal of Management*, **47** (2), 430–455. doi: 10.1177/0149206319833445

Fiset, J. and K. Boies (2018), 'Seeing the unseen: Ostracism interventionary behaviour and its impact on employees', *European Journal of Work and Organisational Psychology*, **27** (4), 403–417.

Flanagan, J. C. (1954), 'The critical incident technique', *Psychological Bulletin*, **51** (4), 327–358.

Glaser, B. (1998), *Doing Grounded Theory: Issues and Discussions*, Mill Valley, CA: Sociology Press.

Harzing, A.-W. and A. J. Feely (2008), 'The language barrier and its implications for HQ–subsidiary relationships', *Cross Cultural Management: An International Journal*, **15**, 49–61.

Harzing, A.-W., K. Köster and U. Magner (2011), 'Babel in business: The language barrier and its solutions in the HQ–subsidiary relationship', *Journal of World Business*, **46** (3), 279–287.

Harzing, A.-W. and M. Pudelko (2013), 'Language competencies, policies and practices in multinational corporations: A comprehensive review and comparison of Anglophone, Asian, Continental European and Nordic MNCs', *Journal of World Business*, **48** (1), 87–97.

Hinds, P. J., T. B. Neeley and C. D. Cramton (2014), 'Language as a lightning rod: Power contests, emotion regulation, and subgroup dynamics in global teams', *Journal of International Business Studies*, **45** (5), 536–561.

Hitlan, R. T., K. M. Kelly, S. Schepman, K. T. Schneider and M. A. Zárate (2006), 'Language exclusion and the consequences of perceived ostracism in the workplace', *Group Dynamics: Theory, Research, and Practice*, **10** (1), 56–70.

Hitlan, R. T., M. A. Zárate, K. M. Kelly and C. M. DeSoto (2016), 'Linguistic ostracism causes prejudice: Support for a serial mediation effect', *The Journal of Social Psychology*, **156** (4), 422–436.

Kees, J., C. Berry, S. Burton and K. Sheehan (2017), 'An analysis of data quality: Professional panels, student subject pools, and Amazon's Mechanical Turk', *Journal of Advertising*, **46**, 141–155.

Klitmøller, A. and J. Lauring (2013), 'When global virtual teams share knowledge: Media richness, cultural difference and language commonality', *Journal of World Business*, **48** (3), 398–406.

Klitmøller, A., S. C. Schneider and K. Jonsen (2015), 'Speaking of global virtual teams: Language differences, social categorisation and media choice', *Personnel Review*, **44** (2), 270–285.

Kulkarni, M. (2015), 'Language-based diversity and faultlines in organisations', *Journal of Organizational Behavior*, **36** (1), 128–146.

Kulkarni, M. and K. Sommer (2015), 'Language-based exclusion and prosocial behaviors in organisations', *Human Resource Management*, **54** (4), 637–652.

Lauring, J. and A. Klitmøller (2015), 'Corporate language-based communication avoidance in MNCs: A multi-sited ethnography approach', *Journal of World Business*, **50**, 46–55.

Lecomte, P., H. Tenzer and L. E. Zhang (2018), 'Working across language boundaries: New perspectives on language-sensitive international management research', *European Journal of International Management*, **12**, 1–7.

Lindhout, P., J. C. Kingston-Howlett and G. Reniers (2019), 'Learning from language problem related accident information in the process industry: A literature study', *Process Safety and Environmental Protection*, **130**, 140–152.

Locke, K. (2001), *Grounded Theory in Management Research*, Thousand Oaks, CA: Sage Publications.

Madera, J. M. (2013), 'Best practices in diversity management in customer service organisations: An investigation of top companies cited by Diversity Inc.', *Cornell Hospitality Quarterly*, **54** (2), 124–135.

Marschan-Piekkari, R., D. Welch and L. Welch (1999), 'Adopting a common corporate language: IHRM implications', *International Journal of Human Resource Management*, **10** (3), 377–390.

Neeley, T. B. and T. Dumas (2016), 'Unearned status gain: Evidence from a global language mandate', *Academy of Management Journal*, **51** (1), 14–43.

Neeley, T. B., P. J. Hinds and C. D. Cramton (2012), 'The (un)hidden turmoil of language in global collaboration', *Organisational Dynamics*, **41**, 236–244.

Neeley, T. B. and R. S. Kaplan (2014), 'What's your language strategy?', *Harvard Business Review*, **92** (9), 70–76.

Padilla, A. M., K. J. Lindholm, A. Chen, R. Duran, K. Hakuta, W. Lambert and G. R. Tucker (1991), 'The English-only movement', *American Psychologist*, **46**, 120–130.

Peer, E., J. Vosgerau and A. Acquisti (2014), 'Reputation as a sufficient condition for data quality on Amazon Mechanical Turk', *Behavior Research Methods*, **46** (4), 1023–1031.

Peltokorpi, V. (2010), 'Intercultural communication in foreign subsidiaries: The influence of expatriates' language and cultural competencies', *Scandinavian Journal of Management*, **26** (2), 176–188.

Peltokorpi, V. (2017), 'Absorptive capacity in foreign subsidiaries: The effects of language-sensitive recruitment, language training, and interunit knowledge transfer', *International Business Review*, **26** (1), 119–129.

Peltokorpi, V. and E. Vaara (2012), 'Language policies and practices in wholly-owned foreign subsidiaries', *Journal of International Business Studies*, **43** (9), 808–833.

Peltokorpi, V. and E. Vaara (2014), 'Knowledge transfer in multinational corporations: Productive and counterproductive effects of language-sensitive recruitment', *Journal of International Business Studies*, **45** (5), 600–622.

Piekkari, R., D. Welch and L. S. Welch (2014), *Language in International Business: The Multilingual Reality of Global Business Expansion*, Cheltenham, UK and Northampton, MA, USA: Edward Elgar Publishing.

Reeves, N. and C. Wright (1996), *Linguistic Auditing: A Guide to Identifying Foreign Language Communication Needs in Corporations*, Clevedon, UK: Multilingual Matters.

Roberts, C. (2010), 'Language socialization in the workplace', *Annual Review of Applied Linguistics*, **30**, 211–227.

Salas, E., C. S. Burke, J. E. Fowlkes and K. A. Wilson (2004), 'Challenges and approaches to understanding leadership efficacy in multi-cultural teams', *Cultural Ergonomics: Advances in Human Performance and Cognitive Engineering Research*, **4**, 341–384.

Tajfel, H. and J. C. Turner (1979), 'An integrative theory of intergroup conflict', in W. G. Austin and S. Worchels (eds), *The Social Psychology of Intergroup Relations* (pp. 33–47). Monterey, CA: Brooks/Cole.

Tenzer, H. and M. Pudelko (2015), 'Leading across language barriers: Managing language-induced emotions in multinational teams', *The Leadership Quarterly*, **26**, 606–625.

Tenzer, H., M. Pudelko and A.-W. Harzing (2014), 'The impact of language barriers on trust formation in multinational teams', *Journal of International Business Studies*, **45** (5), 508–535.

Tenzer, H., M. Pudelko and M. Zellmer-Bruhn (2021), 'The impact of language barriers on knowledge processing in multinational teams', *Journal of World Business*, **56** (2), 101184.

Van Der Zee, K. I. and J. P. Van Oudenhoven (2000), 'The Multicultural Personality Questionnaire: A multidimensional instrument of multicultural effectiveness', *European Journal of Personality*, **14** (4), 291–309.

Van Oudenhoven, J. P., S. Mol and K. I. Van der Zee (2003), 'Study of the adjustment of Western expatriates in Taiwan ROC with the Multicultural Personality Questionnaire', *Asian Journal of Social Psychology*, **6** (2), 159–170.

Volk, S., T. Köhler and M. Pudelko (2014), 'Brain drain: The cognitive neuroscience of foreign language processing in multinational corporations', *Journal of International Business Studies*, **45** (7), 862–885.

Wenzel, M., J. K. Turner and T. G. Okimoto (2010), 'Is forgiveness an outcome or initiator of sociocognitive processes? Rumination, empathy, and cognitive appraisals following a transgression', *Social Psychological and Personality Science*, **1** (4), 369–377.

Yamao, S. and T. Sekiguchi (2015), 'Employee commitment to corporate globalization: The role of English language proficiency and human resource practices', *Journal of World Business*, **50** (1), 168–179.

PART III

Organisations as discursive, polyphonic spaces:
a multidisciplinary approach

9. Introduction to *Organisations as discursive, polyphonic spaces: a multidisciplinary approach*

Betty Beeler

After our focus on multilingual practices in local and global settings in the previous sections, we turn our attention to the intersection between language-sensitive enquiry into the multilingual workplace and OS research which conceptualises organisations as polyphonic, discursive spaces. Developed over the past two decades as part of the 'linguistic turn' (Alvesson and Kärreman, 2000), research on the organisation as a discursive space seeks to uncover processes by which communication shapes the organisation and its performance (Brannen et al., 2014). Some of the themes associated with this stream include dialogical meaning-making (Bakhtin, 1984; Shotter, 2008; Tsoukas, 2009), multivoicedness (Bakhtin, 1984; Kornberger et al., 2006; Belova et al., 2008), the Communicative Constitution of Organisations or CCO (Tsoukas and Chia, 2002; Cooren et al., 2011), the management of discourse (Bruce et al., 2011), managing as a discursive practice (Kornberger et al., 2006), narrativity (Cooren et al., 2014) and the 'storytelling organisation' (Gabriel, 1995; Boje, 2008, 2019).

There has been relatively little dialogue between discourse-oriented OS scholars who study the way multiple *voices* combine and compete within an organisation, on the one hand, and language-oriented IB (and some OS) scholars who focus on the way multiple *languages* compete and combine within an organisation, on the other (Janssens et al., 2004; Tietze, 2008; Brannen et al., 2014; Angouri and Piekkari, 2018; Karhunen et al., 2018). This lack of dialogue is all the more striking as the concept of polyphony implies multiple languages as well as multiple voices, both of which are key to organisational processes, and in particular, to language-based 'circuits of power' (Vaara et al., 2005; Belova et al., 2008). In fact, as Steyaert and Janssens (2013) point out, there is a gaping inconsistency in the idea of exploring the increasingly multilingual workplace from a monolingual world view.

The multivoicedness–multilingualism divide in organisational studies can be attributed to the same factors that inhibit the crossing of any disciplinary divide, such as a reticence to leave the comfort of one's academic 'home base' or an attachment to a particular paradigm to the detriment of all others (Tietze, 2008; Angouri and Piekkari, 2018). In the case of organisational scholars whose background in the social sciences does not include sociolinguistic theory, there may be the assumption that as an object of enquiry, language is limited to its functional or technical properties, which prevents many researchers from seeing it as a social construct shaping social, political and organisational outcomes. This mistaken notion prevents them from recognising the central role of language in dialogical meaning-making, which is to say that meaning emerges from interactive exchanges rather than being mechanically transmitted as chunks of information (Bakhtin, 1984; Cunliffe, 2002; Shotter, 2008).

The chapters presented in this section put the spotlight on the potential benefits of cross-pollination between discourse-centred and language-centred scholars by exploring three questions: First, what themes can be shared by the two research streams? Next, how can a better understanding of the impact of languages on organisational processes advance OS and IB studies in general? And finally, how can current findings on multilingual issues produced by language-oriented scholars contribute to research on the polyphonic organisation? Collectively, the authors aim to stimulate the dialogue that has been missing between the two communities despite calls for interdisciplinary cooperation over the years (Angouri and Piekkari, 2018).

In the first chapter of this section, **Marjana Johansson** and **Wilhelm Barner-Rasmussen** begin by acknowledging the current lack of links between the two research communities at a time when the coexistence of multiple languages is having an impact on all levels of the organisation. To address this gap, they draw on language-centred IB research to propose paths of exploration that could be shared by both streams, and in particular, cross-pollination between IB literature on multilingual issues and that of OS researchers on the Communicative Constitution of Organisations, a theory which puts language at the centre of organisational processes (Cooren et al., 2011). Other themes highlighted in the chapter include the role of language in organisational identities, diversity, and translation.

Beyond the opportunities to cooperate on common areas of inquiry, Johansson and Barner-Rasmussen show how language-sensitive researchers have linked language to methodological issues. They point in particular to a number of challenges that language diversity can pose for researchers, such as the pitfalls of relying on translation without an awareness of potential underlying linguistic biases, or the impact of multiple languages on data-gathering and analysis. The epistemological and ontological implications of managing people of diverse origins are also highlighted.

Next, **Linda Cohen** and **Jane Kassis-Henderson** show how a language-based study of language and identity can contribute to OS research. They use an intersectional perspective to illustrate the manner in which organisational actors can draw on multiple facets of their identity depending on the context and the effect they wish to provoke. The originality of this perspective lies in the emphasis that the authors place on the fluid nature of the multiple voices that we have at our disposal and the role of those voices in shaping our sense of identity. As we acquire more language repertoires in the course of our personal experiences, according to this perspective, our identity takes on new repertoires as well, evolving in a permanent state of 'becoming'.

The concept of an ever-evolving and multifaceted identity that is enhanced by the person's multiple languages helps to explain why a monolingual vision of communication with its linguistic norms and standardised practices fails to reflect the reality of who people are and what skills they actually have. In addition, the practice of granting status to organisational actors according to their proficiency in the dominant language – to the detriment of those who have developed an array of language skills – implies that people's identity is solely based on their language skillset, dismissing their multiple intersecting skills. As the authors explain, when this happens, the organisation misses the opportunity to recognise and call upon those skills.

In the final chapter, **Cihat Erbil**, **Mustafa F. Özbilgin** and **Sercan Hamza Bağlama** propose a plurilingual approach to language in the workplace that aims at eliminating the 'symbolic violence' that prevails when language is used as a tool of domination. Drawing on the cases of language management in Turkey and Britain, they examine the manner in which the hierarchisation of languages today continues to reflect historical power relations, affecting opportunities for employment, marginalising employees along linguistic lines and perpetuating norms that fail to take into account the diversity of humanity. Even in Turkey, they explain, the person's inability to use the right accent can lead to discrimination.

The authors propose several ways to combat the injustice of language-based hegemony and achieve a polyphonic workplace, beginning with recruitment and promotion that favour those with multiple language skills and human resource practices that encourage language learning within the institution. They call for a paradigm shift from a monolingual mindset towards plurilingual openness which will require changes in power relations at all levels. These changes, they argue, necessitate the commitment of global and local organisations.

REFERENCES

Alvesson, M. and D. Kärreman (2000), 'Taking the linguistic turn', *The Journal of Applied Behavioral Science*, **36**, 136–158.

Angouri, J. and R. Piekkari (2018), 'Organising multilingually: Setting an agenda for studying language at work', *European Journal of International Management*, **12** (1/2), 8–27.

Bakhtin, M. M. (1984), *Problems of Dostoyevsky's Poetics*, Minneapolis, USA: University of Minnesota Press.

Belova, O., I. King and M. Śliwa (2008), 'Introduction: Polyphony and organization studies: Mikhail Bakhtin and beyond', *Organization Studies*, **29** (4), 493–500.

Boje, D. M. (2008), *Storytelling Organizations*, London, UK: Sage.

Boje, D. M. (2019), *Organizational Research: Storytelling in Action*, New York, USA: Routledge.

Brannen, M. Y., R. Piekkari and S. Tietze (2014), 'The multifaceted role of language in international business: Unpacking the forms, functions and features of a critical challenge to MNC theory and performance', *Journal of International Business Studies*, **45** (5), 495–507.

Bruce, B. C., J. M. Connell, C. Higgins and J. T. Mahoney (2011), 'The discourse of management and the management of discourse', *International Journal of Strategic Change Management*, **3** (1–2), 141–154.

Cooren, F., T. Kuhn, J. P. Cornelissen and T. Clark (2011), 'Communication, organizing and organization: An overview and introduction to the special issue', *Organization Studies*, **32** (9), 1149–1170.

Cooren, F., E. Vaara, A. Langley and H. Tsoukas (2014), 'Language and communication at work: Discourse, narrativity, and organizing. Introducing the fourth volume of "Perspectives on Process Organization Studies"', in François Cooren, Eero Vaara, Ann Langley and Haridimos Tsoukas (eds), *Language and Communication at Work: Discourse, Narrativity, and Organizing*, Oxford, UK: Oxford University Press, pp. 1–16.

Cunliffe, A. L. (2002), 'Social poetics as management inquiry: A dialogical approach', *Journal of Management Inquiry*, **11** (2), 128–146.

Gabriel, Y. (1995), 'The unmanaged organization: Stories, fantasies and subjectivity', *Organization Studies*, **16** (3), 477–501.

Janssens, M., J. Lambert and C. Steyaert (2004), 'Developing language strategies for international companies: The contribution of translation studies', *Journal of World Business*, **39** (4), 414–430.

Karhunen, P., A. Kankaanranta, L. Louhiala-Salminen and R. Piekkari (2018), 'Let's talk about language: A review of language-sensitive research in international management', *Journal of Management Studies*, **55** (6), 980–1013.

Kornberger, M., C. Carter and S. R. Clegg (2006), 'Rethinking the polyphonic organization: Managing as discursive practice', *Scandinavian Journal of Management*, **22** (1), 3–30.

Shotter, J. (2008), 'Dialogism and polyphony in organizing theorizing in organization studies: Action guiding anticipations and the continuous creation of novelty', *Organization Studies*, **29** (4), 501–524.

Steyaert, C. and M. Janssens (2013), 'Multilingual scholarship and the paradox of translation and language in management and organization studies', *Organization*, **20** (1), 131–142.

Tietze, S. (2008), *International Management and Language*, London, UK: Routledge.
Tsoukas, H. (2009), 'A dialogical approach to the creation of new knowledge in organization', *Organization Science*, **20** (6), 941–957.
Tsoukas, H. and R. Chia (2002), 'On organizational becoming: Rethinking organizational change', *Organization Science*, **13** (5), 567–582.
Vaara, E., J. Tienari, R. Piekkari and R. Säntti (2005), 'Language and the circuits of power in a merging multinational corporation', *Journal of Management Studies*, **42** (3), 595–623.

10. Organizing through and by multilingualism: writing languages into the study and practices of organizations

Marjana Johansson and Wilhelm Barner-Rasmussen

INTRODUCTION

The use of 'language-focused perspectives in organization studies' (Schoeneborn et al., 2019) is by now well established. Examinations of the relation between language and organizing have been concerned with the ways and extent to which language can be seen to represent organizational realities, and how language performatively accomplishes such realities (Alvesson and Kärreman, 2000). Discursive analyses have produced an insightful body of literature which has opened up perspectives on the ambiguities and power struggles inherent in organizations (e.g. Alvesson and Willmott, 2002; Hardy and Thomas, 2015; Iedema and Wodak, 1999; Zanoni and Janssens, 2015). Another important area of language-based organizational inquiry centres on narratives and storytelling, exploring philosophical and methodological aspects of narratology in organizational contexts (Boje, 1991; Czarniawska, 1997, 2004; Gabriel, 1995, 2000). A third significant area of inquiry explores how organizations are constituted in and through communication (Ashcraft and Mumby, 2004; Cooren et al., 2011; Mumby, 1997, 2013; Tsoukas and Chia, 2002). That line of work emphasizes the productive power of linguistic action, recently increasingly vocally in terms of the view that *Communication Constitutes Organization*, or CCO (e.g. Ashcraft et al., 2009; Schoeneborn et al., 2019). The view holds that communication is not 'merely one among many activities occurring inside pre-existing organizational walls [but] the main force that creates, generates and sustains – *constitutes* – what we consider to be organization and organizing practices... communication is not about message transmission, but is a *process of meaning production and negotiation'* (Ashcraft et al., 2009, p. 2, emphases in original).

In this chapter we draw on a CCO perspective to explore communication as organizing, specifically insofar as 'organizations, as well as organizational phenomena, come into existence, persist, and are transformed in and through interconnected communication practices' (Schoeneborn et al., 2019, 476). In doing so, we highlight and explore a glaring and surprisingly fundamental omission of this perspective, namely that CCO has not engaged at any length with the question of *if and how the coexistence of multiple languages shapes organizational practices and processes*. Rather, as Brannen, Piekkari and Tietze (2014, 497) observe in their introduction to the special issue on languages in *Journal of International Business Studies*, the focus of CCO and other language-focused strands within organization studies (OS) is 'primarily on the role of discourse, frames and narratives in sense-making and sensegiving rather than on multiple and different languages per se'. This important lacuna is what the present chapter aims to address. To buttress our point that the coexistence of multiple languages indeed ought to be taken more seriously in OS, we draw upon a lively line of inquiry in international business (IB) studies, namely the subfield that focuses on language-related issues in the organization and management of multinational enterprises (MNEs). This line of work harks back to the seminal paper of Marschan, Welch and Welch (1997) that for the first time explicitly connected language use to strategy, control, and communication in the MNE context. Their groundbreaking observation that language 'permeates virtually every aspect of... [international] business activities' (Marschan et al. 1997, 591) has by now evolved into an established area of research (see e.g. Brannen et al., 2014; Karhunen et al., 2018) that explicitly engages with the coexistence of multiple languages in the very complex organizations that MNEs are, and its implications for their management and organization.

It has repeatedly and authoritatively been argued that MNEs, as some of the most complex organizations ever, constitute special and extreme cases offering unique insights for OS (Ghoshal and Westney, 1993; Roth and Kostova, 2003; Brannen et al., 2014). Roth and Kostova (2003), in their exploration of MNEs as a context with potential to generate novel theoretical contributions for management and organization research, noted their distinctiveness on dimensions notably including 'the spatial separation of subunits, language and cultural diversity, organizational complexity, and multiplicity of environments' (p. 895; see also Gupta and Govindarajan, 1991). Roth and Kostova urged management and organization scholars to draw on these distinctions to spur the development of both existing and new theory, not only by delimiting theory and propositions more clearly, but also by systematically leveraging the tensions and potentially unexpected combinations coexisting inside MNEs to generate and test new theoretical alternatives. This point has been reiterated by international management experts (Piekkari and Westney, 2017; Tenzer et al., 2017) who have specifically emphasized language use and linguistic dynamics as issues where MNEs can act as vanguard sources of learning due to their unique combination of organizational complexity and global reach.

Against this background, there is little doubt of the potential for cross-pollination between two fields that each in their own way are very much preoccupied with language in organizational contexts. Yet, links between the two fields related to languages remain sparse (though see e.g. Vaara et al., 2005; Steyaert and Janssens, 2012; Śliwa and Johansson, 2014 for exceptions), and largely focused on language-focused IB research drawing upon organization studies for inspiration. Potentially critical components of the relation between language(s) and organizing may thus remain obscure. We hope that the present chapter will help mitigate this risk.

Our intention is to extend and develop current research on the dynamics associated with multiple languages in organizations by leveraging language-sensitive IB studies to shed light on issues of particular interest to OS research. Not to throw the baby out with the bath water, we fully recognize that IB research engaging with the theme of language has tended thus far to build on simpler ontological and epistemological assumptions than work inspired by CCO, not least with regard to the nature of language itself. We agree with Karhunen and colleagues (2018) that this constitutes an important challenge for future language-sensitive IB research. Still, it would be shortsighted to ignore the lessons that language-sensitive IB research may hold for OS.

Accordingly, and also echoing the recent call by Geppert and colleagues (2016) for integrating IB and OS perspectives more generally, we set the following interlinked aims for this chapter. First, to articulate the languages-related lacuna in OS through an overview of CCO-informed research. Second, and more specifically, to juxtapose the CCO perspective with empirical findings on language from the IB context. Third, to suggest some future trajectories for OS focusing explicitly on languages, multilingualism, and linguistic diversity. These trajectories include observations on the methodological challenges of conducting empirical research in multilingual contexts (Brannen et al., 2014; Piekkari et al., 2014; Tietze, 2010), an issue of high practical relevance that IB tends to address more explicitly and transparently than comparable OS research. Fulfilling these aims provides the structure of the remainder of this chapter.

CCO: THE COMMUNICATIVE CONSTITUTION OF ORGANIZATIONS

The field of CCO 'seeks to explain the existence, recognition, practice, power, and modification of organization in explicitly communicative terms' (Kuhn, 2012, 550). What is meant by communication encompasses a range of forms; for example, Cooren et al. (2011, 1151) include 'speech acts, turns of talk, discourse, rhetorical tropes, texts, narratives' and 'policies, strategies, operations, values, (formal or informal) relations, or structures' as well as any 'artifact, metaphor, architectural element [and] body' (ibid.). Vasquez, Bencherki, Cooren and Sergi (2018, 419) also mention 'feelings, concerns, principles, [and] collectives'. Communication is thus a broad label that includes but is not limited to verbal or written linguistic forms of expression, although they are central to this chapter. CCO, more specifically the so-called Montreal School of communication studies, views communication as 'the means by which organizations are established, composed, designed, and sustained' (Cooren et al., 2011, 1150). In other words, organizations are constituted through communicative processes – organization(s) *as* communication – rather than communication simply being the means of transmission of information, meaning and ideas *in* organizations.

Such a communicative perspective does not assume convergence; rather, it can be seen as a polyphonic endeavour (Trittin and Schoeneborn, 2017) where the aim is not to reach consensus or assimilation, but to dialogically link 'various dissonant voices' (p. 311). This makes communication 'a process that is uncertain, ambiguous, paradoxical, fragmented, and dilemmatic', yet for these reasons also fluid and ripe with potential. It also brings power into focus, for example by drawing attention to how power makes particular meanings dominant or marginal, or ascribes particular individuals and groups with authority (Kuhn, 2012).

Empirically, CCO has in particular been employed to analyse organizational identity and strategy. Identity-focused research has for example conceptualized how fluid types of organizations such as collectives and social movements may achieve status as an entity or actor through speech acts that function as identity claims (Dobusch and Schoeneborn, 2015); in other words, how language use brings an organizational entity into being. Dawson (2018) similarly focuses on organizational identity in relation to social media interactions, including viewing social media marketers as boundary spanners who translate social media messages into organizational identity-making. Dawson emphasizes 'language, plurivocality and co-authoring' (p. 1) which points towards how multiple actors are involved in linguistic identity constructions. The multiplicity and diversity of organizational actors is also addressed by

Koschmann (2012) who examines the emergence of a collective identity through the communicative processes of interorganizational collaboration. Also related to organizations and identities, but with a focus on individuals' organizational identification, Chaput et al. (2011) examine how identification occurs in everyday interactions. They do this by analysing the development of a political party in Quebec, thus researching an empirical setting which is linguistically different to the dominant national language (French v. English). The paper does mention two languages being used, but it is in relation to translating French-language data into English for research and publication purposes and the authors do not discuss the broader linguistic context within which the party is formed, nor how multiple languages shaped knowledge production.

Related to strategy, Vasquez et al. (2018) draw on a CCO approach to examine the organizational strategic planning process, including interactions between individuals and the role of texts in negotiating meanings surrounding organizational strategy. Importantly, the authors show how such communicative processes are underpinned by power in that 'different matters of concerns are voiced and others are made silent' (p. 429). Similarly acknowledging the processual, communicative character of strategy – or strategizing – Aten and Thomas (2016) examine how technology-enabled crowdsourcing influences strategizing by analysing two cases of strategy generation in one organization in the US Navy. Technology allowed for what the authors call 'the collective construction of multivoice strategic resources' (p. 165), thus framing strategizing as an emergent process involving multiple actors, which shapes the future of the organization. Finally, Kopaneva (2015) draws on CCO to explore how employees construct ownership of the company mission and vision, which can be seen in terms of an authoritative text (Koschmann, 2012) 'through which an organization constitutes itself as an agent' (Kopaneva, 2015, 127). Through a qualitative study, the author shows how company missions and visions are subject to different interpretations and negotiations, which produce different orientations towards the organization. Kopaneva and Sia (2015) further elaborate on the same argument and interestingly include the observation that 'communities of practice essentially speak different languages' (p. 363), pointing to how communicative processes involve translation. In the article 'different languages' refer to worldviews rather than multiple natural languages, but in this chapter the role of different languages for constituting organizations is precisely what we seek to explore.

While studies such as the above shed valuable light on how organizations come into being and are sustained through communicative acts, including speech and text, they have so far not accounted for the coexistence of multiple languages. To start addressing this lacuna, we next turn to language-sensitive research in the field of IB, within which inquiries into the character and effects of managing multiple languages in an organizational context span more than two decades.

LANGUAGE-SENSITIVE IB RESEARCH

Already the earliest language-sensitive IB research addressed the coexistence of multiple languages as constitutive of MNE (informal) organization. In their seminal case study of a large Finnish multinational, Marschan-Piekkari, Welch and Welch (1999) explored how the parallel existence of multiple languages in the firm influenced its *de facto* structure, specifically through the emergence of informal language-based groupings that for example brought German-speaking and Latin units closer together while pulling them apart from units using other languages. This language-based affinity resulted in more interaction, more extensive exchange of information, and a greater sense of affinity within the language-based groups, and correspondingly less identification between them. This gave rise to what Marschan-Piekkari and colleagues termed a 'shadow structure' that had little to do with the formal organizational structure yet played a powerful organizing role.

Marschan-Piekkari and colleagues (1999) also presented early evidence of the links between language skills and organizational members' ability to access organizational resources and influence organizational goals, in highlighting how Finnish-speakers stationed in subsidiary units enjoyed better access to news and knowledge emanating in Finnish from HQ than did other organizational members in similar hierarchical positions but lacking skills in the parent company language. Later research has arrived at similar findings pertaining to the influence of a shared language on interunit knowledge flows (e.g. Barner-Rasmussen, 2003) and trust and shared vision (e.g. Barner-Rasmussen and Björkman, 2007). These findings at the interunit level have subsequently been supported by individual- and group-level studies documenting tendencies towards language-based homosociality (e.g. Mäkelä et al., 2007), and trust between groups being impeded by language-related behaviour such as code switching (Harzing and Feely, 2008; Tange and Lauring, 2009; Hinds et al., 2014).

Language-sensitive IB research has furthermore underlined that also in a hierarchical sense, MNE organizations are constituted (or rather, often fail to be constituted as unitary organizations) by communication carried out in different languages. This is because different employee groups are highly differentiated in their ability to bridge between or move across the multiple language boundaries that typify MNEs (Barner-Rasmussen and Björkman, 2007). A common corporate language (CCL) is often perceived as a solution to such barriers, but its adoption can be significantly impeded by negative political and/or cultural connotations (see e.g. Vaara et al., 2005) pertaining to power relations. Even without such connotations, individuals in different functions, at different hierarchical levels, and with different demographic backgrounds tend to differ in terms of their CCL skills (Barner-Rasmussen and Aarnio, 2011; Yamao and Sekiguchi, 2015). Research on language use in other types of international work communities, for example within academia (Śliwa and Johansson, 2014), add weight to the argument that even those who are highly fluent in the CCL but do not speak it as their native language may be at a disadvantage and may therefore perceive themselves as outsiders. Moreover, even at best, a CCL usually only solves internal language challenges. In external contacts, client requirements, subsidiary legitimacy, and formal demands (e.g. with regard to taxation or accounting procedures) usually force the use of local language/s (Brannen et al., 2014; Feely and Harzing, 2003; Marschan-Piekkari et al., 1999).

The challenges discussed above are all directly related to how the simultaneous existence of multiple natural languages in MNEs influence the possibilities to 'perform' or 'make' shared reality in these organizations. They take on a special poignancy in arduous situations such as restructurings or postmerger integration processes (Vaara et al., 2005), where evidence shows that linguistic challenges hamper the constitutive power of managerial communication in numerous and severe ways. Language may cause misunderstandings regarding goals, practices, processes, and intentions between the merged parties, leading to distrust and open conflict (Hinds et al., 2014). Slogans, visions, metaphors, and figures of speech may turn out wrong or laughable in translation (Barner-Rasmussen et al., 2009; Koveshnikov et al., 2016), decreasing credibility and watering down efforts to build shared visions and goals. Communication efforts may also enmesh with prior historical tensions at country level (Vaara et al., 2005), resulting in deliberate misinterpretations and conflict escalation along demographic faultlines constituting a major block to efforts to forge organizational unity.

When considering the above in light of the previously outlined CCO-based studies of organizational identity and strategy, we see how language-sensitive IB research has emphatically demonstrated that multiple languages are a crucial constitutive component of organizing and its political, social, and material effects. Incorporating a multiple language perspective into OS through a CCO 'entry point' therefore paves the way for enriching the field of OS.

DEVELOPING A RESEARCH AGENDA

Recent calls for increased cross-disciplinary explorations between OS and IB have pointed towards ensuing mutual benefits. Speaking in favour of enhancing such dialogues, Piekkari and Westney (2017) specifically discuss organization theory perspectives on language in MNEs. They show how drawing on theorizing developed within OS in relation to organizational design, identity and power may enrich language-sensitive IB research. Similarly, Karhunen and colleagues (2018) argue that three distinct perspectives (a structural, a functional, and a social practice view) can be outlined within existing IB research on language, and the greatest gaps in current research – as well as the greatest opportunities to genuinely advance our understanding – are in the latter view. They go on to present a number of suggestions for how the view of language as a social practice can be further advanced.

In spite of these positive developments, it is clear that bringing language-focused research in OS and in IB closer together still offers ample opportunities for theoretical and methodological advances. As we have argued above, OS has largely ignored the empirical issue of multiple languages with all its potential corollaries, while IB stands to benefit greatly from more nuanced approaches to language as an organizational issue. In what follows we outline some preliminary suggestions of particular areas of inquiry within OS that stand to gain much from incorporating analyses of multiple languages.

Identities in Organizations

The research on identities in organizational contexts is well developed in OS (see Brown, 2017, 2019, 2021; Knights and Clarke, 2017). The enduring appeal of the concept of identity is that it 'facilitates cross-disciplinary and multi-level research, encourages nuanced, contextual analyses, and focuses squarely on people in *processes of organizing*' (Brown, 2019, 7, added emphasis). The perspective predominantly taken on identities is a processual one, emphasizing their dynamic, non-essentialist and constitutive nature – a perspective that chimes with the ontological tenets of CCO, as seen above in the CCO-based research into identities. One strand of OS identity research is concerned with how identities are shaped by 'situated practices of language use' (Brown, 2019, 9), primarily with a focus on discourse and forms of talk (e.g. Thomas and Davies, 2005; Brown and Toyoki, 2013). How the use of a particular language, or multiple languages, shapes identities and identifications in such processes however remains unjustifiably underexplored. Boussebaa and Brown (2017) present an exception as they draw on IB language-sensitive research on English as a *lingua franca* to critically examine the effects of organizational Englishization on employee identity regulation. Also bridging IB and OS to explore identities, Koveshnikov et al. (2016) discuss managerial identity work in a Finnish–Russian MNE but focus on forms of talk rather than on the use of multiple languages.

Brown (2019) outlines three key strands of organizational identity research, two of which are of particular interest for developing our proposed research agenda. The first of these strands is concerned with how identities are intertwined with organizational processes and outcomes; in other words, a perspective on identities and organizing as mutually constitutive processes. In this strand we can position much of the CCO-inspired work on identities outlined earlier, for example Dobusch and Schoeneborn (2015) and Dawson (2018). A second major strand centres on the micro-politics of identity formation, focusing on power relations and questions of structure and agency. This theme aligns with Chaput et al.'s (2011) investigation into how identity is constructed through micro-level interactions. In relation to both these strands we see opportunities for enrichment through cross-fertilization with IB language-sensitive research. First, the exploration of such research into how languages shape the structuring (both formally and informally) and managing of MNEs (e.g. Barner-Rasmussen and Björkman, 2007) presents an existing body of research which has the potential to open up avenues for bringing languages into CCO research focused on identity, and by extension more broadly into OS identity research focused on organizational processes. Second, language-sensitive IB research concerned with how languages are implied in power relations (Vaara et al., 2005) and how language skills shape employees' status positions (Neeley, 2013; Neeley and Dumas, 2016) and access to information and knowledge (Marschan-Piekkari et al., 1999; Barner-Rasmussen, 2003) provides a means to broaden CCO/OS inquiries on power and self-identities to include the role of multiple languages in such processes.

Organizational Diversity

Another area within OS which readily lends itself to further exploration through paying attention to languages, is organizational diversity. This proposed development potentially encompasses two perspectives: (a) multilingualism as a form of diversity, and (b) research into how languages contribute to constituting organizational differences, neither of which has so far been considered in any significant extent in relation to organizational diversity. Ogbonna and Harris (2009) and van Laer and Janssens (2011) are rare examples which in some form account for how language is implied in processes of discrimination and marginalization in relation to diversity. In these papers, language is however merely viewed as a sub-dimension of the broader issue of ethnic diversity. Interestingly, Trittin and Schoeneborn (2017) propose a communications-focused reconceptualization of diversity management as a 'plurality of voices' which articulate meanings of diversity. They view language in use in terms of discourse, but their framework could form the foundation for incorporating a multiple language perspective into diversity research.

Especially within critical diversity studies, the focus is concerned with the production of diversity and 'diverse subjects' (e.g. Ahonen et al., 2014; Brewis, 2019; Zanoni and Janssens, 2007). Such studies often employ discursive analyses to show what kinds of differences are made available through discourses of diversity. For example, Ostendorp and Steyaert (2009, 375) explore how ideas of diversity are 'repeated locally and translated in specific contexts' in a Swiss multilingual organization, but do not per se focus on the practices or effects involving different languages. It is our contention that research into organizational diversity would be enriched by broadening the issue of language beyond discourse to account for how difference and diversity are multilingually performed. This would include viewing language as a 'diversity category' which shapes opportunities and access, which IB research has begun to address in terms of careers and participation in decision-making (Piekkari, 2008; Tietze, 2008), but the field of diversity research within OS has so far not paid attention to. Here, burgeoning work which draws on sociolinguistics for understanding social evaluations of speakers of different languages might be further developed (Śliwa and Johansson, 2014). Language-sensitive explorations of organizational diversity may also extend into examinations of the simultaneous use, blending, and 'making' of languages, hitherto exemplified by concepts such as *multilingua franca* (Janssens and Steyaert, 2014), translanguaging (García, 2009), and code switching (Nunan and Carter, 2001). The mixing of multiple languages is seen to carry benefits related to inclusivity and creativity (Lüdi et al., 2013), another aspect that might provide useful insights into developing organizational diversity research.

Translation

A third area of considerable potential is exploring how processes of translation shape organizing and organizations. Within OS, the concept of translation is not new in that it has been borrowed from the philosophy of science and notably the work of Latour (1987) to describe processes of organizational change (Czarniawska and Sévon, 1996) and the spread of management theories (fashions) (Czarniawska, 2011). In these texts, translation – as opposed to diffusion – signifies the processes by which ideas and practices travel and change as they are adopted and adapted into local contexts. Translation is of course also used in the context of languages and constitutes an existing area of research in IB in relation to managing the multilingual MNE (e.g. Ciuk et al., 2018; Tréguer-Felten, 2017). Here, we see the potential for OS to broaden existing conceptualizations of translation to incorporate a multilingual dimension, including a consideration of the (im)possibility of translating management and organization phenomena into different languages (see e.g. Holden and Michailova, 2014).

Epistemological and Methodological Challenges: How IB Can Help

To this list we can add some insights from the border zone between epistemology and methodology, where IB scholars have expended much effort – perhaps due to the international and cross-cultural nature of their field where translation and its positivist sister, construct equivalency, have long been regarded as key issues of empirical quality. Welch and Piekkari (2006) were early to point out the importance of what language interviews are conducted in, as well as the limitations of most researchers and research teams in these regards. They particularly warned of the potential hidden consequences of interviewing respondents, especially non-elite ones, in languages that they may be less comfortable with than the interviewers (see also, e.g. Aichhorn and Puck, 2017 on 'foreign language anxiety'). In this context we emphasize that this issue is significant especially if the resulting data – including metaphors and nuances such as personal pronouns which may be interpreted as signals of, for example, organizational identification – are then subjected to in-depth interpretive analysis, as the risk for misunderstandings and misattributions is evident. In terms of solutions to this vexed challenge, Tenzer and colleagues (2017) identify 'enormous potential' in multi-language research teams providing an intimate understanding of languages relevant to the research context at hand, especially in emerging economies.

Welch and Piekkari (2006) also raised a warning flag regarding potential biases and outright errors in the translation of interview data into the reporting language (usually English), an argument subsequently elaborated by Chidlow, Plakoyiannaki and Welch (2014). Criticizing 'technicist' approaches to translation as word-by-word transfers of meaning, Chidlow and colleagues advocate the reframing of translation as a process of intercultural interaction, arguing that this can provide insights relevant far beyond IB, in all disciplines that collect data from more than one linguistic context.

Although much of language-sensitive IB research tends to take a functionalist perspective on languages, there is also a growing stream of research which conceptualizes languages in more nuanced tones; as fluid, practised in action and as having hybrid characteristics (Karhunen et al., 2018). Especially these latter lines of inquiry may be valuable for developing CCO-research in understanding the dynamic, constitutive role of languages.

CONCLUSION

To conclude, as we have begun to outline in this chapter, we see ample opportunities for furthering language-centred approaches to organizations and organizing through considering how the coexistence of languages, which has been studied in the organizational context of MNEs, might inform research within the field of organization studies. Furthermore, integrating novel perspectives from fields such as critical sociolinguistics and translation studies has the potential to open up new vistas for both fields. More generally, drawing on insights from the broader social sciences could help us develop a richer understanding of the effects of languages on the processes of organizing, and of the effects of organizations and organizing process on language-related phenomena.

REFERENCES

Ahonen, P., Tienari, J., Meriläinen, S. and Pullen, A. (2014), Hidden contexts and invisible power relations: A Foucauldian reading of diversity research. *Human Relations*, 67(3), 263–286.

Aichhorn, N. and Puck, J. (2017), 'I just don't feel comfortable speaking English': Foreign language anxiety as a catalyst for spoken-language barriers in MNCs. *International Business Review*, 26(4), 749–763.

Alvesson, M. and Kärreman, D. (2000), Taking the linguistic turn in organizational research: Challenges, responses, consequences. *The Journal of Applied Behavioural Science*, 36(2), 136–158.

Alvesson, M. and Willmott, H. (2002), Identity regulation as organizational control: Producing the appropriate individual. *Journal of Management Studies*, 39(5), 619–644.

Ashcraft, K.L., Kuhn, T.R. and Cooren, F. (2009), Constitutional amendments: 'Materializing' organizational communication. In J.P. Walsh and A.P. Brief (eds), *The Academy of Management Annals, Vol. 3*. London: Routledge, pp. 1–64.

Ashcraft, K.L. and Mumby, D.K. (2004), *Reworking Gender: A Feminist Communicology of Organization*. Thousand Oaks, CA: Sage.

Aten, K. and Thomas, G.F. (2016), Crowdsourcing strategizing: Communication technology affordances and the communicative constitution of organizational strategy. *International Journal of Business Communication*, 53(2), 148–180.

Barner-Rasmussen, W. (2003), *Knowledge sharing in multinational corporations. A social capital perspective*. Doctoral thesis. Helsinki: Hanken School of Economics.

Barner-Rasmussen, W. and Aarnio, C. (2011), Shifting the faultlines of language. A quantitative functional-level exploration of language use in MNC subsidiaries. *Journal of World Business*, 46(3), 288–295.

Barner-Rasmussen, W. and Björkman, I. (2007), Language matters! Language fluency, socialization mechanisms and their relationship to interunit trustworthiness and shared vision. *Management and Organization Review*, 3(1), 105–128.

Barner-Rasmussen, W., Björkman, I., Ehrnrooth, M., Koveshnikov, A., Mäkelä, K., Vaara, E. and Zhang, L. (2009), *Cross-Border Competence Management in Emerging Markets: Voices from China and Russia*. Research reports of Hanken School of Economics, Helsinki.

Boje, D. (1991), The storytelling organization: A study of story performance in an office-supply firm. *Administrative Science Quarterly*, 36, 106–126.

Boussebaa, M. and Brown, A.D. (2017), Englishization, identity regulation and imperialism. *Organization Studies*, 38(1), 7–29.

Brannen, M.Y., Piekkari, R. and Tietze, S. (2014), The multifaceted role of language in international business: Unpacking the forms, functions and features of a critical challenge to MNC theory and performance. *Journal of International Business Studies*, 45(5), 495–507.

Brewis, D. (2019), Duality and fallibility in practices of the Self: The 'inclusive subject' in diversity training. *Organization Studies*, 40(1), 93–113.

Brown, A.D. (2017), Identity work and organizational identification. *International Journal of Management Reviews*, 19(3), 296–317.

Brown, A.D. (2019), Identities in organization studies. *Organization Studies*, 40(1), 7–21.

Brown, A.D. (2021), Identities in and around organizations: Towards an identity work perspective. *Human Relations*, DOI: 10.1177/0018726721993910.

Brown, A.D. and Toyoki, S. (2013), Identity work and legitimacy. *Organization Studies*, 34(7), 875–896.

Chaput, M., Brummans, B.H.J.M. and Cooren, F. (2011), The role of organizational identification in the communicative constitution of an organization: A study of cosubstantialization in a young political party. *Management Communication Quarterly*, 25(2), 252–282.

Chidlow, A., Plakoyiannaki, E. and Welch, C. (2014), Translation in cross-language international business research: Beyond equivalence. *Journal of International Business Studies*, 45, 562–582.

Ciuk, S., James, P. and Śliwa, M. (2018), Micropolitical dynamics of interlingual translation processes in an MNC subsidiary. *British Journal of Management*, 30(4), 926–942.

Cooren, F., Kuhn, T., Cornelissen, J.P. and Clark, T. (2011), Communication, organizing and organization: An overview and introduction to the special issue. *Organization Studies*, 32(9), 1149–1170.

Czarniawska, B. (1997), *A Narrative Approach to Organization Studies*. London: Sage.

Czarniawska, B. (2004), *Narratives in Social Science Research*. London: Sage.

Czarniawska, B. (2011), Fashion in research and management. *Organization Studies*, 32(5), 599–602.

Czarniawska, B. and Sévon, G. (eds) (1996), *Translating Organizational Change*. Berlin: De Gruyter.

Dawson, V.R. (2018), Fans, friends, advocates, ambassadors, and haters: Social media communities and the communicative constitution of organizational identity. *Social Media + Society*, 4(1), 1–11.

Dobusch, L. and Schoeneborn, D. (2015), Fluidity, identity, and organizationality: The communicative constitution of *Anonymous*. *Journal of Management Studies*, 52(8), 1005–1035.

Feely, A. J. and Harzing, A. W. (2003), Language management in multinational companies. *Cross Cultural Management: An International Journal*, 10(2), 37–52.

Gabriel, Y. (1995), The unmanaged organization: Stories, fantasies and subjectivity. *Organization Studies*, 16(3), 477–501.

Gabriel, Y. (2000), *Storytelling in Organizations: Facts, Fictions and Fantasies*. Oxford: Oxford University Press.

García, O. (2009), Education, multilingualism and translanguaging in the 21st century. In A. Mohanty, M. Panda, R. Phillipson and T. Skutnabb-Kangas (eds), *Multilingual Education for Social Justice: Globalising the Local*. New Delhi: Orient Blackswan, pp. 128–145.

Geppert, M., Becker-Ritterspah, F. and Mudambi, R. (2016), Politics and power in multinational companies: Integrating the International Business and Organization Studies perspectives. *Organization Studies*, 37(9), 1209–1225.

Ghoshal, S. and Westney, E. (eds) (1993), *Organization Theory and the Multinational Corporation*. New York: St Martin's Press.

Gupta, A.K. and Govindarajan, V. (1991), Knowledge flows and the structure of control within multi-national corporations. *Academy of Management Review*, 16(4), 768–792.

Hardy, C. and Thomas, R. (2015), Discourse in a material world. *Journal of Management Studies*, 52(5), 680–696.

Harzing, A.-W. and Feely, A.J. (2008), The language barrier and its implications for HQ–subsidiary relationships. *Cross Cultural Management: An International Journal*, 15(1), 49–61.

Hinds, P.J., Neeley, T.B. and Cramton, C.D. (2014), Language as a lightning rod: Power contests, emotion regulation, and subgroup dynamics in global teams. *Journal of International Business Studies*, 45(4), 536–561.

Holden, N. and Michailova, S. (2014), A more expansive perspective on translation in IB research: Insights from the Russian *Handbook of Knowledge Management*. *Journal of International Business Studies*, 45(5), 906–918.

Iedema, R. and Wodak, R. (1999), Introduction: Organizational discourses and practices. *Discourse and Society*, 10(1), 5–19.

Janssens, M. and Steyaert, C. (2014), Re-considering language within a cosmopolitan understanding: Toward a multilingual franca approach in International Business Studies. *Journal of International Business Studies*, 45(5), 623–639.

Karhunen, P., Kankaanranta, A., Louhiala-Salminen, L. and Piekkari, R. (2018), Let's talk about language: A review of language-sensitive research in international management. *Journal of Management Studies*, 55(6), 980–1013.

Knights, D. and Clarke, C. (2017), Pushing the boundaries of amnesia and myopia: A critical review of the literature on identity in management and organization studies. *International Journal of Management Reviews*, 19, 337–356.

Kopaneva, I.M. (2015), Left in the dust: Employee constructions of mission and vision ownership. *International Journal of Business Communication*, 56(1), 122–145.

Kopaneva, I. and Sia, P.M. (2015), Lost in translation: Employee and organizational constructions of vision and mission. *Management Communication Quarterly*, 29(3), 358–384.

Koschmann, M.A. (2012), The communicative constitution of collective identity in interorganizational collaboration. *Management Communication Quarterly*, 27(1), 61–89.

Koveshnikov, A., Vaara, E. and Ehrnrooth, M. (2016), Stereotype-based managerial identity work in multinational corporations. *Organization Studies*, 37(9), 1353–1379.

Kuhn, T. (2012), Negotiating the micro–macro divide: Thought leadership from organizational communication for theorizing organization. *Management Communication Quarterly*, 26(4), 543–584.

Latour, B. (1987), *Science in Action: How to Follow Scientists and Engineers through Society*. Cambridge, MA: Harvard University Press.

Lüdi, G., Höchle, K. and Yanaprasart, P. (2013), Multilingualism and diversity management in companies in the Upper Rhine Region. In A.C. Berthoud, F. Grin and G. Lüdi (eds), *Exploring the Dynamics of Multilingualism: The DYLAN Project*. Amsterdam and Philadelphia: John Benjamins, pp. 59–82.

Mäkelä, K., Kalla, H.K. and Piekkari, R. (2007), Interpersonal similarity as a driver of knowledge sharing within multinational corporations. *International Business Review*, 16(1), 1–22.

Marschan, R., Welch, D. and Welch, L. (1997), Language: The forgotten factor in multinational management. *European Management Journal*, 15(5), 591–598.

Marschan-Piekkari, R., Welch, D.E. and Welch, L.S. (1999), In the shadow: The impact of language on structure, power and communication in the multinational. *International Business Review*, 8(4), 421–440.

Mumby, D.K. (1997), Modernism, postmodernism, and communication studies: A rereading of an ongoing debate. *Communication Theory*, 7(1), 1–28.

Mumby, D.K. (2013), *Organizational Communication: A Critical Approach*. Los Angeles, CA: Sage.

Neeley, T.B. (2013), Language matters: Status loss and achieved status distinctions in global organizations. *Organization Science*, 24(2), 476–497.

Neeley, T.B. and Dumas, T.L. (2016), Unearned status gain: Evidence from a global language mandate. *Academy of Management Journal*, 59(1), 14–43.

Nunan, D. and Carter, R. (2001), *Teaching English to Speakers of Other Languages*. Cambridge: Cambridge University Press.

Ogbonna, E. and Harris, L.C. (2006), The dynamics of employee relationships in an ethnically diverse workforce. *Human Relations*, 59(3), 379–407.

Ostendorp, A. and Steyaert, C. (2009), How different can differences be(come)?: Interpretative repertoires of diversity concepts in Swiss-based organizations. *Scandinavian Journal of Management*, 25(4), 374–384.

Piekkari, R. (2008), Language and careers in multinational corporations. In S. Tietze (ed.), *International Management and Language*. London: Routledge, pp. 128–137.

Piekkari, R., Welch, D.E. and Welch, L.S. (2014), *Language in International Business: The Multilingual Reality of Global Business Expansion*. Cheltenham, UK and Northampton, MA, USA: Edward Elgar Publishing.

Piekkari, R. and Westney, E.D. (2017), Language as a meeting ground for research on the MNC and organization theory. In Christoph Dörrenbächer and Mike Geppert (eds), *Multinational Corporations and Organization Theory: Post Millennium Perspectives (Research in the Sociology of Organizations, Volume 49)*. Bingley, UK: Emerald Publishing, pp. 193–232.

Roth, K. and Kostova, T. (2003), The use of the multinational corporation as a research context. *Journal of Management*, 29(6), 883–902.

Schoeneborn, D., Kuhn, T.R. and Kärreman, D. (2019), The communicative constitution of organization, organizing and organizationality. *Organization Studies*, 40(4), 475–496.

Śliwa, M. and Johansson, M. (2014), How non-native English speaking staff are evaluated in linguistically diverse organizations: A sociolinguistic perspective. *Journal of International Business Studies*, 45(5), 1133–1151.

Steyaert, C. and Janssens, M. (2012), Multilingual scholarship and the paradox of translation and language in management and organization. *Organization*, 20(1), 131–142.

Tange, H. and Lauring, J. (2009), Language management and social interaction within the multilingual workplace. *Journal of Communication Management*, 13(3), 218–232.

Tenzer, H., Terjesen, S. and Harzing, A-W. (2017), Language in international business: A review and agenda for future research. *Management International Review*, 57(6), 815–854.

Thomas, R. and Davies, A. (2005), Theorizing the micro-politics of resistance: New Public Management and managerial identities in the UK public services. *Organization Studies*, 26(5), 683–706.

Tietze, S. (2008), The work of management academics: An English language perspective. *English for Specific Purposes*, 27(4), 371–386.

Tietze, S. (2010), International managers as translators. *European Journal of International Management*, 4(1–2), 184–199.

Tréguer-Felten, G. (2017), The role of translation in the cross-cultural transferability of corporate codes of conduct. *International Journal of Cross-Cultural Management*, 17(1), 137–149.

Trittin, H. and Schoeneborn, D. (2017), Diversity as polyphony: Reconceptualizing diversity management from a communication-centered perspective. *Journal of Business Ethics*, 144(2), 305–322.

Tsoukas, H. and Chia, R. (2002), On organizational becoming: Rethinking organizational change. *Organization Science*, 13(5), 567–582.

Vaara, E., Tienari, J., Piekkari, R. and Säntti, R. (2005), Language and the circuits of power in a merging multinational corporation. *Journal of Management Studies*, 42(3), 595–623.

van Laer, K. and Janssens, M. (2011), Ethnic minority professionals' experiences with subtle discrimination in the workplace. *Human Relations*, 64(9), 1203–1227.

Vasquez, C., Bencherki, N., Cooren, F. and Sergi, V. (2018), From 'matters of concern' to 'matters of authority': Studying the performativity of strategy from a communicative constitution of organization (CCO) approach. *Long Range Planning*, 51(3), 417–435.

Welch, C. and Piekkari, R. (2006), Crossing language boundaries: Qualitative interviewing in International Business. *Management International Review*, 46(4), 417–437.

Yamao, S. and Sekiguchi, T. (2015), Employee commitment to corporate globalization: The role of English language proficiency and human resource practices. Journal of World Business, 50(1), 168–179.

Zanoni, P. and Janssens, M. (2007), Minority employees engaging with (diversity), management: An analysis of control, agency, and micro-emancipation. *Journal of Management Studies*, 44(8), 1371–1397.

Zanoni, P. and Janssens, M. (2015), The power of diversity discourses at work: On the interlocking nature of diversities and occupations. *Organization Studies*, 36(11), 1463–1483.

11. Revisiting identity construction in the multilingual workplace: an intersectional approach

Linda Cohen and Jane Kassis-Henderson

INTRODUCTION

In this chapter we use an intersectional lens to challenge widely held assumptions about the role of language and identity in organizational processes, focusing in particular on the way language and identity shape power, position and performance. Drawing on language-oriented organizational studies, we seek to disrupt accepted narratives about linguistic norms and standards, and to show why these norms are not adapted to the needs of today's multilingual workplace. These traditional narratives reflect the general acceptance of dominant linguistic norms based on a standardized national language in processes of socialization. Individuals tend to internalize these standardized norms and mistakenly consider superior this standard style of speech over others. This can have a negative impact on organizational and individual performance and cause companies to view language and cultural diversity as a 'problem'.

The approach to language and identity to which we adhere is based on a dynamic co-construction between the individual and the specific context in which individuals interact to focus on 'becoming' as they negotiate identity construction by and through social interactions (Alvesson et al., 2008), rather than on 'being' in terms of a homogenous and deterministic model. Hence, we situate and analyse language and culture in the interstices between people, as well as within individuals themselves. According to this perspective, the interplay of language and identity is not only negotiated and situated (Blommaert, 2010; Martin-Jones et al., 2012); it underpins a view of languages as hybrid, fluid and situational codes (Primecz et al., 2009; Zanoni et al., 2010; Janssens and Steyaert, 2014; Holmes, 2015; Steyaert and Janssens, 2015). Due to the fact that different facets of identity condition expectations and reactions within the context of specific encounters, consciously deploying a change of voice according to context can have a positive impact on empowerment (Kramsch, 2012; Steyaert and Janssens, 2015).

This alternative conception of identity construction draws on the theoretical framework of intersectionality (Zander et al., 2010) which allows for a broader delineation of identity determination, enabling 'becoming' by refocusing attention on the multiple cultural and linguistic facets of each individual that play out differently according to the needs of each encounter. If people were to discontinue the deterministic model which consists in routinely reproducing their sense of self-identity as if they were grounded in a stable, pre-defined setting they would better position themselves to adapt to changing contexts which characterize the workplace today (Alvesson et al., 2008; Coupland and Brown, 2012). Through this dialogic process of identity construction that is based on an awareness of self in co-relation to the external social forces at a given time, individuals are able to adopt a critical and more flexible approach to language, both as observers and as observed, and through agency and reflexivity, become conscious of the ways language (or voice) can be used to empower, cope with change, resist constraints and manage stigmatization in order to fit in – or indeed to opt out of – the dominant mode in organizations.

A NEGLECTED AREA IN ORGANIZATIONAL STUDIES

Mainstream research on management and organizations, we contend, has not paid sufficient attention to the 'language factor' resulting in the failure to question the values inherent in the dominant narrative in research and institutions. Based on the premise of 'one country/one culture/one language', as we will show, this standardized essentialist paradigm leads to de facto exclusions by imposing and maintaining the dominant codes of linguistic and cultural behaviour, 'othering' those who do not conform to, or who have not adequately integrated, this idealized model. This view of language as static explains the tendency of organizations to implement policies based on simplified solutions to a complex set of issues, such as imposing a *lingua franca* as a way to overcome communication barriers and facilitate operations. Pretending the problem no longer exists does not eradicate its manifestations and this solution itself has created a new set of problems. As will be shown below, acquiring the linguistic code alone does not necessarily lead to successful interaction; equally important are the meta-cognitive skills that determine how to use the code in context.

Indeed, organizational inquiry has explored the role played by communication in constituting organizations (Ashcraft and Mumby, 2004; Cooren et al., 2011). In certain streams of inquiry, communication is considered to be equivalent to organizing, as an organization is shaped and transformed by communication practices (Schoeneborn et al., 2019). One aspect of this is the investigation of how power struggles are played out through discourse (Alvesson and Willmott, 2002; Zanoni and Janssens, 2015). Research has brought to light the diverse functions of language that play a part in organizational life by showing its symbolic function and its role as a marker of individual or group identity or as a factor of exclusion or instrument of power. However, what has not been sufficiently analysed is the coexistence of multiple languages and the consequences both for the individual and the increasingly multilingual organization.

Paradoxically, the dynamic role of language is equally overlooked in organizational studies on identity (Mughan, 2015) where the focus tends to be more on the study of age, gender or ethnicity as differentiating factors and hence identity markers. Although 'language' is of course present in identity studies as they rely on interviews and discourse analysis for research data, the impact of the ways an individual uses language in context is not sufficiently addressed. In summary, commonly held assumptions about language and identity reflect the general acceptance of dominant linguistic norms which has led to the adoption of normative practices within organizations. We take a closer look at the consequences of assuming that 'language' and 'culture' conform to a deterministic model in the next section.

MAINSTREAM MODEL BASED ON ESSENTIALISM: LIMITS OF NORMATIVE PRACTICES

Based on the view that individuals can be fitted into measurable categories, institutions commonly resort to standardized tests to determine people's language proficiency and suitability for employment. Such tests, however, do not sufficiently evaluate language use in context and therefore do not reflect the true linguistic and communicative competencies of the individual (Pilcher and Richards, 2017). This is because they test an individual's test-taking ability, that is, their familiarity with the dominant test-taking mode, rather than the potential to use language in a specific context, resulting in the exclusion of otherwise well-qualified individuals. In addition, these standardized tests assume a uniform national identity and form of language, which does not account for the diversity that exists within the population as a whole, as manifested in varied grammatical and lexical usages as well as in different dialects and accents. On the personal, or individual, level, the standardized norm does not account for the various identity markers which influence language use or the socially constructed nature of identities as they play out in context. So, whether on the collective or individual level, standardized language requirements are a normalizing device which reinforces the status quo.

Indeed, criteria founded on the monolingual model – whereby languages are seen as strictly separate codes epitomized by the ideal native speaker – prevail and marginalize the different language and communication competencies of bi- and multi-linguals. This means that models of language proficiency are based on the performance of a given speaker in one particular language, regardless of the particular language profile of this speaker. Relying on standards that use monolingualism as a yardstick, individuals attribute to themselves and to others specific language identities such as native speaker, bilingual, or multilingual which are then linked to expectations of practices and competencies. Even those who are 'bilingual' or speak several languages without attaining the level of the 'ideal' native speaker may be stigmatized in contexts dominated by monolinguals (who often accumulate this privilege with that of being a 'native speaker' of the dominant language). The monolingual and mono-cultural bias amplifies an enduring state of privilege that benefits speakers of the dominant language (Neeley, 2012; Gaibrois and Nentwich, 2020).

Adherence to this status quo creates boundaries between language groups, creating winners and losers and the formation of in-groups and out-groups based on perceived language skills. This often leads to misunderstandings in the multilingual workplace linked to performance anxiety or over-confidence.

The predominant solution for dealing with the complexity of this diverse workforce has been to adopt a *lingua franca*, most often English. This impacts recruitment and promotion processes and provides justification for excluding 'otherness' found in groups and individuals who do not correspond to dominant criteria. Low tolerance for diversity in accent, register, or grammatical practices results in making sure the marginalized remain marginalized. This effort to eliminate diversity is based on the fiction of the efficacy of standardized language usage, which does not take into account the micro-variations that exist, whether *intra* or *inter*-nationally, when individuals interact in context.

The shift from an over-reliance on standardized language usage towards an emphasis on meta-cognitive skills and the interplay between multiple linguistic codes in interaction is long overdue (Kassis-Henderson et al., 2018).

The following excerpt from data collected in our research on multilingual teams (Cohen and Kassis-Henderson, 2017) demonstrates the importance of calling into question the idealized native speaker model and standardized speech and showing how the realignment of status positions among the members of the multilingual team can help them to focus on the efficacy of communication.

> It's true we have no English speaker in the sense of English/English; so we don't have any complexes – so to speak – in expressing ourselves with our accents, our not quite perfect vocabulary, in fact speaking a common language puts us on a more equal footing. We work together in English, but it is not really English. The English we use is a working language, a language of communication, not the language of Shakespeare!

From these comments, we can see that the interviewee has internalized the dominant power distribution and is sensitive to the possible imbalance that results from the presence of native speakers. Interestingly, although team members may initially accept the dominant role often (self)-assigned to native speakers, as teamwork progresses there is a potential for realignment as clusters play out differently, which may even sideline the native speaker (Cohen and Kassis-Henderson, 2012).

INTERSECTIONALITY AND THE 'MULTILINGUAL TURN': GIVING VOICE TO DIVERSITY

The preceding section has made clear that there is a need for a better understanding of the ways organizations mobilize or impede the coexistence of several languages in the workplace in organizational studies (Johansson and Barner-Rasmussen, 2019). The increasing frequency of interactions between people of diverse cultural and linguistic backgrounds in organizations described above has already given rise to what has been labelled the 'linguistic turn', characterized by greater recognition within the social sciences of the important role of language in the social construction of reality (Vaara et al., 2005). The field of applied linguistics has further evolved by operating a 'multilingual turn', which calls into question the monolingual bias as discussed above and emphasizes the performative role of language in its multiple forms.

However, when international organizations or MNCs do address the 'problem' of linguistic diversity, it is often with the stated purpose of overcoming the difficulties it creates for communication, which results in their arguably simplistic solution of imposing a common working language. Recent research has revealed the shortcomings of this homogenizing monolingual *lingua franca* approach (i.e. imposing the use of English in MNCs) and lays the groundwork for a new model drawing on intersectionality and what has been called the 'multilingual turn' (Kramsch, 2012; May, 2013; Cohen and Kassis-Henderson, 2017) which gives voice to diversity and allows for another, more effective way of being inside organizations – both for the individual as well as the group.

This multilingual/multicultural identity work enables an individual to 'be' differently in an organization and, through agency, to transform what would otherwise be felt and seen as a position of exclusion. For example, given the monolingual bias that commonly exists in mainstream organizations, individuals with hybrid identities tend to silence or self-censor facets of their identity that they consider not valued in the dominant corporate culture – such as failing to mention Tamoul or Arabic on a CV. This shows a systemic lack of awareness of the added-value multilingual individuals bring to the organization both in terms of the languages they speak as well as the meta-cognitive skills associated with multilingualism (Hong and Doz, 2013). Such individuals silence themselves, and are too often silenced by, the dominant language and culture.

By drawing on the concept of intersectionality (Crenshaw, 1991; Boogaard and Roggeband, 2010; Zander et al., 2010; Frame, 2016) to revisit the constructs of linguistic and national identity, this chapter adopts a *multiple culture* and *multilingual* perspective that includes group affiliations – beyond the national – that influence the identity and behaviour of individuals (Sackmann, 1997). These broader, fluid and non-exclusive group affiliations impacting the construction of personal identity fall into three main categories – demographic, geographic and associative – forming a 'cultural mosaic' with each facet of identity, or 'tile' (Chao and Moon, 2005) positioned and repositioned according to the needs of each interaction. This constant repositioning impacts language usage as it entails drawing upon different linguistic resources and modifying 'voice'. The ability to use these different linguistic resources is key to agency as it lays the groundwork to negotiate the social world and to create socially constructed meaning for more effective communication (Bakhtin et al., 1981; Ahearn, 2001).

It is important to note that from a multiple culture and multilingual perspective, sociocultural identities are not static, deterministic constructs resulting only from membership in social, cultural or linguistic groups; rather, they are dynamic and changing and are reflected in the different 'voices' within each individual. Our approach disconnects the relationship between language and national identity and 'dis-invents' language by focusing more on speech and repertoire rather than language as a set or fixed category (Makoni and Pennycook, 2012; Busch, 2012). This is in line with the work of scholars who have conceptualized language as "translingual practices to express voice" (Steyaert and Janssens, 2015:137). An awareness of intersectionality as an analytical framework will help an individual understand the origin of these different voices and accept their importance in the continual process of 'becoming' as identity-construction unfolds in social interactions.

From a multiple culture perspective, all individuals have hybrid voices, but do not necessarily know how to tap into them. Indeed, research has shown that people with awareness of this hybridity identify with one or more 'cultures', or adopt elements of particular 'cultures', depending on the context at any given time (Brannen and Thomas, 2010; Jameson, 2007). This liminality allows the individual to exist in a state of hybridity and change voice as they shift through the intersections of gender, race, class, ethnicity, religion, age, and so on (Ozkazanç-Pan, 2015; Gaibrois, 2018). Hybridity is therefore not simply the sum of two or more cultures or voices. It follows that as each individual has a unique set of linguistic and cultural resources, all workplaces are inherently 'multilingual' and 'multicultural'.

THE 'MULTILINGUAL' PERSPECTIVE AND EMPOWERMENT

This multilingual/multicultural perspective has opened up research avenues for organizational and cross-cultural scholars aiming to understand how individuals and organizations can transform these often hidden resources into productive practices. Some studies focus on the micro-variation manifest in the use of styles, accents and words within what appears on the surface to be the same 'language' – often English – but is in fact a hybrid code. In what is called the 'multilingual franca' approach, words assume new meanings and connotations which are shared momentarily within specific exchanges as speakers tap into their own and others' multilingual repertoires or resources (Makoni and Pennycook, 2012; Janssens and Steyaert, 2014). In this light, English as a *lingua franca* – which is different from standardized English – is conceptualized as a multilingual way of using English which allows people to express voice by mobilizing multiple linguistic resources. This *lingua franca* multilingualism results in languages being "so deeply intertwined and fused into each other that the level of fluidity renders it difficult to determine any boundaries that may indicate that there are different languages involved" (Makoni and Pennycook, 2012:447) and allows the less dominant, or marginalized voices, to come into play.

The excerpt below (Cohen and Kassis-Henderson, 2017:17) demonstrates how speakers may use their varied linguistic resources corresponding to different facets of their identity in order to build a common communication practice which is conducive to building relations and enhancing performance. Translanguaging often becomes the norm in multilingual groups, even when organizations try to impose a *lingua franca* (Makoni and Pennycook, 2012; Steyaert and Janssens, 2015).

> Sometimes I try to use words in Spanish, so we have English words and French words, so we have a mixed phrase and it's fun! And if I use a word in Spanish, sometimes it may be the wrong word, but they understand – and then they reuse the word in the way I said it and becomes a useful team word! It works because we're all using languages in the same way! It is a source of effectiveness; we have to create processes and we learn every time.

Through this quote we understand that communicative competencies should not only be defined by the standardized criteria dictated by the mainstream approach, but also by the meta-cognitive skills resulting from using multiple linguistic codes as resources in interaction.

Research on heteroglossia (Bakhtin et al., 1981) can be seen as a precursor to the multilingual perspective by highlighting the diversity of voice as the essence of verbal performance. In order to create meaning a speaker may switch languages, alternate between a dialect and a national standard, shift register, or speak monolingually (Bailey, 2012). Meaning – created through a negotiated chain of hybrid utterances – is based on the ability to summon different sets of linguistic resources, in response to a specific set of circumstances. Effective communication and the ability to negotiate the social world stem from an individual's use of these 'heteroglossic' sets of linguistic resources (Bakhtin et al., 1981).

To a similar end, and by applying the theory of 'thirdness' to linguistics and communication, Claire Kramsch (2009) expands on the concept of 'third culture' to understand how language is negotiated to build a common culture in interaction. This author provides a model other than the traditional dichotomy of native/non-native speaker to focus on what is created through the relation between speakers and the dynamic of the event itself. Group interaction creates a common sense of identity resulting from "a relational process-oriented disposition that is built in time through habit" (Kramsch, 2009:234). This place of contact or encounter informs language choices to create what Kramsch has conceptualized as a 'third place' in communication. Accordingly, the way language is used and communicative practice are both the result of and necessary to the process of building rapport, essential in all work settings (Cohen and Kassis-Henderson, 2012).

Research into language practices in multilingual teams has revealed that there is great flexibility in language use, even within a workplace setting with an official working language, or *lingua franca* (Cohen and Kassis-Henderson, 2017). This same flexibility, or fluidity, is described in studies on the use of English as a *lingua franca* which show parallels with the features of multilingual communities where performance strategies are constantly adapted to suit changing communicative contexts (Canagarajah, 2007). These practices are conceptualized in terms of 'voice' rather than 'language' differences (Steyaert and Janssens, 2015). Depending on the context, one aspect or another of a person's history or narrative will be foregrounded, and s/he will tap into their language repertoire to empower the appropriate 'voice'. Thus a linguistic repertoire is not something static but rather is achieved situationally in communicative interaction with others (Busch, 2012). Through agency and a reflexive positioning within identity construction, an individual will come to an understanding of the interest of drawing on the various aspects of identity though 'voice'. This in turn will influence communication by a shift in the rapport with the other, thereby impacting agency and empowering the individual to modify the dynamics of the interaction.

DEVELOPING COMPETENCES IN CORRELATION WITH THE CONCEPTUAL FRAMEWORK ABOVE

A standardized, homogenized view of a 'common' culture – be it national or corporate – stifles or excludes any sign of difference, but does not do away with it. Taken from this perspective, constructing identity is a continual dialectical process (Martin and Nakayama, 2015), realigned according to context and, as said above, in a continuous state of 'becoming'. Such active self-questioning, of how we see ourselves and how others see us, is the essence of the "dialogic construction of the self" (Beech, 2010:290) and is a vital meta-cognitive skill for the enhancement of communicative practices.

In order to form a cohesive team, it is essential for co-workers to build rapport in order to be able to work together. Understanding the multiple facets of one's own cultural identity by using the conceptual framework of intersectionality changes the way one acknowledges cultural differences in the other. This broader, more inclusive view contributes to rapport building as it facilitates the finding of commonalities where on the surface only the differences were apparent (Cohen and Kassis-Henderson, 2012). Common speech acts – normally considered as culturally determined – such as greetings, orders and requests, apologies and compliments are important from a rapport management perspective (Spencer-Oatey, 2008:20) but must be critically reframed.

FACEWORK AT THE INTERSECTION OF LANGUAGE AND IDENTITY

Under the guise of respect for traditional ways of doing things, individuals perpetuate assumptions about how things should be done, what is appropriate behaviour and what is not, about who deserves respect in the pecking order or who does not, and recreate automatic verbal and behavioural responses. Through a critical intersectional approach to oneself and the situation, individuals can assert themselves differently by breaking with routine which will disrupt the traditional order of things and bring about the disconfirmation of expectations (Yagi and Kleinberg, 2011). Such a reflexive stance is essential when it comes to working in multilingual–multicultural organizations. This is aptly illustrated by the following example: A young German woman of mixed ethnicity with an Indian surname joins a team in a German company mainly comprised of middle-aged men. The fact that she refrains from the morning handshake ritual led to the misplaced assumption that this was due to a supposed religious tradition colleagues associated to her ethnicity. As she was able to reflexively reframe this incident, rather than taking offence she affirmatively addressed the situation. This reflexive stance allowed her to avoid conflict and save face for herself and others. If such an incident, which was in fact simply due to a generational difference when it comes to daily greetings in the workplace, is not contained – or if the disconfirmation of expectations is not correctly framed – this type of misunderstanding can have important negative consequences leading to stigmatization, exclusion and loss of face (Mahadevan, 2017).

As this example shows, facework is a crucial part of identity work leading as it does to identity respect in the context of interactions (Ting-Toomey, 2005). And as Goffman explained in his founding article on facework: "There is no occasion of talk so trivial as not to require each participant to show serious concern with the way in which he handles himself and the others present" (Goffman, 1967:33). Research shows that 'rapport threat' and 'rapport enhancement' are subjective evaluations which not only depend on the content of the message but on "interpretations and reactions to who says what under what circumstances" (Spencer-Oatey, 2008:20) as well as how one says it and how it is heard.

FACEWORK AND ACCENTS

Accent – and the correlating assumptions related to identity – also plays an important role in how identity is constructed and perceived, as illustrated by the experience of a lawyer from the United States working in an international organization in France (Kassis-Henderson and Cohen, 2020:13–14):

I speak French, have always tried to keep up with French culture … but this is the first time I've lived outside of the US. One of the first things that surprised me in dealing with the French on a daily basis, in day-to-day life, was that the first thing they would say is: 'oh! you're American!' They immediately identified me – because of my accent – as being 'American'. I was at first taken aback as it was the first time I could say – to others, as well as to myself! – 'yes, I'm American'! Because in the US, I'm 'African-American' – and my belonging to the black community has always *identified* me first. … Then something changed. My French became more proficient, more natural, I felt I was finally losing my American accent that French people quickly recognized. Personally I was looking forward to better exchanges, communication with the French. But instead I realized I was getting certain looks, there was a certain hesitation in interactions, and certain kinds of questions started coming up more frequently. It wasn't 'oh, you're American!' but 'where are you from, the *Antilles* – the French West Indies?' And little by little I started connecting the dots – the strange reaction I was getting – or what I felt was a strange reaction – was due to my losing the 'American' status as I was losing the American accent and with it the privilege of being the 'American in Paris'. Instead I realized I was being seen – and treated – as 'black'! So I started a survival experiment – I exaggerated my 'US' accent and indeed, I was again treated with the 'respect' I felt when I first arrived in Paris! I recovered my privileged status! I once again became the 'American in Paris'!

This case shows how identity is in a perpetual state of construction with different facets coming to the fore in the interstices of interaction. An awareness of language/voice as a dimension of intersectionality enables the shift from stigmatization to empowerment, allowing an individual to affirmatively react to prevent marginalization (Boogaard and Roggeband, 2010).

IMPLICATIONS AND CONCLUSIONS

This chapter has addressed the critical role of languages in organizations which has been too often neglected in organizational studies (Johansson and Barner-Rasmussen, 2019). It highlights the value of intersectionality to obtain a fuller understanding of the multi-faceted nature of identity and how this is impacted by language – and vice versa. Based on our exploration of intersectionality, we have shown the complex interplay of language and identity and the resulting power effects (Zanoni et al., 2010; Primecz et al., 2016; Mahadevan, 2017). Depending on the desired outcome, an individual draws on various aspects of their identity behind which lie a multiplicity of voices. These voices in turn compose the varied language repertoires, or resources, derived from the experiences and background of each individual.

An intersectional approach in combination with the multilingual perspective provides many benefits for organizational processes. As discussed above, excellent proficiency in a given language may be less significant than wider meta-cognitive skills gained through exposure to multiple languages and cultures, an aspect which is too often overlooked (Holmes, 2015; Kassis-Henderson et al., 2018). Individuals tend to be identified in the workplace by labels – nationality, native speaker, monolingual, bilingual – which hide the multiple intersecting aspects of their identity. If these were to be taken into account, the diversity within and between individuals could be tapped as a resource rather than be seen as an organizational problem. For this reason, this chapter calls for greater attention to cross-fertilization between organizational studies, international business and language-based research, which could constitute in itself a multivoiced platform supporting a shift from the dominant monolingual narrative towards an intersectional approach, one which empowers organizational actors of diverse skills and origins.

REFERENCES

Ahearn, L.M. (2001), Language and agency. *Annual Review of Anthropology*, 30, 109–137.

Alvesson, M., Ashcraft, K.K. and Thomas, R. (2008), Identity matters: Reflections on the construction of identity scholarship in organization studies. *Organization*, 15(1), 5–28.

Alvesson, M. and Willmott, H. (2002), Identity regulation as organization control: Producing the appropriate individual. *Journal of Management Studies*, 39(5), 619–644.

Ashcraft, K.L. and Mumby, D.K. (2004), *Reworking Gender: A Feminist Communicology of Organization*, Thousand Oaks, CA: Sage.

Bailey, B. (2012), Heteroglossia. In Martin-Jones, M., Blackledge, M. and Creese, A. (eds), *The Routledge Handbook of Multilingualism* (pp. 499–507), Abingdon: Routledge.

Bakhtin, M.M., Holquist, M. and Emerson, C. (1981), *The Dialogic Imagination: Four Essays by M. M. Bakhtin*, Austin: University of Texas Press.

Beech, N. (2010), Liminality and the practices of identity reconstruction. *Human Relations*, 64(2), 285–302.

Blommaert, J. (2010), *The Sociolinguistics of Globalization*, Cambridge: Cambridge University Press.

Boogaard, B. and Roggeband, C. (2010), Paradoxes of intersectionality: Theorizing inequality in the Dutch police force through structure and agency. *Organization*, 17(1), 53–75.

Brannen, M.-Y. and Thomas, D. (2010), Bicultural individuals in organizations: Implications and opportunity. International Journal of Cross Cultural Management, 10(1), 5–16.

Busch, B. (2012), The linguistic repertoire revisited. *Applied Linguistics*, 33(5), 503–523.

Canagarajah, S. (2007), Lingua franca English, multilingual communities and language acquisition. *The Modern Language Journal*, 91(1), 923–939.

Chao, G.T. and Moon, H. (2005), The cultural mosaic: A meta theory for understanding the complexity of culture. *Journal of Applied Psychology*, 90(6), 1128–1140.

Cohen, L. and Kassis-Henderson, J. (2012), Language use in establishing rapport and building relations: Implications for international teams and management education. *Revue Management et Avenir*, 55, 185–207.

Cohen, L. and Kassis-Henderson, J. (2017), Revisiting culture and language in global management teams: Toward a multilingual turn. *International Journal of Cross-Cultural Management*, 17(1), 7–22.

Cooren, F., Kuhn, T., Cornelissen, J.P. and Clark, T. (2011), Communication, organizing and organization: An overview and introduction to the special issue. *Organization Studies*, 32(9), 1149–1170.

Coupland, C. and Brown, A.D. (2012), Identities in action: Processes and outcomes. *Scandinavian Journal of Management*, 28(1), 1–4.

Crenshaw, K. (1991), Mapping the margins: Intersectionality, identity politics, and violence against women of color. *Stanford Law Review*, 43(6), 1241–1299.

Frame, A. (2016), Intersectional identities in interpersonal communication. In Ciepiela, K. (ed.), *Identity in Communicative Contexts* (pp. 21–38), Berlin: Peter Lang.

Gaibrois, C. (2018), 'It crosses all the boundaries': Hybrid language use as an empowering resource. *European Journal of International Management*, 12(1–2), 82–110.

Gaibrois, C. and Nentwich, J. (2020), The dynamics of privilege: How employees of a multinational corporation construct and contest the privileging effects of English proficiency. *Canadian Journal of Administrative Sciences*, 37(4), 468–482.

Goffman, E. (1967), *Interaction Ritual*, New York: Doubleday.

Holmes, P. (2015), Intercultural encounters as socially constructed experiences: Which concepts? Which pedagogies? In Holden, N., Michailova, S. and Tietze, S. (eds),

The Routledge Companion to Cross-Cultural Management (pp. 237–247), London and New York: Routledge.

Hong, H.-J. and Doz, Y. (2013), L'Oréal masters multiculturalism. *Harvard Business Review*, June, 14–18.

Jameson, D. (2007), Reconceptualizing cultural identity and its role in intercultural business communication. *Journal of Business Communication*, 44(3), 199–235.

Janssens, M. and Steyaert, C. (2014), Re-considering language from a cosmopolitan understanding: Toward a multilingual franca approach in international business studies. *Journal of International Business Studies*, 45(5), 623–639.

Johansson, M. and Barner-Rasmussen, W. (2019), Organizing through and by multilingualism: Writing languages into the study and practices of organizations. Conference paper, 13th GEM&L International Conference on Management and Language, Sheffield Hallam University, June 3–9, 2019.

Kassis-Henderson, J. and Cohen, L. (2020), The paradoxical consequences of the perfect accent! A critical approach to cross-cultural interactions. In Mahadevan, J., Primecz, H. and Romani, L. (eds), *Cases in Critical Cross-Cultural Management: An Intersectional Approach to Culture* (pp. 12–21), London: Routledge.

Kassis-Henderson, J., Cohen, L. and McCulloch, R. (2018), Boundary crossing and reflexivity: Navigating the complexity of cultural and linguistic identity. *Business and Professional Communication Quarterly*, 81(3), 304–327.

Kramsch, C. (2009), Third culture and language education. In Cook, V. and Wei, L. (eds), *Contemporary Applied Linguistics* (pp. 233–254), London: Continuum.

Kramsch, C. (2012), Authenticity and legitimacy in multilingual SLA. *Critical Multilingualism, an Interdisciplinary Journal*, 1(1), 107–128.

Mahadevan, J. (2017), *A Very Short, Fairly Interesting and Reasonably Cheap Book about Cross-Cultural Management*, London: Sage.

Makoni, S. and Pennycook, A. (2012), Disinventing multilingualism: From monological multilingualism to multilingual franca. In Martin-Jones, M., Blackledge, A. and Creese, A. (eds), *The Routledge Handbook of Multilingualism* (pp. 439–453), Abingdon: Routledge.

Martin, J.N. and Nakayama, T.K. (2015), Reconsidering intercultural (communication) competence in the workplace: A dialectical approach. *Language and Intercultural Communication*, 15(1), 13–28.

Martin-Jones, M., Blackledge, A. and Creese, A. (2012), Introduction: A sociolinguistics of multilingualism for our times. In Martin-Jones, M., Blackledge, A. and Creese, A. (eds), *The Routledge Handbook of Multilingualism* (pp. 1–26), Abingdon: Routledge.

May, S. (2013), *The Multilingual Turn, Implications for SLA, TESOL, and Bilingual Education*, London: Routledge.

Mughan, T. (2015), Language and languages: Moving from the periphery to the core. In Holden, N., Michailova, S. and Tietze, S. (eds), *The Routledge Companion to Cross Cultural Management* (pp. 79–84), London: Routledge.

Neeley, T.B. (2012), Status loss and achieved status in global organizations. *Organization Science*, 24(2), 476–497.

Ozkazanç-Pan, B. (2015), Postcolonial perspectives on cross-cultural management knowledge. In Holden, N., Michailova, S. and Tietze, S. (eds), *The Routledge Companion to Cross-Cultural Management* (pp. 371–379), London and New York: Routledge.

Pilcher, N. and Richards, K. (2017), Challenging the power invested in the International English Language Testing System (IELTS): Why determining 'English' preparedness needs to be undertaken within the subject context. *Power and Education*, 9(1), 3–17.

Primecz, H., Mahadevan, J. and Romani, L. (2016), Why is cross-cultural management scholarship blind to power relations? Investigating ethnicity, language, gender and religion in power-laden contexts. *International Journal of Cross Cultural Management*, 16(2), 127–136.

Primecz, H., Romani, L. and Sackmann, S.A. (2009), Cross-cultural management research. Contributions from various paradigms. *International Journal of Cross Cultural Management*, 9(3), 267–274.

Sackmann, S.A. (ed.) (1997), *Cultural Complexity in Organizations: Inherent Contrasts and Contradictions*, Newbury Park: Sage Publications.

Schoeneborn, D., Kuhn, T.R. and Kärreman, D. (2019), The communicative constitution of organization, organizing and organizationality. *Organization Studies*, 40(4), 475–496.

Spencer-Oatey, H. (2008), *Culturally Speaking, Culture, Communication and Politeness Theory*, London: Continuum International Publishing Group.

Steyaert, C. and Janssens, M. (2015), Translation in cross-cultural management: A matter of voice. In Holden, N., Michailova, S. and Tietze, S. (eds), *The Routledge Companion to Cross-Cultural Management* (pp. 131–141), London and New York: Routledge.

Ting-Toomey, S. (2005), The matrix of face: An updated face-negotiation theory. In Gudykunst, W.B. (ed.), *Theorizing about Intercultural Communication* (pp. 71–92), Thousand Oaks, CA: Sage.

Vaara, E., Tienari, J., Piekkari, R. and Säntti, R. (2005), Language and the circuits of power in a merging multinational corporation. *Journal of Management Studies*, 42(3), 595–623.

Yagi, N. and Kleinberg, J. (2011), Boundary work: An interpretive ethnographic perspective on negotiating and leveraging cross-cultural identity. Journal of International Business Studies, 42(5), 629–653.

Zander, U., Zander, L., Gaffney, S. and Olsson, J. (2010), Intersectionality as a new perspective in international business research. *Scandinavian Journal of Management*, 26(4), 457–466.

Zanoni, P. and Janssens, M. (2015), The power of diversity discourses at work: On the interlocking nature of diversities and occupations. *Organization Studies*, 36(11), 1463–1483.

Zanoni, P., Janssens, M., Benschop, Y. and Nkomo, S. (2010), Guest editorial: Unpacking diversity, grasping inequality: Rethinking difference through critical perspectives. *Organization*, 17(1), 9–29.

12. Duality of language as a tool for integration versus mobility at work: utility of a polyphonic perspective

Cihat Erbil, Mustafa F. Özbilgin and Sercan Hamza Bağlama

INTRODUCTION

Learning a language is a powerful tool for seeking inclusion and integration in a workplace. Knowing a national or local/official language well is often considered to be essential criteria for workplace integration. In some countries, the ability to speak the native language in standardised or sophisticated ways signals talent and educational attainment to potential employers. In those cases, one's ability to learn the native language serves a dual mechanism as privileged entry into jobs and employment for native speakers and as a rite of passage for learners of that language for workplace integration. There is a hierarchy of utility in learning the native language. There is a hierarchical order between the value of a native language between the Global North and the Global South, and between the coloniser and the colonised. While the countries in the Global North have retained and valorised their native languages, some of the countries in the Global South have been linguistically dominated, and suffered from the devaluation of their native languages. Thus, there remain hierarchies of desirability among languages in a neo-colonial world. For example, some languages, such as English, are valorised both in English-speaking countries and internationally. In contrast, mastery of other languages, such as Turkish, would help workplace integration in Turkey, but would have little currency abroad. Other languages, such as Welsh or Kurdish, could be stigmatised and devalued outside very local settings where they are commonly spoken (Baysu and Agirdag, 2019; Elliott et al., 2020).

Studies show that there are more than 7100 languages in the world today (Dasgupta et al., 2021). Many of these languages run the risk of extinction due to the dominance of some languages in inter-community exchanges. Loss of a language entails a major loss of meanings and cultural artefacts produced in that language. The extinction of languages and cultures is happening at an alarming rate today as only a small number of languages are considered to be worthy of learning for access to employment and work for individuals in the international arena. Many languages are not considered as valuable. There is a domination of languages, such as English, Spanish, French, Chinese and German, in the international business field. Learning foreign languages also has multiple outcomes, such as improving one's chances of employment, signalling social and economic standing, and allowing an individual to move between jobs, organisations or countries (Gazzola and Mazzacani, 2019). Particularly in the field of international business, where expatriate employment and transnational staff are the norms, linguistic abilities are considered to be the critical measures of talent.

Language ability also signals other forms of social and economic status (Wilmot, 2017). For example, in the UK, the ability to read Latin and, to some extent, French is associated with an upper-class education. Similarly, multiple languages often signal high social and economic status. Such signalling using language reveals that language ability is a site of power, constructed at the nexus of culture, resources, status beliefs and hierarchies in societies.

DEFINITIONS OF KEY TERMS

We operationalise the terms of linguistic capital, symbolic violence, and integration and mobility, drawing on a sociological approach. Bourdieu (1991) focuses on using language as one tool of cultural capital that determines individuals' privileged positions and capacity to access desirable resources. We can define linguistic capital as fluency in the language used by groups that hold status power over their economic, social, and political resources. Concerning the evaluation of individuals' language skills, Bourdieu associates the concept of capital with the ability to use language in a semantic order acceptable to the parties holding social resources, beyond grammatical mastery. He points out that cultural capital is also present in linguistic capital. For example, a language that is desirable in any country may provide linguistic capital to the individual at the local level and weaken the individual's cultural capital at the international level if it is not considered to be an internationally recognised language, as in the example of the English language. Individuals who cannot use them to connect with the semantic order of the dominant group face not only a symbolic barrier in social terms but also actual barriers that cause them to be deprived of public resources and hinder their access. Individuals without linguistic capital restrict their relationships with their social environment, remain content with the information provided by secondary sources, and cannot access opportunities to take part in the study (Smits and Gündüz-Hoşgör, 2003).

Privileged groups can turn language into a tool of domination to enable access to social resources to maintain their positions because language is an apparatus of symbolic violence that expresses the use of cultural, social, and political resources in maintaining the power gained against groups subjected to systematic discrimination (Bourdieu, 1989). Dominant groups exercise their strength by depriving individuals of language skills or not allowing the polyphonic nature of multilingualism in three ways. First, possibilities for individuals to strengthen their linguistic capital may be economically or socially restricted. Consequently, highly industrialised and segmented education can be a barrier to language learning because of individuals' poor socioeconomic conditions (Matear, 2008). Language is a method of violence that causes class-based exploitation for individuals who have to accept low-status and low-paid jobs because they may not strengthen their linguistic competence (Dick and Nadin, 2011). Second, individuals may lack the possibility of existing in their language. Neo-colonialism may create an obstacle in social systems for individuals to achieve status with their local indigenous languages which may not be sufficient for inclusion in economic systems (Kamasak et al., 2020a). For example, as a postcolonial state, South Africa's higher education curriculum even undermines the officially recognised local languages with the neoliberal hegemonic discourse that propagates neoliberalism in connection with 'internationalisation', 'employability' and 'acquiring of skills' (Gyamera and Burke, 2018). Therefore, indigenous people are indirectly dictated to use English at the expected level to be included in economic systems (Nudelman, 2020). Third, hegemony can use language to assimilate or exploit individuals by controlling various learning methods to control uneven power relations. For example, the state keeps ethnic minority Uighurs in China and uses forced labour in various factories as part of its economic and social agenda, while forcing them to learn the Chinese language, which is part of the official ideology with assimilation-oriented motivations (Xu et al., 2020). This is an example of symbolic violence in language use at work.

Individuals seek to strengthen their linguistic capital, not only to avoid the hegemony and symbolic violence of the dominant language, but also to integrate into the social structure (Huot et al., 2020). Integration takes place when newcomers incorporate the norms, values and systems of the social and macro-national or meso-organisational structure to gain access to opportunities and resources and to feel safe and belonging (Ager and Strang, 2008; Hynie, 2018). There is a relational interplay between workplace integration at meso-organisational and macro-national levels. A workplace environment, which is multilingual and inclusive, facilitates the integration of individuals with their linguistic capacities and provides them with access to economic and social resources and a repertoire of status. However, policies aimed at blocking, excluding or not recognising certain languages, including the lack of social and legal regulations or the inability to protect the dominance of languages, lead to sociolinguistic exclusion (Lønsmann, 2014) and can hamper workplace integration. Thus, the official/national language is often essential for workplace integration. Hence, individuals in vulnerable groups, such as immigrants, refugees and ethnic minorities, have to accept low-status, low-paid and precarious jobs that are out of proportion to their skillsets (Lee et al., 2020; Risberg and Romani, 2021).

Linguistic capital also determines mobility. Mobility implies intra-organisational movement, such as promotion, or inter-organisational movements, such as finding new positions for individuals and international mobility. In monolingual working environments which silence linguistic diversity, the dominance of the delegitimate language adversely affects the internal mobility for out-group members such as ethnic and religious minorities. A monolingual working language can enfranchise members who have mastered the language and the cultural and symbolic elements of language while restricting others' career prospects and hindering their mobility by preventing them from using skillsets and analytical repertoires with the language barrier (Janssens and Brett, 2006).

NATIONAL LANGUAGE REQUIREMENT AT WORK: THE CASES OF BRITAIN AND TURKEY

English is the official language in Britain, with little regional variations in words and expressions allowed from other languages in the UK. Britain has a complex colonial history which was shaped by uneven trade relations which often took the form of the extraction and movement of resources from the colonies to the UK. Colonial subjects were given certain rights to settle in the UK, and they mainly adopted English as a national language (Pennycook, 1998). In Britain's colonial and neo-colonial territories, the English language was used extensively in social and political spheres for trade. The uneven relations of power between the coloniser and those in the colonised territories have also been marked as a symbolic way of learning languages (Hornberger and Vaish, 2009). Starting with the dominant prevalence of the English language in Britain, linguistic diversity has been lost to the dominant force of the English language. Today, in Britain, Scots, Welsh, Gaelic, Irish, Angloromani and Cornish are still spoken by very small groups of people who are largely limited to their highly ethnicised territories.

Although the Welsh language has been defended to an extent and offered in schools in Wales as a language, Welsh language education remains limited to Wales (Gorrara et al., 2020). It has been subject to considerable debate and controversy between demands for the conservation of the language despite the symbolic violence that it has been subjected to throughout history, and questions regarding its ultimate utility for learners in access to jobs and work in a world order where linguistic hierarchies do exist. In the same way, it is very uncommon for people to speak a second language in Britain. Children are encouraged to learn European languages and Latin only in elite schools and upper-class families. Compared to European countries, Britain fares extremely poorly in second language learning (Eurostat, 2021).

While English dominated the British territories, it has become the lingua franca of business in the international sphere. English domination at home and abroad has meant that being a native speaker is not only valuable in Britain but also abroad as a way of engaging in international business to a large extent (Hejazi and Ma, 2011). What appears entirely warped in this picture is the pre-dicament of the non-native speakers of the English language. As the English language has gained international currency, learning English (Nickerson, 2005) or an alternatively dominant language, such as Spanish, Chinese, and French, has become a means for gaining international mobility and accessing international employment and work opportunities for non-English speakers who would like to pursue international careers (Oakes, 2013). The gap between the native and non-native speakers of English in terms of choices and chances has widened over time. For example, the native speakers of English are not required to speak a second language in order to pursue expatriate careers. However, a second language requirement would be enforced for non-English language speakers, as English has become a semi-official language for inter-national business (Leung et al., 2014). The uneven nature of the requirements of language learning in order to access work and employment in international business entrenches the distinction between the colonial countries and the col-onised territories, lending support to Fanon's (1963/2004) arguments on 'the colonised mind', where the language at work becomes a site of macro-national level power relations in a neo-colonial world order.

The movements towards the acceptance of Turkish as a national language started in the period of the westernisation policies followed in the Ottoman Empire to prevent the decline of the Empire (Aydingün and Aydingün, 2004). Throughout its history, in the Ottoman Empire, which had multi-ethnic and multi-religious individuals, nearly ten languages were spoken only on the streets of Istanbul (Öncü, 2007). The state administration, on the other hand, used Ottoman Turkish. Although the official language of the state was Turkish, the problems in the educational system made it hard to learn the Ottoman language (i.e. using the Arabic script) both for the Turks and ethnic minorities. Moreover, the difficulty of writing in Ottoman Turkish using the Arabic alphabet and the vibrancy of literacy in other languages in the Ottoman Empire caused many ethnic minorities to write Turkish with their own scripts, such as Armenian, Cyrillic, Greek, Hebrew and Latin, which were the scripts commonly used in the Ottoman Empire (Uygur, 2021).

In the last period of the Empire, intellectuals began to voice their demands for the simplification of Ottoman Turkish, which included the Persian and Arabic scripts and languages. In order to create national sentiment (Aydingün and Aydingün, 2004). In the same period, learning the French language was considered to be an upper-class endeavour that signalled social and economic status. Therefore, upper-class families sent their children to France for education or arranged French lessons for them. In fact, those individuals who were educated in France with republican ideals were called Young Turks, who were the significant players in the reformation of the Ottoman Empire in its years of decline. After the collapse of the Ottoman Empire, the first constitution prepared before the announcement of the Turkish Republic accepted Turkish as the official language. The constitutions renewed in the following periods, 1924 and 1961, also recognised Turkish as the official language. The constitution, which was adopted after the military coup in 1980 and has still been in force, defines Turkish as the language of the state (Gençkaya and Özbudun, 2009). From the early 1960s, learning the French language left its place to English language learning as the second language which became a marker of social and economic standing in modern Turkey. Other local languages, which are still spoken in Turkey, gradually diminished as a result of the ethnic and religious structure based on a dominant group, Turkish Sunni Muslims, in the country over the same period (Çelik, 2012).

In tandem with the enforcement of Turkish as the official language in Turkey with limited recognition for Kurdish and other minority ethnic languages across Turkey, there was also the process of economic liberalisation which brought in foreign investment in the country. Many people from Turkey sought migration abroad for better economic, social and political conditions in other countries in that period. With the entrenchment of the neoliberal ideology in Turkey, learning English, German, French and later Russian and Arabic (Di Paolo and Tansel, 2015; Ulum, 2020) at the school and university level has become not only the signifiers of socioeconomic standing but also instrumental demands for talent acquisition for labour market participation or international mobility out of Turkey.

Considering the cases of Britain and Turkey, it is an interesting detail that speaking English or Turkish is not enough since speaking English/Turkish in a 'proper' way is also significant. Concisely focusing on the 'accent/ dialect' aspect of the two cases might help bring theoretical insights into the (de)legitimation of a certain accent/dialect within a discursive space. There are, for example, many different accents and dialects of English, such as Yorkshire, Cockney, Geordie, Brummie, Scottish, and Northern Irish, across Britain (Kortmann et al., 2004); however, the Queen's/King's English is traditionally considered to be the standard/proper one for British English. The Queen's/King's English still functions as an indirect signifier of an individual's educational background, class position, or social status, and is therefore accepted to be elegant, elevated, noble, and sophisticated. Excellence in the Queen's/King's English is perceived as a particular requirement of being an integral part of the dominant society which would allow individuals to actualise themselves as middle-class persons. Those who are able to speak the Queen's/King's English are celebrated, while those who are unable to speak the 'proper' English are ridiculed and mocked. A similar case also exists in Turkey. As in Britain, there are different accents and dialects in Turkey; however, the İstanbul Turkish is conceived as the 'proper' accent and thus identified with refinement and cultural and educational superiority. Inability to use the 'proper' accent leaves individuals vulnerable to an array of negative perceptions and images.

In this context, 'asking' individuals to conform to using the 'proper' accent/ dialect either in Turkish and English actually leads to monoculturalism/ monophony since other local accents/dialects are ignored and de-legitimated. The voluntary desire to use the 'proper' accent functions as cultural/linguistic capital for mobility both in the dominant society and at work since it is one of those 'linguistic' rituals of being a middle-class person, which also exemplifies the operation of symbolic violence in postmodern capitalism (Bourdieu and Passeron, 1990).

LEGITIMATION AND DELEGITIMATION OF LANGUAGES AT WORK

When discussing the issue of linguistic ability at work, it is possible to ask a number of questions to explore the dynamics of power relations that under-pin language learning. First, whose language is more valuable? This simple question fleshes out the uneven power relations and politics of language which often remain silent in the way linguistic ability is defined, measured and used in order to provide access to work and employment (Tenzer and Pudelko, 2017). This question also brings attention to the issue of historical and con-temporary forms of privilege and disadvantage afforded to different groups of ethnic and linguistic majority and minority groups.

Second, which languages are desirable/undesirable? There is an explicit hierarchy of languages in the world of work and the international business field in terms of their supposed desirability and undesirability (Lønsmann, 2014). However, as Bourdieu (1991) argues, it is not the language itself that creates power asymmetry. The desirability of language is affected by power relations between interlocutors. Therefore, some languages of the Global North, which control economic tools, are considered to be desirable for language learning, while the other languages of the Global South are devalued and considered to be trivial, unnecessary or undesirable. These power hierarchies in terms of desirability and undesirability offer different routes of (de)legitimation for different forms of linguistic capital.

Legitimation and delegitimation of certain forms of linguistic capital at work happen in a sociohistorical setting in which historical social injustice manifests in the way a language is valorised or dismissed as a form of resource (capital) at work (Kamasak et al., 2020b). In order to understand how this process of legitimation happens, it is possible to examine whether the nation state adopts a purist and hegemonic or pluralist and democratic stance in terms of languages. The culture of national languages presents a primary barrier in the legitimation and valorisation of multiple languages (Tange and Lauring, 2009). Furthermore, second language learning is subject to legitimation and delegitimation depending on the economic, social and political relations of power based on both historical and contemporary relations. The social desirability of a second language is closely mirrored by its valorisation and legitimation at work.

From a different perspective, the two questions regarding the unconscious desirability of a European language seem to be an extension of the legacies and practices of the neo-colonial discourse in contemporary societies. Since language is a medium through which "the conceptions of truth, order, and reality become established" and "a hierarchical structure of power is perpetuated" (Ashcroft et al., 1989, 7), it functions like a battleground and explains why European languages, especially English, are spoken according to the cultural and linguistic requirements of being a refined and civilised person. In a post-colonial framework, speaking a more standardised form of the language of the coloniser helps the colonial subject become more visible in the neo-colonial centre. The desire of the colonial subject to get 'whiter' in direct proportion to the ability to speak the language of the coloniser, which is associated with civilisation and progress, creates a dialogical cultural space and leads the colonial subject to enjoy a position of honour, integration and dignity which would only be bestowed upon them by those in the mainstream 'white' society. The pathological obsession with the mastery of the language of the coloniser helps them not only illusorily overcome the feeling of unbelongingness, rootlessness and inferiority complex, but also sound intellectually credible, which actually functions as cultural/linguistic capital for economic and cultural mobility (Bağlama, 2019). In other words, the colonial subject voluntarily celebrates the civilisational superiority of the West and mimics whatever is presented as proper in order to be a recognisable 'other' and to sustain their political existence in the neo-colonial centre, which socioculturally orients them to the operation of a financialised world order and thus makes them more 'proper' and 'efficient' to be employed in the labour market.

In order to articulate the desirability of a 'proper' accent, for example the Queen's English in the UK or the İstanbul Turkish in Turkey, the concept of class should be taken into account since what is imposed as the 'true' and 'real' accent through different agencies and apparatuses on different platforms is *that* of the upper-class. Conforming to the use of a more 'proper' speech pattern and prioritising the language of the bourgeoisie are indicative of the internalisation of the cultural and linguistic hegemony of the upper-class. Such a hierarchy of discourse, operating through the oppositional distinction between the working class and the upper-class, imposes the narratives of the powerful and reconstitutes working-class individuals in an indirect way. To put it in a different way, despite welcoming and including *anyone* irrespective of her/his class position in theory, postmodern capitalism assigns a 'proper' identity to individuals and promotes those who represent the 'proper' in terms of actions, thoughts, manners and *accent*. This is how the material practices of the money-oriented world are voluntarily perpetuated within a discursive space: "We're moving toward control societies that no longer operate by confining people but through continuous control and instant communication" (Deleuze, 1995, 174). Considering these arguments, using the 'proper' accent is presented as a way of self-actualisation, visibility and recognition, and thus operates as cultural/linguistic capital instrumental for mobility at work, which again exemplifies the process of sociocultural interpellation.

TOWARDS A POLYPHONIC AND PLURILINGUAL APPROACH AT WORK

If we examine the reasons why international joint ventures and other forms of international businesses fail, human errors such as failures of communication due to misunderstandings and lack of linguistic abilities appear as primary reasons (Ristolainen et al., 2021). In fact, many international, multinational and global organisations today declare interest in staff who are polyphonic and plurilingual in order to avoid such failures in the future (Piekkari et al., 2014). Yet many of the linguistic hierarchies which we outlined above remain intact. Many organisations, thus, continue to operate dual systems where the dominance of certain forms of language continues and there is recognition of linguistic ability as part of a talent repertoire that individuals bring to work (Welch and Welch, 2018).

We posit that in order to transcend the current hierarchies of power in the acquisition of linguistic capital and the symbolic forms of violence associated with historical forms of injustice induced by colonisation and other forms of domination, we need to move towards polyphonic and plurilingual approaches that recognise talent. The fact that workplaces do not culturally support plurilingual approaches or develop appropriate tools prevents the talent from emerging in favour of those included in dominant groups. However, talent is a set of language-based practices (Nair-Venugopal, 2013), and the lack of actual plurilingualism leads workplaces to monophony (Bothorel-Witz and Tsamadou-Jacoberger, 2013), which disconnects their dialogue with stakeholders, diverts ethical space, and hampers innovative potential (Trittin and Schoeneborn, 2017). Workplaces should abandon the monolinguistic tendency, which synchronises integration with the use of the legitimate language, and encourage polyphony in a way that allows individuals to actualise their life projects and self-authentic identities, as required by the talent inherent in expression (Painter-Morland et al., 2019).

There is an urgent need to protect the linguistic diversity in the world and the cultural heritage that we owe to it (Lüdi et al., 2016). We need to embody diversity beyond sociodemographic differences (Tatli and Özbilgin, 2012) and achieve a redefinition of talent and merit beyond classical status beliefs which put neo-colonial and ethnic biases into the definition of international talent and merit, particularly for expatriates and third nationals in global organisations. For example, global organisations designing and using plurilingual, culturally sensitive and responsive communication channels that include employees, especially in underdeveloped host countries, can save them from being limited by the cultural bond of expatriates (Thomas, 2007) and support the polyphonic working environment. Communication channels should include marginalised and missing voices, and cover all views and values to recognise the talent in order not to allow the power asymmetry symbolised by language. Companies should also integrate plurilingual-led policies, be flexible in their HRM strategies, and implement practices such as promotion and recruitment aimed at supporting polyphony in a way that enables mobility and integration for linguistic diversity (van den Born and Peltokorpi, 2007; Trittin and Schoeneborn, 2017).

DISCUSSION

Linguistic capital is widely used as a measure of talent and merit at work internationally. However, as we outlined above, linguistic capital is often imbued with uneven relations of power due to the historical domination of some languages and the exclusion and subjugation of others based on a large set of reasons such as colonial history, discrimination of certain ethnic and linguistic groups, and domination in economic, social and political fields. Drawing on two distinct examples, Turkey and Britain, we illustrated how linguistic capital was historically shaped, why in both countries linguistic capital became a site of negotiation of power relations, and where historical and contemporary battles for domination were settled. In the current world order, the domination of a limited number of languages, while there are over 7000 languages in the world, needs redress. We identified that this could come in the form of a paradigm shift from a monolingual and neo-colonial model of language learning to polyphonic perspectives.

There are multilevel measures that could be taken in order to move from current linguistic hierarchies in contemporary organisations to a plurilingual and polyphonic paradigm. Global organisations, such as the United Nations, could play a role in accounting for and valorising the linguistic heritage of the world. There could also be drives, such as the European Union DYLAN (Language Dynamics and Management of Diversity) project, for the protection of languages at the international level, which encourages nation states to reconsider their official language policies in more inclusive ways. At the heart of many linguistic hierarchies are power inequities and imbalances between nation states and communities (Ristolainen et al., 2021). Thus, moving to a polyphonic paradigm at a deeper level would require a shift of power relations and the reconstruction of the value and respectability of languages that are marginalised in the current linguistic order of power relations. At the meso level of organisations, definitions of linguistic capital could be captured in a richer way with the recognition and inclusion of a broader range of languages. As we explained in this chapter, there are uneven power relations in the way the diversity of languages is valued or devalued. In order to address biases and discrimination which render some languages less valuable, diversity and equality education could be offered and enforced in schools (Bell et al., 2009). More importantly, at the individual level, there is a need for empowerment of individuals who speak multiple languages to recognise the value of their linguistic abilities and to help others see the significance of language learning in their organisations.

REFERENCES

Ager, A. and Strang, A. (2008), Understanding integration: A conceptual framework. *Journal of Refugee Studies*, *21*(2), 166–191.

Ashcroft, B., Griffiths, G. and Tiffin, H. (1989), *The Empire Writes Back: Theory and Practice in Post-Colonial Literatures*, London: Routledge.

Aydingün, A. and Aydingün, I. (2004), The role of language in the formation of Turkish national identity and Turkishness. *Nationalism and Ethnic Politics*, *10*(3), 415–432.

Bağlama, S. H. (2019), Zadie Smith's *White Teeth*: The interpellation of the colonial subject in multicultural Britain. *Journal of Language, Literature and Culture*, *66*(2), 77–90.

Baysu, G. and Agirdag, O. (2019), Turkey: Silencing ethnic inequalities under a carpet of nationalism shifting between secular and religious poles. In Stevens, P. A. J. and Dworkin, A. G. (eds), *The Palgrave Handbook of Race and Ethnic Inequalities in Education* (pp. 1073–1096), New York: Palgrave Macmillan.

Bell, M. P., Connerley, M. L. and Cocchiara, F. K. (2009), The case for mandatory diversity education. *Academy of Management Learning and Education*, *8*(4), 597–609.

Bothorel-Witz, A. and Tsamadou-Jacoberger, I. (2013), Representations of multilingualism and management of linguistic diversity in companies. In Berthoud, A. C.,

Grin, F. and Lüdi, G. (eds), *Exploring the Dynamics of Multilingualism: The DYLAN Project, Vol. 2* (pp. 83–100), Amsterdam: John Benjamins Publishing Company.

Bourdieu, P. (1989), Social space and symbolic power. *Sociological Theory*, *7*(1), 14–25.

Bourdieu, P. (1991), *Language and Symbolic Power*, Cambridge, MA: Harvard University Press.

Bourdieu, P. and Passeron, J. C. (1990), *Reproduction in Education, Society and Culture* (Vol. 4), London: SAGE.

Çelik, A. B. (2012), Ethnopolitical conflict in Turkey: From the denial of Kurds to peaceful co-existence? In Landis, D. and Albert, R. D. (eds), *Handbook of Ethnic Conflict: International Perspectives* (pp. 241–260), Boston, MA: Springer.

Dasgupta, A. N. Z., Makoka, D., Dudha, Z., Stephenson, N. and Crampin, A. C. (2021), Fish hooks and gumboots: The language of pregnancy prevention in northern Malawi. *Bulletin of the World Health Organization*, *99*(1), 67–68.

Deleuze, G. (1995), *Negotiations 1972–1990*. Trans. Martin Joughin. New York: Columbia University Press.

Di Paolo, A. and Tansel, A. (2015), Returns to foreign language skills in a developing country: The case of Turkey. *The Journal of Development Studies*, *51*(4), 407–421.

Dick, P. and Nadin, S. (2011), Exploiting the exploited: The psychological contract, workplace domination and symbolic violence. *Culture and Organization*, *17*(4), 293–311.

Elliott, E., Thomas, G. M. and Byrne, E. (2020), Stigma, class, and 'respect': Young people's articulation and management of place in a post-industrial estate in south Wales. *People, Place and Policy Online*, *14*(2), 157–152.

Eurostat (2021), Foreign language skills statistics. https://ec.europa.eu/eurostat/statistics-explained/pdfscache/44913.pdf (accessed on 11 April 2021),

Fanon, F. (1963/2004), *The Wretched of the Earth*. Trans. Richard Philcoxtr. New York: Grove Press.

Gazzola, M. and Mazzacani, D. (2019), Foreign language skills and employment status of European natives: Evidence from Germany, Italy and Spain. *Empirica*, *46*(4), 713–740.

Gençkaya, Ö. F. and Özbudun, E. (2009), *Democratization and the Politics of Constitution-making in Turkey*, Budapest and New York: Central European University Press.

Gorrara, C., Jenkins, L., Jepson, E. and Llewelyn Machin, T. (2020), Multilingual perspectives: Preparing for language learning in the new curriculum for Wales. *The Curriculum Journal*, *31*(2), 244–257.

Gyamera, G. O. and Burke, P. J. (2018), Neoliberalism and curriculum in higher education: A post-colonial analyses. *Teaching in Higher Education*, *23*(4), 450–467.

Hejazi, W. and Ma, J. (2011), Gravity, the English language and international business. *Multinational Business Review*, *19*(2), 152–167.

Hornberger, N. and Vaish, V. (2009), Multilingual language policy and school linguistic practice: Globalization and English-language teaching in India, Singapore and South Africa. *Compare*, *39*(3), 305–320.

Huot, S., Cao, A., Kim, J., Shajari, M. and Zimonjic, T. (2020), The power of language: Exploring the relationship between linguistic capital and occupation for immigrants to Canada. *Journal of Occupational Science*, *27*(1), 95–106.

Hynie, M. (2018), Refugee integration: Research and policy. *Peace and Conflict: Journal of Peace Psychology*, *24*(3), 265–276.

Janssens, M. and Brett, J. M. (2006), Cultural intelligence in global teams: A fusion model of collaboration. *Group and Organization Management*, *31*(1), 124–153.

Kamasak, R., Özbilgin, M. and Atay, D. (2020a), The cultural impact of hidden curriculum on language learners: A review and some implications for curriculum design. In Slapac, A. and Coppersmith, S. A. (eds), *Beyond Language Learning Instruction: Transformative Supports for Emergent Bilinguals and Educators* (pp. 104–125), Hershey, PA: IGI Global.

Kamasak, R., Özbilgin, M. F., Yavuz, M. and Akalin, C. (2020b), Race discrimination at work in the United Kingdom. In Vassilopoulou, J., Brabet, J., Kyriakidou, O. and Shovunmi, V. (eds), *Race Discrimination and the Management of Ethnic Diversity at Work: European Countries' Perspective. Vol. 6, International Perspectives on Equality, Diversity and Inclusion* (pp. 107–127), Bingley, UK: Emerald Publishing.

Kortmann, B., Burridge, K., Mesthrie, R., Schneider E. W. and Upton, C. (2004), *A Handbook of Varieties of English*, Berlin: Mouton de Gruyter.

Lee, E. S., Szkudlarek, B., Nguyen, D. C. and Nardon, L. (2020), Unveiling the Canvas Ceiling: A multidisciplinary literature review of refugee employment and workforce integration. *International Journal of Management Reviews*, *22*(2), 193–216.

Leung, C., Davison, C. and Mohan, B. (2014), *English as a Second Language in the Mainstream: Teaching, Learning and Identity*, London: Routledge.

Lønsmann, D. (2014), Linguistic diversity in the international workplace: Language ideologies and processes of exclusion. *Multilingua*, *33*(1–2), 89–116.

Lüdi, G., Meier, K. H. and Yanaprasart, P. (eds) (2016), *Managing Plurilingual and Intercultural Practices in the Workplace: The Case of Multilingual Switzerland* (Vol. 4), Amsterdam: John Benjamins Publishing Company.

Matear, A. (2008), English language learning and education policy in Chile: Can English really open doors for all? *Asia Pacific Journal of Education*, *28*(2), 131–147.

Nair-Venugopal, S. (2013), Linguistic ideology and practice: Language, literacy and communication in a localized workplace context in relation to the globalized. *Linguistics and Education*, *24*, 454–465.

Nickerson, C. (2005), English as a lingua franca in international business contexts. *English for Specific Purposes*, *24*(4), 367–380.

Nudelman, G. (2020), The hidden curriculum in two employability skills development courses in a South African electrical engineering degree programme. *Journal of Education and Work*, *33*(5–6), 360–374.

Oakes, L. (2013), Foreign language learning in a 'monoglot culture': Motivational variables amongst students of French and Spanish at an English university. *System*, *41*(1), 178–191.

Öncü, A. (2007), The politics of Istanbul's Ottoman heritage in the era of globalism. In Drieskens, Barbara, Mermier, Franck and Wimmen, Heiko (eds), *Cities of the South: Citizenship and Exclusion in the Twenty-First Century* (pp. 233–264), London: Saqi Books.

Painter-Morland, M., Kirk, S., Deslandes, G. and Tansley, C. (2019), Talent management: The good, the bad, and the possible. *European Management Review*, *16*(1), 135–146.

Pennycook, A. (1998), *English and the Discourses of Colonialism*, London: Routledge.

Piekkari, R., Welch, D. and Welch, L. S. (2014), *Language in International Business: The Multilingual Reality of Global Business Expansion*, Cheltenham, UK and Northampton, MA, USA: Edward Elgar Publishing.

Risberg, A. and Romani, L. (2021), Underemploying highly skilled migrants: An organizational logic protecting corporate 'normality'. *Human Relations*, *75*(4), 655–680.

Ristolainen, J., Outila, V. and Piekkari, R. (2021), Reversal of language hierarchy and the politics of translation in a multinational corporation. *Critical Perspectives on International Business*, doi.org/10.1108/cpoib-06-2020-0086.

Smits, J. and Gündüz-Hoşgör, A. (2003), Linguistic capital: Language as a socio-economic resource among Kurdish and Arabic women in Turkey. *Ethnic and Racial Studies*, *26*(5), 829–853.

Tange, H. and Lauring, J. (2009), Language management and social interaction within the multilingual workplace. *Journal of Communication Management*, *13*(3), 218–232.

Tatli, A. and Özbilgin, M. F. (2012), An emic approach to intersectional study of diversity at work: A Bourdieuan framing. *International Journal of Management Reviews*, *14*(2), 180–200.

Tenzer, H. and Pudelko, M. (2017), The influence of language differences on power dynamics in multinational teams. *Journal of World Business*, *52*(1), 45–61.

Thomas, C. A. (2007), Language policy in multilingual organizations. *Working Papers in Educational Linguistics (WPEL)*, *22*(1), 81–104.

Trittin, H. and Schoeneborn, D. (2017), Diversity as polyphony: Reconceptualizing diversity management from a communication-centered perspective. *Journal of Business Ethics*, *144*(2), 305–322.

Ulum, O. G. (2020), Neoliberal policies and English language education in Turkey. *English Language Teaching*, *13*(9), 63–71.

Uygur, K. (2021), *Understanding a Hybrid Print Media and Its Influence on Public Opinion: The Case of Armeno-Turkish Periodical Press in the Ottoman Empire, 1850–1875*. (Unpublished doctoral dissertation), University of Birmingham: Birmingham, UK.

van den Born, F. and Peltokorpi, V. (2010), Language policies and communication in multinational companies: Alignment with strategic orientation and human resource management practices. *The Journal of Business Communication*, *47*(2), 97–118.

Welch, D. E. and Welch, L. S. (2018), Developing multilingual capacity: A challenge for the multinational enterprise. *Journal of Management*, *44*(3), 854–869.

Wilmot, N. V. (2017), Language and the faces of power: A theoretical approach. *International Journal of Cross Cultural Management*, *17*(1), 85–100.

Xu, V. X., Cave, D., Leibold, J., Munro, K. and Ruser, N. (2020), *Uyghurs for Sale*. Australian Strategic Policy Institute. https://www.aspi.org.au/report/uyghurs-sale

PART IV

Different critical perspectives on the power of language in international business

13. Introduction to *Different critical perspectives on the power of language in international business*

Philippe Lecomte

In line with the performative role of language (see Chapters 7, 10 and 11), this section approaches different aspects of the power of language in organisations. This topic is not new. Since Clegg's seminal article on the language of power and the power of language (1987), a lot of scholars have contributed to studies into the link between power and language in IB and organisations (Vaara et al., 2005; Hinds et al., 2014; Gaibrois and Steyaert, 2017; Tenzer and Pudelko, 2017; Wilmot, 2017). Many authors have addressed the question of language policies and its relation to power struggles around the dominance of English as a *lingua franca* and in organisations (Fredriksson et al., 2006; Harzing and Pudelko, 2013; Aichhorn and Puck, 2017; Lønsmann, 2017; Peltokorpi and Yamao, 2017; Sanden and Kankaanranta, 2018; Linn et al., 2018). Scholars coming from the stream of critical discourse analysis have taken a critical discourse perspective in order to highlight the ties between language and strategy (Vaara et al., 2010; Mantere, 2013; Balogun et al., 2014), and between language, power and identity regulation (Boussebaa and Brown, 2017). Geppert and Dörrenbächer (2014) have addressed the link between power and politics, while other authors examine the role of discourse on organisational decision-making (Wodak, 2014; Wodak and Savski, 2018).

This non-exhaustive literature review shows that the concept of the power of language has been studied from multiple perspectives. However, according to IB and organisational scholars, traditional methodological approaches to language in IB lack a multilevel perspective to better understand the close relation between language use and power issues. There is a need to investigate the relationship between macro- and micro-levels (Kwon et al., 2009), while examining the power effects of language on organisations and individuals (Tsoukas and Chia, 2002). According to Cooren et al. (2015, 2), we need to 'understand the role of language in unfolding organizational processes and as part of organizational action'.

Chapter 14 opens with **Sanden's** literature review and three emerging themes: language misuse in organisations, the conflictual relationship between language policies and practices and the interconnectedness between top-down and bottom-up language regulation processes. First, in a knowledge-based economy, the notions of language nodes and of gatekeepers become crucial, as the power struggle in the organisations revolves around the communication of information or its retention. Second, Sanden points out the discrepancy between language policies and practices in organisations, and between *de jure* and *de facto* language usages. There is a gap between the language policy decisions of organisations and the everyday reality. In terms of power, this means that management cannot always impose its decisions and that the grassroots have a say. In this respect, Sanden's arguments are in line with Tienari's analysis (Chapter 16) of the ambiguity of power, which involves both the power to decide and the power to resist. Closely related to the preceding analyses, the question of the effectiveness of the implementation of a company's language policy is posed in terms of coherence between the strategy of the organisation (macro-level) and its human resources (micro-level). Novel conceptual insights are provided by the author around notions that are related to language planning such as linguistic auditing, the Language Management Theory, and linguascapes.

In **Chapter 15**, **Kastberg** and **Ditlevsen** look at how companies shape employee identities. They analyse how power manifests itself through the concepts of voice and voicer, using the internal communication magazine of the Grundfos group, the world's leading pump and water solutions manufacturer. Choosing one specific issue of the magazine that deals with Grundfos' new corporate strategy, they show how the employee magazine is a powerful instrument of identity formation and regulation and therefore a site of power and control of this social identity. The originality of this chapter is the synthesis operated between two streams of research, the literatures on voice and on the CCO (communication as constitutive of organisation) approach. By analysing the presence and/or absence of voicers and what is voiced in the magazine, Kastberg and Ditlevson show who has the power and how this power is used to form an identity for the employees of the international group. The CCO approach of organisations and of organising claims that organisations are constituted through communication. This organisational process does not occur on equal terms, because not every voice and/or voicer is legitimate. The analysis shows who has a voice and who counts as a legitimate organisational voicer, in order to identify which actors of the organisation contribute to shaping employee identity formation.

Tienari's (Chapter 16) contribution is a personal testimony experienced by an international management researcher at the crossroads of a partially shared national bilingualism and the assumed hegemonic monolingualism of the academic *lingua franca*. The case of the Hanken School of Economics in Helsinki provides an exemplary context for Tienari's analysis of his own experience as a researcher in the field of international management, and as a Finnish-speaking Finn in a business school where the official languages are Swedish and English. The author analyses the power games between the academic language of management research dominated by the hegemony of English, the Swedish corporate identity of the business school, and the national language (Finnish) of the researcher, using a multilevel analysis. At two levels of analysis (organisational and individual), Tienari demonstrates how language issues are embedded in power relations and how ambivalent both language and power are. His analysis of this ambivalence is a navigation between power and resistance around questions of language. The author draws on Foucault (1980), who sees power as transformative and not only as limiting. Resistance is viewed positively and dynamically as a driver of organisational change. If tradition sees power as a resource, Tienari argues for a different approach that favours processual and relational phenomena. The originality of this chapter is that both levels of analysis (the organisational and the individual) mirror the subjective experience of an international scholar.

REFERENCES

Aichhorn, N. and Puck, J. (2017), 'I just don't feel comfortable speaking English': Foreign language anxiety as a catalyst for spoken-language barriers in MNCs. *International Business Review 26*, 749–763.

Balogun, J., Jacobs, C., Jarzabkowski, P., Mantere, S. and Vaara, E. (2014), Placing strategy discourse in context: Sociomateriality, sensemaking, and power. *Journal of Management Studies 51*(2), 175–201.

Boussebaa, M. and Brown, A-D. (2017), Englishization, identity, regulation and imperialism. *Organization Studies 38*(1), 7–29.

Clegg, S. R. (1987), The language of power and the power of language. *Organization Studies 8*(1), 61–70.

Cooren, F., Vaara, E., Langley, A. and Tsoukas, H. (2015), *Language and Communication at Work: Discourse, Narrativity, and Organizing.* Oxford, UK: Oxford University Press.

Foucault, M. (1980), *Power/Knowledge: Selected Interviews and Other Writings 1972–1974*, ed. C. Gordon. Brighton: Harvester Press.

Fredriksson, R., Barner-Rasmussen, W. and Piekkari, R. (2006), The multinational corporation as a multilingual organization: The notion of a common corporate language. *Corporate Communications: An International Journal 11*(4), 406–423.

Gaibrois, C. and Steyaert, C. (2017), Beyond possession and competition: Investigating cooperative aspects of power in multilingual organizations. *International Journal of Cross Cultural Management 17*(1), 69–84.

Geppert, M. and Dörrenbächer, C. (2014), Politics and power within multinational corporations: Mainstream studies, emerging critical approaches and suggestions for future research. *International Journal of Management Reviews 16*, 226–244.

Harzing, A.-W. and Pudelko, M. (2013), Language competencies, policies and practices in multinational corporations: A comprehensive review and comparison of Anglophone, Asian, Continental European and Nordic MNCs. *Journal of World Business 48*, 87–97.

Hinds, P. J., Neeley, T. B. and Cramton, C. D. (2014), Language as a lightning rod: Power contests, emotion regulation, and subgroup dynamics in global teams. *Journal of International Business Studies 45*(5), 536–561.

Kwon, W., Clarke, I. and Wodak, R. (2009), Organizational decision-making, discourse, and power: Integrating across contexts and scales. *Discourse and Communication 3*(3), 273–302, 10.1177/1750481309337208.

Linn, A., Sanden, G. R. and Piekkari, R. (2018), Language standardization in sociolinguistics and international business: Theory and practice across the table: English in Europe Volume 5, in Sherman, T. and Nekvapil, J. (eds), *English in Business and Commerce. Interactions and Policies.* Berlin and Boston: De Gruyter Mouton Publishing, pp. 19–45.

Lønsmann, D. (2017), Embrace it or resist it? Employees' reception of corporate language policies. *International Journal of Cross Cultural Management 17*(1), 101–123.

Mantere, S. (2013), What is organizational strategy? A language-based view. *Journal of Management Studies 50*(8), 1408–1426.

Peltokorpi, V. and Yamao, S. (2017), Corporate language proficiency in reverse knowledge transfer: A moderated mediation model of shared vision and communication frequency. *Journal of World Business 52*, 404–416.

Sanden, G-R. and Kankaanranta, A. (2018), 'English is an unwritten rule here': Non-formalised language policies in multinational corporations. *Corporate Communications: An International Journal 23*(4), 544–566.

Tenzer, H. and Pudelko, M. (2017), The influence of language differences on power dynamics in multinational teams. *Journal of World Business 52*, 45–61.

Tsoukas, H. and Chia, R. (2002), On organizational becoming: Rethinking organizational change. *Organization Science 13*(5), 567–582.

Vaara, E., Tienari, J., Piekkari, R. and Säntti, R. (2005), Language and the circuits of power in a merging multinational corporation. *Journal of Management Studies 42*(3), 595–623.

Vaara, E., Sorsa, V. and Pälli, P. (2010), On the force potential of strategy texts: A critical discourse analysis of a strategic plan and its power effects in a city organization. *Organization 17*(6), 685–702.

Wilmot, N-V. (2017), Language and the faces of power: A theoretical approach. *International Journal of Cross Cultural Management 17*(1), 85–100.

Wodak, R. (2014), Analyzing interaction in meetings, perspectives from critical discourse studies and the discourse-historical approach, in Cooren, F., Vaara, E., Langley, A. and Tsoukas, H. (eds), *Language and Communication at Work.* Oxford: Oxford University Press, pp. 39–70.

Wodak, R. and Savski, K. (2018), Critical discourse-ethnographic approaches to language policy, in Tollefson, James W. and Milans, Miguel Perez (eds), *Oxford Handbook of Language Policy and Planning.* Oxford: Oxford University Press, pp. 93–112.

14. Language in multilingual organizations: power, policies and politics

Guro R. Sanden

INTRODUCTION

Regardless of employees' positions in the organizational hierarchy, their job tasks, location, background and career goals, they all have one thing in common; they need to communicate and they do so through the use of language. A company's language policy affects everyone who works or will work for that company (Thomas, 2008). It is possibly the most wide-ranging policy that any corporation can implement, and it does not come without consequences.

Since the late 1990s (see Marschan et al., 1997), numerous empirical studies have demonstrated the importance of language in and for international business activities. Language has gone from being a relatively narrow topic in international business research, to one which is widely accepted as a critical component when studying companies and organizations that operate internationally (Brannen et al., 2014; Tenzer et al., 2017).

This book chapter focuses on power struggles around language use in multilingual organizations, particularly multinational corporations (MNCs). By drawing on theory and empirical evidence from existing language-sensitive research in international business and management, the chapter starts by examining the power of language, and the ways in which language can be misused in organizational contexts. The chapter then critically examines the relationship between language policies and language practices, with a particular focus on how managerial attempts to regulate employees' language practices can lead to discrepancies between *de jure* and *de facto* language policies. The chapter ends with a discussion on how language practices at the front-line level feed into macro-level politics concerning language use, and vice versa.

THE POWER OF LANGUAGE

In order to understand the power dynamics associated with language, it is crucial to first understand why language gives power. Let's go back to the very beginning; the very beginning of human communication. Although there is no agreement in the literature as to when humans first started talking to each other – estimates range from 2 million years to 50,000 years ago (Balter, 2005) – it is likely that our ancestors did not all speak the same language, to the extent that we use the term 'language' to refer to our ancestors' form of communication.

As stated by Calvet (1998, 15), the world has been multilingual ever since humans first started communicating with one another. Even the most basic, rudimentary use of language could distinguish one group of people from another; their different linguistic codes implied that they were in semiological conflict with each other. Ever since the invention of language, its use has been associated with power, prestige, ability to obtain and act on knowledge, negotiations over status, reputation and identity. In essence, the evolution of language is a story of power. It is also a story of powerlessness, because wherever there are people with power, there will always be people with less power, or no power at all. Thus, the story is defined by the relationship between the powerful and the powerless.

In the words of Bourdieu (1991), we can think of linguistic exchange as a form of economic exchange. The exchange is established between a producer of linguistic capital – an aspect of symbolic power that has become routinized in social life (Bourdieu, 1991, 23) – and a consumer of linguistic capital, who is capable of procuring the symbolic good (Bourdieu, 1991, 66). By following this argument, power can be defined based on unequal distribution of linguistic capital (Bourdieu, 1991, 57). In other words, some people have more linguistic capital than others, and are therefore able to spend their capital on symbolic products and services that less affluent people cannot afford. As a result, people's linguistic capital can determine their position in the wider society of which they are a part. It can also prevent people from being part of certain societies, or in other ways control who gets to be part of a society.

Language can both divide and unite people. It can create and maintain group boundaries, and it can determine who we think of as 'insiders' or 'outsiders' (Bourdieu, 1991; Harzing and Feely, 2008). We recognize people who speak like us and we think of them as one of us, in the same way that we reject people who speak differently as not being one of us (Calvet, 1998, 66). On a symbolic level, language can be seen as a mechanism of social inclusion and exclusion. But there is also a very practical side to language. Its communicative function means that it can serve as an effective mechanism of discrimination, by excluding certain people or groups of people from access to information (Sanden, 2020; Tietze et al., 2003).

When discussing why language yields power, it is hard to avoid mentioning the different dimensions or perspectives that language entails. It is clear that language is a medium of communication that enables exchange of information between interlocutors. This can be referred to as the instrumental dimension of language. Equally important is the expressive or symbolic dimension of language, as language serves as a bearer of identity, belonging and social capital (Kraus, 2008, 78–80). In this way, language constitutes a compound, value-laden marker of cultural and social identity (Harzing and Feely, 2008; Hinds et al., 2014), while at the same time, presenting itself in a way that Welch, Welch and Piekkari (2005, 11) label 'the brutal simplicity of language as a potential barrier to communication', meaning; if people are unable to understand each other 'simply' because they cannot find a common language to communicate in, the communicative function of language has little value. Both dimensions of language – that is, the instrumental and expressive – contain a number of power-related questions. Where the instrumental dimension of language concerns who gets to know what, when and how, the expressive dimension can lead to more philosophical discussions about identity and belonging.

In a corporate context, the instrumental dimension of language will often come across as more obvious and profound than the expressive dimension, due to the nature of workplace communication. That does not mean that issues related to employees' professional identity are less important than meaningful interactions. In fact, the two dimensions of language are often interrelated, and the extent to which employees are able to effectively communicate with each other can determine how they feel about themselves in a work situation (Neeley, 2013). However, any successful collaboration between employees is dependent on their ability to communicate in a common language. For this reason, language practices in business organizations clearly intersect with economic motives. The current economic climate increases the importance of language for business organizations. In contrast to the 'old economy', which is typically described as a labor-intensive economy striving to achieve maximum production effectiveness, the 'new economy' is characterized by information-driven organizations and global networks (Duchêne and Heller, 2012). Rather than focusing on the means and methods of production, the new economy is a knowledge-based economy, built up around accessibility and usability of information (Dhir, 2005).

Duchêne (2009) discusses how the new economy ultimately places language at the forefront of a corporation's business activities. For a start, communication and exchange of information is a key factor in the new economic landscape. For companies operating within a service-based industry, information is often part of the service that they deliver to their customers, which means that language skills become a selling point and a part of the end product. The characteristics of the new economy mean that companies often operate on the global market, across national and linguistic borders. As a result, any company with international aspirations will be faced with the multilingual reality of international business at some point, either through their external communication practices, or by attracting foreign professionals with multiple linguistic backgrounds (Piekkari et al., 2014). Multilingualism has become the new norm of the new economy.

MISUSE OF LANGUAGE

Just as there are several reasons as to why language gives power, there are several ways in which the power of language can be misused. As argued by Tange and Lauring (2009, 218), the language practices of employees in the multilingual workplace cannot be explained only with reference to language skills, but must also be analyzed in relation to theories on social identity and power (see also Lauring, 2008; Lauring and Klitmøller, 2014). For one thing, the instrumental dimension of language as a medium of communication entails that language skills can be used to obtain access to information. A corporate language policy that regulates the company's language of reporting will to some extent also determine who gets to benefit from easy access to corporate documentation (Thomas, 2008).

Language-skilled employees often take on a role as 'language nodes', either as part of, or in addition to, their normal job tasks (Marschan-Piekkari et al., 1999). Language nodes are employees who function as communication channels for people who otherwise would have problems understanding each other, for example in headquarters–subsidiary communication. Bilingual expatriates, who are assigned to work at a foreign subsidiary and report back to the corporate headquarters, can for example serve as an important link between the headquarters and the subsidiary in which they work (Barner-Rasmussen and Björkman, 2005; see also Barner-Rasmussen et al., 2014). Once these employees return to the headquarters, they may be able to take on an intermediate role as repatriates if they have acquired language skills in the host country during their foreign assignment. The same goes for inpatriates, who are foreign employees, for example from one of the company's international subsidiaries, that have been assigned into the domestic management (Feely and Harzing, 2003).

Although language nodes often perform an important role as the main communication channel between the headquarters and its network of subsidiaries, this role puts the language nodes in a potentially powerful position. If employees with certain language skills choose to filter, distort or withhold information to other colleagues without the same language skills, they are acting as 'gatekeepers' of information (Marschan et al., 1997; see also Charles and Marschan-Piekkari, 2002). Gatekeeping-behavior is particularly problematic if the gatekeeper is the only person who can communicate corporate information to another group of employees, for example subsidiary staff. As such, relying on language nodes as a channel for disseminating corporate information may lead to abuse of power at the subsidiary level (Welch et al., 2001).

This is exactly what Peltokorpi and Vaara (2014) found in their study on the role of language-sensitive recruitment for knowledge transfer in MNCs. In this case, newly recruited host-country national employees were acting as language nodes in the MNCs' subsidiaries due to their English language skills. As English skills were limited in the subsidiaries, they were able to promote or impede knowledge transfer across language boundaries, for example by controlling the information transferred from the subsidiary to the headquarters as well as other MNC units. This tendency was particularly evident in small and newly established subsidiaries, as the language nodes could easier bypass hierarchies and thereby transfer, develop, and share information with colleagues in other parts of the MNC network.

Peltokorpi and Vaara's (2014) study reveal how communication through language nodes can have counterproductive effects on intra-organizational knowledge transfer. Yet, the consequences of relying on employees with certain language skills can have more wide-ranging implications for the organization overall, as demonstrated by Marschan-Piekkari et al. (1999). In their pioneering study on the impact of language on structure, power and communication in a Finnish MNC, Kone Elevators, Marschan-Piekkari et al. (1999) found that communication and collaboration among employees were largely dependent on employees' language preferences. In fact, a new organizational structure appeared on the basis of individual language skills, because employees formed clusters with other speakers of their native language. Consequently, a new 'shadow structure' emerged from the various language clusters and individuals who were acting as language nodes in the organization. The existence of this shadow structure demonstrates the power of language to the extent that it not only influences the internal communicative environment, but actually challenges the functioning of the official chain of command and formal communication lines.

Even if shadow structures do not appear on the basis of language use in multilingual organizations, the existence of multiple languages will in itself have an effect on power relationships in the organization. Harzing and Feely (2008) discuss how the language barrier in MNCs can lead to a power-authority distortion, especially for parent companies located in countries with less widely spoken languages. Their two coupled vicious cycles model illustrates how lack of a common language between headquarters and subsidiary influences the way in which MNCs manage their subsidiary operations. Communication problems such as loss of rhetorical skills and misunderstandings can lead to uncertainty, anxiety and mistrust between the headquarters and its subsidiary. As a result, attitudes harden, group identities polarize and the risk of conflict intensifies. This increases separation between the headquarters and subsidiary, which again renders communication more formal and guarded. Both headquarters and subsidiary are challenged by their inability to communicate effectively with the other part, and the headquarters–subsidiary relationship is affected in terms of strategic decision-making, organization and personnel selection, global integration strategies, and autonomy and control procedures.

While much of the existing language-sensitive literature in international business focuses on how language affects the relationship between employees and organizational units, it is clear that language can also affect potential and future employees and their role in the organizational hierarchy. Piekkari et al. (2005; see also Piekkari, 2008) discuss how career paths are prone to being language-dependent. On the one hand, language skills may advance individual career development and make it easier to climb the corporate ladder, if the person possesses the right language skills. Knowing a foreign language is an asset that adds to a person's career capital (Terjesen, 2005). On the other hand, lack of language skills can severely limit career opportunities, hamper career advancement, or steer individuals' career paths in a different direction. In both cases, language skills may have broad career implications by shaping, steering or diverting career paths.

Companies' language policy initiatives are inevitably an important piece of this puzzle. The implementation of a common corporate language can act as a glass ceiling, and prevent promising individuals from advancing in the organization. Piekkari (2008) argues that the top management may not be able to observe this effect, as they are likely to be competent in the common corporate language or other key languages commonly used within the firm. As such, the glass-ceiling effect is out of sight for the company's top echelons, and individuals without the necessary language skills remain effete.

LANGUAGE POLICIES IN MULTILINGUAL ORGANIZATIONS: DE JURE VS. DE FACTO

Although multilingualism in many cases is a practical necessity for multinational companies (Duchêne, 2009), there is often a need to streamline communication and decide on some common language practices among linguistically diverse employees. The dominance of English as the global lingua franca means that English often is seen as the most prevalent solution for efficient internal communication (Tietze, 2010).

It is now common practice for MNCs to implement English language policies in order to facilitate smoother and faster exchange of information within the multilingual organization (Neeley, 2017; Nurmi and Koroma, 2020). Language policies can be formalized through official language policy documents, or they can be left unstated, and exist as a common understanding about language use in the organization, so-called non-formalized policies (Sanden and Kankaanranta, 2018). Regardless of what form they come in, language policies usually contain some element of control or regulation, for example by establishing English as a common corporate language, or by explicitly stating what language or languages are to be used in what situations (Baldauf, 2006).

As with any corporate policy, there is always a risk that employees resist or ignore the policy initiative. If employees disregard the content of a company's language policy to the extent that the policy is not fully implemented in practice, there will be a discrepancy between de jure and de facto language policy. Previous empirical studies suggest that the official language policy may be undermined for several different reasons, for example due to high workload or time pressure (Sanden and Lønsmann, 2018), or because of more cunning reasons, as deliberate acts of power (Logemann and Piekkari, 2015).

A study conducted by Sanden and Lønsmann (2018) in Scandinavian MNCs found that the companies' monolingual English language policies were inconsistent with the multilingual reality of front-line employees. The three companies included in the study had all implemented English as the common corporate language, but the qualitative interviews with employees revealed that they had to deal with a large number of different languages on an everyday basis. As a result, employees found it necessary to use their 'discretionary power' – a term that refers to employees' ability to make a choice among possible courses of action and inaction (Davis, 1969; see also Lipsky, 2010) – to divert from the companies' English language policies. In this way, employees exercised their discretionary power in order to get their job done.

In other cases, as in the study conducted by Logemann and Piekkari (2015), findings revealed that language can be used deliberately to exercise power. Logemann and Piekkari (2015) investigated headquarters–subsidiary interactions in a European MNC where the implementation of English as a common corporate language resulted in a big change in language and communication practices, largely at the expense of other European languages. Their observations show that any process of communication can be sensitive to the power of language. In this particular case, employees both at headquarters and in the subsidiary made use of language and translation to exercise power over meanings. Where the corporate headquarters used their power to communicate corporate mindsets and codes of practice, subsidiary managers used language and translation to resist control from headquarters, for example through local interpretation of standardized rules and norms. At both ends, translation became a political act that led to shifting power positions.

Several other studies demonstrate that the introduction of a corporate language policy often raises a number of issues related to power and powerlessness (Ehrenreich, 2010; Fredriksson et al., 2006; Vaara et al., 2005). Discrepancies between de jure and de facto language policy can for example occur if employees have different interpretations and expectations of what the language policy actually entails, as observed by Fredriksson et al. (2006) in the German manufacturing company Siemens. In Ehrenreich's (2010) study of another German company, English was seen as the de facto lingua franca, but non-native speakers of English felt that their native English speaking colleagues used their language skills as an 'instrument of power' (Ehrenreich, 2010, 422).

Another case which clearly outlines how a language policy can affect power relations in a multilingual workplace is Vaara et al.'s (2005) study of the Finnish–Swedish merger MeritaNordbanken. In this company, Swedish was selected as the common corporate language, which reproduced post-colonial conceptions of Swedish superiority among the Finnish-speaking employees. The Swedish language policy quickly empowered Swedish-speaking Finns who benefitted from easy access to information, whereas those with limited Swedish skills felt disempowered and handicapped by the language policy. By drawing on Clegg (1989), Vaara et al. (2005) refer to this phenomenon as the 'circuits of power'. The expression conveys the idea that corporate language policies inevitably come with certain power implications, which will empower some employees and disempower others.

A similar observation was made by Neeley (2013) in a French MNC that had implemented English as a common corporate language. Neeley (2013) examined how non-native English speakers responded to the new language policy, and found that all non-native English-speaking employees experienced a status loss regardless of their English fluency level. Employees with medium English level fluency were found to be more anxious than their low and high fluency speaking co-workers. The findings from Neeley's study demonstrate that non-native speakers of the corporate language can find themselves in a linguistically subordinate position compared to native speakers. In contrast, native speakers of the corporate language can experience an 'unearned status gain' (Neeley and Dumas, 2016). This status gain occurs due to 'an unexpected or unsolicited increase in relative standing, prestige, or worth attained not through individual effort or achievement but from a shift in organizationally valued characteristics' (Neeley and Dumas, 2016, 14).

While a company's language policy can benefit some employees and place them in a more powerful position than before, it is important to also consider the ways in which these employees can exercise the power given to them. Having employees in potentially powerful positions is not necessarily a problem, but it can become a problem if someone decides to use that power at the expense of someone else. Native speakers of a common corporate language can for example easily obtain information in that language, which in itself is unproblematic. But if they choose to engage in gatekeeping-behavior, the situation quickly turns.

On the other hand, being a language-competent employee is not necessarily only an advantage. In Vaara et al.'s (2005) study of MeritaNordbanken, many Swedish-speaking Finns expressed that they were often overloaded with communication and translation tasks, as there were few people who were able to complete these tasks. Furthermore, due to the political connotation of the Swedish language policy, Swedish speakers were sometimes associated with Swedish dominance, and even blamed for some of the problems resulting from the company's language policy.

Other studies support Vaara et al.'s (2005) observation that employees commonly rely on language-skilled colleagues when faced with the need to communicate in a foreign language (CILT, 2011; Piekkari et al., 2005; Piekkari et al., 2013; Sanden and Lønsmann, 2018). In Piekkari et al.'s (2013) study of translation behavior in a financial service company, the authors found that the translation demands largely were forced on employees regardless of whether or not they possessed the relevant language skills. As a result, many employees relied on their networks in order to solve specific translation tasks. These findings show that even though language may empower some employees, this empowerment may imply an increase in workload and expectations to take on additional work tasks. Being in a powerful position also has its drawbacks.

THE MICRO PROCESSES AND MACRO POLITICS OF LANGUAGE

In sociolinguistic literature, the term language planning is commonly used to refer to deliberate efforts to influence the behavior of others regarding the acquisition, structure, or function of their language use (Cooper, 1989, 45). The decision-makers or authority in charge of the language planning, also known as the language planner (Baldauf, 2006) or language manager (Spolsky, 2009), is in a position to develop laws, regulations, rules, pronouncements or statements of intent about language use that apply to others. As discussed by Sanden (2016a), the authority in charge can include a wide range of people in various positions, dependent on which context the language planning initiative is directed towards. In a corporate context, the tasks typically performed by the language planner/language manager will often fall under the responsibility of a business manager or the company's communication department (Sanden, 2016a, 530).

Regardless of how, where and by whom the language planning is conducted, those in charge of the initiative will possess a great deal of power. In the words of Calvet (1998, 203) 'all planning is carried out by a handful of planners possessing all the power over a people who are planned'. It is quite common that language planning results in unfortunate results for some language speakers. As the goal of a language planning initiative often is to standardize language use in a multilingual community by selecting one language as the standard language, some people will most likely be dispossessed of using their own language (see Linn et al., 2018, for a discussion on language standardization). This observation is true also in international business, as the implementation of corporate language policies often is triggered by the need to facilitate communication between employees with different language backgrounds (Piekkari and Tietze, 2011). Even though the implementation of a common corporate language is meant as a pragmatic decision by the company's leadership, the decision is nevertheless one that will affect employees differently, dependent on their language competences.

This does not mean that those who are subjected to language planning are left without any means to influence the decision-making process. For companies operating across national borders, employees' language practices can be a valuable source of information for strategic language management. According to Reeves and Wright's (1996) linguistic auditing methodology – which provides a set of analytical tools for establishing the strengths and weaknesses of an organization's foreign language communication – a strategic approach to languages should start with mapping the language needs of employees, for example when communicating with external partners and customers. Reeves and Wright (1996) argue that linguistic audits must be incorporated as part of the management's strategic planning; if the company's vision, mission or objectives include international business ventures, a linguistic audit should be the first step in the planning process. The result of the audit would indicate the company's foreign language capabilities, and match these with the company's strategic aspirations (see also Sanden, 2016b).

Another framework that emphasizes the relationship between micro and macro processes is the Language Management Theory (LMT), originally developed by Jernudd and Neustupný (1987). The distinction between simple language management, performed at the micro level, and organized language management, performed at the macro level, is a central component of LMT. Micro and macro planning are two distinct but interrelated mechanisms of language management. While simple language management refers to corrections of individual language use, for example through self-correction, organized language management acts are usually implemented due to language corrective measures defined by a social network or an organization (Nekvapil and Sherman, 2009). Unlike simple language management, organized language management is transsituational, and the implementation of this type of language management requires some degree of organizational control. Yet, while macro planning influences micro planning through top-down measures, micro planning also influences macro planning as language use at the individual level forms the basis for macro-level planning initiatives (Nekvapil, 2006; Nekvapil and Nekula, 2006).

What these frameworks have in common is that even though language planning often is thought of as large-scale macro-level initiatives, what goes on at the micro level, among individual employees, can be equally important. As stated by Louhiala-Salminen and Kankaanranta (2011), macro and micro levels of international business communication are not distinctly separate. The two levels are heavily intertwined, and together they constitute the communicative environment of internationally operating businesses.

Multinational corporations can be seen as multilingual communities. Like other multilingual communities, organizations are made up of people who gradually develop communicative patterns and behaviors specific to the linguistic-communicative environment of which they are a part. By drawing on the transnational anthropology developed by Appadurai (1996), Steyaert, Ostendorp and Gaibrois (2010) observe how organizations tend to form specific linguistic landscapes. The term 'linguascapes' describes 'the flow of languages that cross a specific organisational space' (Steyaert et al., 2010, 270). Language and communication practices within the organizational space are discursively mediated by those who make up the linguascape, which means that the formation of the linguascape often is related to power relationships in the organization. The introduction of a common corporate language can for example create an imbalance between different languages and lead to an internal negotiation process between various language practices (see also Steyaert et al., 2016). To avoid high tension between employees with different language backgrounds, Steyaert et al. (2010) argue that it is necessary to understand the position of the new lingua franca vis-à-vis other languages, and how the internal language hierarchy is related to other organizational processes.

The notion of linguascapes suggests that an organization's language and communication practices are constructed by language users as they engage with each other over time. This implies that the language management initiatives implemented at the corporate level alone cannot determine the formation of the linguascape. Instead, the management's attempt to regulate language use must be seen in direct relation to the way in which individual employees communicate as part of their everyday work life. A corporate language policy can stipulate rules or guidelines for appropriate language use, but its practical value may be limited if language choices are managed on a pragmatic basis at the front-line level (Andersen and Rasmussen, 2004; Piekkari et al., 2013; Sanden and Lønsmann, 2018).

As argued by Ferguson (2012), one cannot assume widespread use of English even in MNCs that have adopted English language policies, as MNCs often consist of subsidiaries with different language needs. In the corporate network, English is often confined to particular employees, interactions or genres in the company's internal communication. An English language policy could mean that English is used in formal communication and at the higher management levels, whereas other languages are more common in informal interactions and among employees at lower hierarchical levels. This would imply a mismatch between the company's official language policy and de facto practices, but previous research suggests that such discrepancies are common in multilingual organizations (see e.g. Fredriksson et al., 2006).

CONCLUSION

As this brief overview has shown, the power of language plays out in many different ways. Language is a resource that can be used to gain power, and exercise power over others without the same resource. It is a power-yielding tool that can be abused if left in the hands of people with ill intentions.

At the same time, any attempt to control language is also an act of power. Multilingual organizations like MNCs exercise power through language when implementing language policies that stipulate how employees with different linguistic backgrounds should communicate with each other. In this way, language and power can be seen as inseparable entities. With a particular focus on the existing literature's coverage of the relationship between language policies and language practices, the insights discussed in this chapter have shown that it is impossible to circumvent power struggles around language use in multilingual organizations.

Another useful insight from language-sensitive research in international business is the connection between micro and macro processes. A complete understanding of the power of language in multilingual organizations must acknowledge both of these processes and how they feed into each other for the simple reason that language policies and other language management initiatives affect everyone in the entire organization. It is not possible to fully understand the effects of top-down initiatives without examining the implications of these initiatives at the front-line level. In the same way, it is necessary to consider how front-line employees navigate multiple languages in order to understand why companies develop top-down initiatives concerning language use. The power of language affects the entire organizational hierarchy, from top to bottom. And for both sides of the spectrum, the struggle is real.

REFERENCES

Andersen, H., and Rasmussen, E. S. (2004), The role of language skills in corporate communication. *Corporate Communication: An International Journal*, 9(3), 231–242.

Appadurai, A. (1996), *Modernity at large. Cultural dimensions of globalization.* Minneapolis: University of Minnesota Press.

Baldauf, R. B. Jr. (2006), Rearticulating the case for micro language planning in a language ecology context. *Current Issues in Language Planning*, 7(2 and 3), 147–170.

Balter, M. (2005), Human language may have evolved to help our ancestors make tools. *Science*. https://www.sciencemag.org/news/2015/01/human-language-may-have -evolved-help-our-ancestors-make-tools#:~:text=Researchers%20have%20long %20debated%20when,than%202%20million%20years%20ago.

Barner-Rasmussen, W., and Björkman, I. (2005), Surmounting interunit barriers: Factors associated with interunit communication intensity in the multinational corporation. *International Studies of Management and Organization*, 35(1), 28–46.

Barner-Rasmussen, W., Ehrnrooth, M., Koveshikov, A., and Mäkelä, K. (2014), Cultural and language skills as resources for boundary spanning within the MNC. *Journal of International Business Studies*, 45(5), 886–905.

Bourdieu, P. (1991), *Language and symbolic power*. Cambridge: Harvard University Press.

Brannen, M. Y., Piekkari, R., and Tietze, S. (2014), The multifaceted role of language in international business: Unpacking the forms, functions and features of a critical challenge to MNC theory and performance. *Journal of International Business Studies*, 45(5), 495–507.

Calvet, L. J. (1998), *Language wars and linguistic politics*. Oxford: Oxford University Press.

Charles, M., and Marschan-Piekkari, R. (2002), Language training for enhanced horizontal communication: A challenge for MNCs. *Business Communication Quarterly*, 65(2), 9–29.

CILT. (2011), *Report on language management strategies and best practice in European SMEs: The PIMLICO Project*. Brussels: European Commission.

Clegg, S. R. (1989), *Frameworks of power*. London: Sage.

Cooper, R. L. (1989), *Language planning and social change*. Cambridge: Cambridge University Press.

Davis, K. C. (1969), *Discretionary justice: A preliminary inquiry*. Baton Rouge: Louisiana State University Press.

Dhir, K. S. (2005), The value of language: Concept, perspectives, and policies. *Corporate Communication: An International Journal*, 10(4), 358–382.

Duchêne, A. (2009), Marketing, management and performance: Multilingualism as commodity in a tourism call centre. *Language Policy*, 8(1), 27–50.

Duchêne, A., and Heller, M. (2012), Language policy in the workplace. In B. Spolsky (ed.), *The Cambridge handbook of language policy* (pp. 323–334), Cambridge: Cambridge University Press.

Ehrenreich, S. (2010), English as a business lingua franca in a German multinational corporation. *Journal of Business Communication*, 47(4), 408–431.

Feely, A. J., and Harzing, A. W. (2003), Language management in multinational companies. *Cross Cultural Management: An International Journal*, 10(2), 37–52.

Ferguson, G. (2012), English in language policy and management. In B. Spolsky (ed.), *The Cambridge handbook of language policy* (pp. 475–498), Cambridge: Cambridge University Press.

Fredriksson, R., Barner-Rasmussen, W., and Piekkari, R. (2006), The multinational corporation as a multilingual organization. The notion of a common corporate language. *Corporate Communication: An International Journal*, 11(4), 406–423.

Harzing, A. W., and Feely, A. J. (2008), The language barrier and its implications for HQ–subsidiary relationships. *Cross Cultural Management: An International Journal*, 15(1), 49–61.

Hinds, P. J., Neeley, T. B. and Cramton, C. D. (2014), Language as a lightning rod: Power contests, emotion regulation, and subgroup dynamics in global teams. *Journal of International Business Studies*, 45(5), 536–561.

Jernudd, B., and Neustupný, J. (1987), Language planning: For whom? In L. Laforge (ed.), *Proceedings of the international colloquium on language planning* (pp. 69–84), Québec: Les presses de L'Université Laval.

Kraus, P. (2008), *A union of diversity: Language, identity and polity-building in Europe*. Cambridge: Cambridge University Press.

Lauring, J. (2008), Rethinking social identity theory in international encounters. Language use as a negotiated object for identity making. *International Journal of Cross-cultural Management*, 8(3), 343–361.

Lauring, J., and Klitmøller, A. (2014), Corporate language-based communication avoidance in MNCs: A multi-sited ethnography approach. *Journal of World Business*, 50(1), 46–55.

Linn, A., Sanden, G. R., and Rebecca Piekkari, R. (2018), Language standardization in sociolinguistics and international business: theory and practice across the table. In T. Sherman and J. Nekvapil (eds.), *English in business and commerce: Interactions and policies* (pp. 19–45), Berlin: Mouton de Gruyter.

Lipsky, M. (2010), *Street-level bureaucracy, 30th anniversary expanded edition: Dilemmas of the individual in public services*. New York: Russell Sage Foundation.

Logemann, M., and Piekkari, P. (2015), Localize or local lies? The power of language and translation in the multinational corporation. *Critical Perspectives on International Business*, 11(1), 30–53.

Louhiala-Salminen, L., and Kankaanranta, A. (2011), Language matters: An introduction. *Journal of Business Communication*, 47(2), 91–96.

Marschan, R., Welch, D., and Welch, L. (1997), Language: The forgotten factor in multinational management. *European Management Journal*, 15(5), 591–598.

Marschan-Piekkari, R., Welch, D., and Welch, L. (1999), In the shadow: The impact of language on structure, power and communication in the multinational. *International Business Review*, 8(4), 421–440.

Neeley, T. B. (2013), Language matters: Status loss and achieved status distinction in global organization. *Organizational Science*, 24(4), 476–497.

Neeley, T. B. (2017), *The language of global success. How a common tongue transforms multinational organizations*. Princeton: Princeton University Press.

Neeley, T. B., and Dumas, T. L. (2016), Unearned status gain: Evidence from a global language mandate. *Academy of Management Journal*, 59(1), 14–43.

Nekvapil, J. (2006), From language planning to language management. *Sociolinguistica*, 20, 92–104.

Nekvapil, J., and Nekula, M. (2006), On language management in multinational companies in the Czech Republic. *Current Issues in Language Planning*, 7(2 and 3), 307–327.

Nekvapil, J., and Sherman, T. (2009), Pre-interaction management in multinational companies in Central Europe. *Current Issues in Language Planning*, 10(2), 181–198.

Nurmi, N., and Koroma, J. (2020), The emotional benefits and performance costs of building a psychologically safe language climate in MNCs. *Journal of World Business*, 55(4), 1–15.

Peltokorpi, V., and Vaara, E. (2014), Knowledge transfer in multinational corporations: Productive and counterproductive effects of language-sensitive recruitment. *Journal of International Business Studies*, 45(5), 600–622.

Piekkari, R. (2008), Language and careers in multinational corporations. In S. Tietze (ed.), *International management and language* (pp. 128–137), Abingdon: Routledge.

Piekkari, R., and Tietze, S. (2011), A world of languages: Implications for international management research and practice. *Journal of World Business*, 46(3), 267–269.

Piekkari, R., Vaara, E., Tienari, J., and Säntti, R. (2005), Integration or disintegration? Human resource implications of a common corporate language decision in a cross-border merger. *International Journal of Human Resource Management*, 16(3), 330–344.

Piekkari, R., Welch, D. E., Welch, L. S., Peltonen, J. P., and Vesa, T. (2013), Translation behaviour: An exploratory study within a service multinational. *International Business Review*, 22(5), 771–783.

Piekkari, R., Welch, D. E., and Welch, L. S. (2014), *Language in international business: The multilingual reality of global business expansion.* Cheltenham, UK and Northampton, MA, USA: Edward Elgar Publishing.

Reeves, N., and Wright, C. (1996), *Linguistic auditing: A guide to identifying foreign language communication needs in corporations.* Clevedon: Multilingual Matters.

Sanden, G. R. (2016a), Language management × 3: A theory, a sub-field, and a business strategy tool. *Applied Linguistics*, 37(4), 520–535.

Sanden, G. R. (2016b), Language: The sharpest tool in the business strategy toolbox. *Corporate Communications: An International Journal*, 21(3), 274–288.

Sanden, G. R. (2020), Ten reasons why language policies can create more problems than they solve. *Current Issues in Language Planning*, 21(1), 22–44.

Sanden, G. R., and Kankaanranta, A. (2018), 'English is an unwritten rule here': Non-formalised language policies in multinational corporations. *Corporate Communications: An International Journal*, 23(4), 544–566.

Sanden, G. R., and Lønsmann, D. (2018), Discretionary power on the front line: A bottom-up perspective on corporate language management. *European Journal of International Management*, 12(1–2), 111–137.

Spolsky, B. (2009), *Language management.* Cambridge: Cambridge University Press.

Steyaert, C., Ostendorp, A., and Gaibrois, C. (2010), Multilingual organizations as 'linguascapes': Negotiating the position of English through discursive practices. *Journal of World Business*, 46(3), 270–278.

Steyaert, C., Ostendorp, A., and Gaibrois, C. (2016), Multilingual organizations as 'linguascapes' and the discursive position of English. In C. Steyaert, J. Nentwich, and P. Hoyer (eds.), *A guide to discursive organizational psychology* (pp. 168–190), Cheltenham, UK and Northampton, MA, USA: Edward Elgar Publishing.

Tange, T., and Lauring, J. (2009), Language management and social interaction within the multilingual workplace. *Journal of Communication Management*, 13 (3), 218–232.

Tenzer, H., Terjesen, S., and Harzing, A. W. (2017), Language in international business: A review and agenda for future research. *Management International Review*, 57, 815–854.

Terjesen, S. (2005), Senior women managers' transition to entrepreneurship: Leveraging embedded career capital. *Career Development International*, 10(3), 246–259.

Thomas, C. A. (2008), Bridging the gap between theory and practice: Language policy in multilingual organisations. *Language Awareness*, 17(4), 307–319.

Tietze, S. (2010), International managers as translators. *European Journal of International Management*, 4(1/2), 184–199.

Tietze, S., Cohen, L., and Musson, G. (2003), *Understanding organizations through language*. London: Sage Publications.

Vaara, E., Tienari, J., Piekkari, R., and Säntti, R. (2005), Language and the circuits of power in a merging multinational corporation. *Journal of Management Studies*, 42(2), 595–623.

Welch, D., Welch, L., and Piekkari, R. (2001), The persistent impact of language on global operations. *Prometheus*, 19(3), 193–209.

Welch, D., Welch, L., and Piekkari, R. (2005), Speaking in tongues: The importance of language in international management processes. *International Studies of Management and Organization*, 35(1), 10–27.

15. Voices in the employee magazine: a critical investigation

Peter Kastberg and Marianne Grove Ditlevsen

INTRODUCTION AND RESEARCH AGENDA

From the point of view of critical organizational communication (e.g., Mumby and Kuhn, 2019), 'organizations are [seen as] key sites of human identity formation in modern society' (Mumby, 2013, 47). This makes the organization 'the primary institution for the development of our identities, surpassing the family, church, government, and education systems in this role' (Deetz, 1992; Mumby, 2013, 47) . A feature of late modernity that has led Deetz to coin the phrase 'corporate colonization' of the individual's life world (Deetz, 1992). In that sense organizations are dominant sites of power and control (Mumby, 2013, 47), that is, institutions which affect individuals' identity and life in a direct and fundamental way. Pairing this with Foucault's idea that language, knowledge and power are inextricably linked (Foucault, 1974), has led us to wonder who actually has a voice and what is voiced in organizational environments where communications are executed as a function of management (Cornelissen, 2011). As a function of management, organizational communication is a means with which the organization seeks to 'align its employees with its overarching vision, mission, values, purposes, strategies, and priorities' (Kounalakis et al., 1999, 9). More specifically, organizational communication provides means with which management 'shape the identities of their employees to achieve managerial goals' (Boussebaa and Brown, 2017, 9). Although one of the primary tools in the organizational communicator's toolbox is the employee magazine, the employee magazine is an under-researched field. What little research there is pertains mostly to the journalistic aspects of the employee magazine (Kounalakis et al., 1999) and its value and usage as an internal PR media (Koch et al., 2018). Both strands of research focus on instrumental aspects of the employee magazine as a vehicle for successful managerial communication (e.g., Kastberg, 2020). Unsurprisingly, this has led both strands of research to favor the perspective of management, at the expense of other perspectives and other stakeholders. Whereas we do not question the legitimacy of the prevailing managerial perspective, we do contest its being taken for granted as the only perspective of relevance when investigating employee magazines. Generalizing crudely, the employee magazine features three core stakeholders, namely management, the editors, and the employees (Clampitt et al., 1986; Koch et al., 2018). In an age in which the tenets of 'corporate governance' (e.g., Solomon, 2007), 'corporate social responsibility' (e.g., Morsing and Schultz, 2006) as well as 'diversity' (Konrad et al., 2006), underpin any organization's 'license to operate' (Gehman et al., 2017) and permeates its practices, employees are relevant and legitimate stakeholders in their own right – and so are investigations into the employee magazine as seen from their perspectives. With an employee perspective as our point of departure, we turn to the field of research that best caters to this view, namely that of critical organizational communication (e.g., Mumby and Kuhn, 2019). At this point, however, it may be important to emphasize that

> [...] the critical approach does not argue that processes such as [...] identification are by definition problematic. Clearly, collective action and members' identification with an organization are necessary. Rather, the concern is with the extent to which the assumptions upon which identification are based is both open to examination and freely arrived at. (Mumby and Kuhn, 2019, 52)

Our research into the employee magazine mirrors that very concern, that is, to what extent the basis of the employee identification aimed at by management is open to examination by employees as well as freely arrived at. Consequently, we are not interested in the extent to which a particular feature of an employee magazine serves its managerial purposes; that would be the case in the two research strands mentioned earlier. In tune with our critical organizational communication perspective (Mumby and Kuhn, 2019), we investigate the employee magazine in its capacity of being a primary vehicle for 'identity formation' and hence as a 'site of power and control' (cf. above). More specifically, we are pursuing answers to two core research questions: who has a voice in the first place, that is, who counts as a legitimate, organizational 'voicer' (Bashshur and Oc, 2015, 1531) and what messages, what contents, are voiced. In order to do so, we introduce and discuss select, research agenda-relevant aspects of cross sections of voice research literatures and then present the communication-as-constitutive approach as the communication-theoretical foundation of this chapter. This funnels into a brief presentation of identity as communicatively constituted (section 2). Empirically, our research design revolves around in-depth investigations into an instance of strategic corporate journalism. We will present, analyze, and discuss an issue of the *G Magazine*, that is, the international employee magazine for the Grundfos Group, a world-leading pump and water solutions manufacturer (section 3).

Our findings are systematically recapitulated in section 4; and in section 5, we isolate, discuss, and reflect upon the core learnings from our investigations.

EMPLOYEE VOICE FROM A CCO PERSPECTIVE

The concept of 'employee voice' is conventionally attributed to Hirschman (1970). According to Hirschman, voice is 'any attempt at all to change rather than to escape from an objectionable state of affairs' (1970, 30). What seems to be central to most ensuing definitions is that employee voice is made to refer to employees' possibility 'to have a say regarding work activities and decision making issues within the organization in which they work' (Wilkinson and Fay, 2011, 65). The possibility for having a say is often referred to as 'upward employee voice' (Ruck et al., 2017, 904) or as 'upward communication from employees' (Ruck et al., 2017, 906). Even if there is a consensus in the extant literature of viewing voice as upward employee communication aiming at changing an objectionable state of affairs, 'there are competing visions and expectations of employee voice' (Wilkinson and Fay, 2011, 71). This is no surprise since no less than four main strands of literature are dealing with employee voice, that is, literature on HRM, on industrial relations, on organizational behavior, and on organizational justice (Wilkinson and Fay, 2011, 66). As it is not within the scope of this chapter to recapitulate the discussions of four literatures, we have extracted and established two illustrative dichotomies that we regard as formative cross sections of literatures dealing with employee voice.

The first is a perspectival dichotomy, that is, employee voice as seen either from a management-centric or from an employee-centric perspective. The '*management-centric* view conceptualizes voice as something management bestows on employees, they are allowed to contribute'; whereas the '*employee-centric* view of voice may conceptualize voice [...] as discretionary employee communication behavior, they decide whether to contribute' (Ruck et al., 2017, 906). The second is more of a conceptual dichotomy stipulating that the 'opposite of voice is silence' (Logan and Tindall, 2018, 1). If we look at the perspectival dichotomy, the management-centric view of employee voice tends to focus on how 'employee voice can be a source of competitive advantage', that is, how employee voice may be guided and managed in order to serve as 'a powerful source of organizational change' (Bowen and Blackmon, 2003, 1394). The second dichotomy, that is, voice vs. silence, offers a different cross section of the field's literatures. Employees can speak up in different ways, for example, they can participate in 'issue selling, whistle-blowing, championing, dissent and boat-rocking' and so on (Morrison and Milliken, 2003, 1354); not all of which may be endorsed by management. Employee silence, on the other hand, effectively 'stops communication [and hence] opportunities to modify routines and knowledge sharing' (Gambarotto and Cammozzo, 2010, 166).

Although these cross sections of relevant literatures form the background of our understanding of employee voice, we opt for going back to basics, as it were. For the purpose of this chapter, having a voice is *not* a matter of speaking up. Having a voice is fundamentally the right to speak in the first place. This means, that we gravitate towards the view favored by organizational justice literature. We will return to central implications of this perception of voice (section 6). In the following section, we will deal with the communication-theoretical fabric of our analytical lens, that is, the so-called CCO principle, and its links to voice and voicer.

The linguistic turn (Rorty, 1992 [1967]), the main tenet of which holds that language is not merely reflecting social reality, but is involved in producing it, spurred fruitful theory building in many fields – among them the field of organizational communication. Especially the proposition that social reality is 'communicated into being' (Ashcraft et al., 2009, 5) gave rise to a significant shift in the appreciation of what communication is and what it does, that is, a shift from a functional or instrumental view to an interpretative one. In a seminal 1974 paper, Karl Weick proposed a paradigmatic shift from organi*zation* to organi*zing*, that is, treating 'the concept of "organization" as a verb and not as a noun' (Putnam et al., 2008, 1). For organizational communication the two most significant ideas stemming from the linguistic turn were the decisive break with the container metaphor of the organization and the transmissive view of communication, respectively. Viewing organization not as a container, that is, not as a place within which communication occurs, builds on the realization that:

> Just as the skin is a misleading boundary for marking off where man ends and the environment starts, so are the walls of an organization. Events inside organizations and organisms are locked into circuits that extend beyond these artificial boundaries. (Weick, 1974, 358)

Viewing communication as constitutive implies that communication is much more than the sending and receiving of messages. Seen as constitutive, communication 'is a process of meaning creation or social construction' and that, as such, 'communication is assumed to be the basic building block for social entities' (Nicotera, 2009, 176). Within current organizational communication theory and practice, the two insights regarding organization and communication, respectively, have merged and crystalized into a coherent view labeled the CCO principle, that is, communication constitutes organization (e.g., Putnam and Fairhurst, 2015, 376). According to the CCO principle

> [...] organizations can no longer be seen as objects, entities, or 'social facts' inside of which communication occurs. Organizations are portrayed, instead, as ongoing and precarious accomplishments realized, experienced, and identified primarily – if not exclusively – *in* communication processes. (Cooren et al., 2011, 1150)

Apart from acknowledging that the organization is communicated into being, we will not be pursuing the ontology of the organization any further. What we will be pursuing, however, are '[c]ommunication processes' that, when enacted, 'constitute organizational life' (Putnam et al., 2008, 6) and, as a central aspect of this, how voice is constituted communicatively. According to the CCO principle

> [...] communication becomes explicitly 'organizational' (in the pragmatic sense of the word) at precisely the moment when a collective agency finds expression in an identifiable actor, and the actor is recognized by his or her community as a legitimate expression of such agency. (Taylor and Cooren, 1997, 435)

From this point of view, voice is constituted '[a]s soon as one acts for another' (Taylor and Cooren, 1997, 429), that is, when an organizational member (identifiable actor) speaks for the organization (collective agency) in a mode sanctioned (recognized as legitimate) by said organization (the actor's community). It follows that not only is voice communicatively constituted, but so is both voicer and the content voiced. This, in turn, links the CCO principle to the formation of employee identity. It does so in the sense that the constitution of voice as 'the ability to make one's self heard, or visible, to others through self-expression' (cf. above) becomes the nexus of the kind of communicatively constituted identity formation that we are investigating. When an organizational member's identity *as* an organizational member is constituted in the flux of communication, it becomes an entity that can no longer be seen as a stable 'essence', aligned once and for all with the organization's values and policies, for example, through an organizational onboarding process (Wanberg, 2012), but a mutable 'existence' in communication. As such employee identity is 'achieved' (Cheney et al., 2011, 110), that is, carefully constructed and continuously reconstructed.

As is the case for all instances of 'social identification', it is a process that 'occurs between unequal partners' (DiSanza and Bullis, 1999, 348). The relationship in question is one in which the organizational member is 'enjoined to incorporate [...] managerial discourses into narratives of self-identity' (Alvesson and Willmott, 2002, 622). Whereas the process of forging 'a oneness' may be targeted directly at specific groups of employees in specific situations, for example, at newcomers during the onboarding phase, it may also 'be accomplished, in more or less focused ways, through diverse media of control' (Alvesson and Willmott, 2002, 632). From the point of view of critical organizational communication, all managerially sanctioned instances of organizational communication, among them the employee maga- zine, are seen as contributing to the communicative constitution of 'oneness' in this broad sense of the word. The phenomenon of speaking *for* an organi- zation as its sanctioned or recognized voice is by no means a trivial matter. Organizational practice as well as theory tells us that voice constituted in this sense is a privilege not bestowed on all organizational members. We are thereby able to enrich our basic appreciation of having a voice with the critical addition that 'on the whole, managers decide whether or not workers have a voice' (Ruck, 2015, 51).

In sum, what we are proposing is a new perspective on strategic corporate journalism. Our theoretical aggregation allows us to look critically at how an organization, as a key site of identity formation, utilizes its employee magazine to facilitate employee alignment – more specifically social identification.

RESEARCH DESIGN

Our research design is problem-driven and fundamentally informed by a constructivist worldview (e.g., Berger and Luckmann, 1996 [1966]), that is, featuring a relativistic ontology and an (inter)subjective epistemology. Our empirical analysis is rooted in a social semiotic perspective on language (e.g., van Leeuwen, 2005; Ledin and Machin, 2020) and is qualitative in nature. Concretely, we conduct in-depth examinations of select, research agenda-relevant instances of organizational communication as these make themselves manifest in the constitution of voice.

The data for the analysis stem from *G Magazine*, the employee magazine of Grundfos – a global pump company with its headquarters in Denmark. Grundfos employs around 19,280 people in 56 countries. The employee mag- azine is a strategic corporate medium (Kastberg, 2020) that helps management reach the entire company with a consistent message (FitzPatrick, 2016).

The employee magazine is widely known as a publication that is 'produced on behalf of an organisation's management to cover organisation-related news to its internal stakeholders' (Koch et al., 2018, 52). It is not only mandated by the organization's management but also controlled by the organization with respect to what it contains and when and how often it is published (Kastberg, 2020). Being strategic, it serves as an instrument – or even as the anchor of all internal communication – with the aim of ensuring alignment between the stra- tegic, the tactical, and the operational level of management strategy (Kastberg, 2020). The *G Magazine* serves as a strategic corporate medium, reaching out to all its employees and being published in eight different languages, makes it accessible to as many employees as possible, including employees without proficiency in English. One of the main purposes of the employee magazine as a strategic corporate medium is to contribute to the employees' identification with the organization (Koch et al., 2018; Kastberg, 2020).

The employee magazine analyzed is the English version of the *G Magazine* that was distributed in July 2019. The issue is 40 pages long and counts approximately 8,100 words and 36 color-pictures of which 15 cover one page or more. The excessive use of pictures reflects that employee magazines 'have visual strengths and [therefore can] activate emotions better than other channels' (Grabuschnig and Vizgirdaité, 2015, 37). Visuals in employee magazines are of particular interest as they form part of emotional factors of the medium like shared identity, engagement, and proximity (Grabuschnig and Vizgirdaité, 2015). The extensive use of visuals is therefore a strong testimony to the main objective 'to contribute to the employees' identification' with the organization.

The July 2019-issue of *G Magazine* was singled out for examination as this issue was dedicated to introducing the new corporate strategy. What makes this issue particularly suitable for the purposes of our chapter is the fact that the corporate strategy lays the ground for where the organization is going and, consequently, has a huge impact on employee identity formation. In lieu of this, the issue features the new Grundfos Strategy 2025, it presents the new Group Management Team that 'gives more power to strategy' (Grundfos, 2019, 6), as well as focuses on the concept of quality. These articles make up the first one third of the magazine. Besides short news stories related to Grundfos, the other two thirds of the magazine include reports on Grundfos' presence at a trade fair, their approach to the Indian market, a prestige project in China, as well as feature articles on selected individuals (a manager, an employee, and a partner) and a development and innovation team.

Overall, the *G Magazine* of July 2019 covers a wide range of strategically relevant aspects of Grundfos as a global organization that emphasizes close relationships with employees, partners, and customers. Debates and controversial or delicate topics relating to the organization, that would otherwise form part of an employee magazine demonstrating a sensitivity to employee concerns, are not present.

Based on these observations, the *G Magazine* of July 2019 serves as a strategic communication platform. It is thus to be expected that strategic management tools form the basis of the employee magazine. This includes the mission, that is, 'the pursuit of a goal that is unique to an organization's competitive advantage' (Bowen, 2018, 3) and the core values, that is, 'fundamental principles and operating philosophies that inform decisions and behaviors'

(Seeger and Seeger, 2018, 1). Grundfos' mission or 'overriding purpose of the organization' (Cornelissen, 2004, 24) is:

> We pioneer solutions to the world's water and climate challenges and improve quality of life for people. (Grundfos, 2020a)

Closely related to the mission of Grundfos is its promise to society and customers, that is, 'be [responsible] think [ahead] innovate' (Grundfos, 2020b) – a promise that doubles as its slogan. The core values decided by management are: 'sustainable', 'open and trustworthy', 'focused on people', 'independent', 'partnership', and finally 'relentlessly ambitious' (Grundfos, 2020a). In addition, corporate strategies for reaching corporate goals that management have chosen are expected to be part of the strategic basis of the magazine. Such strategies are traditionally based on strengths of the organization identified by management. In Grundfos' case, the strengths are identified to relate to 'products, innovation, quality and customer knowledge' (Grundfos, 2019, 4).

Analytically speaking, we have developed and applied a method assemblage (Law, 2004, 14). This assemblage mirrors the complex nature of our research agenda and allows us to integrate the two different, yet interdependent aspects of the phenomenon of voice, that is, the who (the voicer), the what (the topic or content), and to synthesize them into a coherent argument. As for the voicer, we are interested in identifying the aforementioned actors in the sense of a real person, in the here and now of some real situation, with a name, a circumstantial identity and a real personal history' (Taylor and Cooren, 1997, 426). When it comes to the what, that is, content or topic, a topic analysis (Li and Yamanishi, 2000; Ditlevsen et al., 2007) is applied.

FINDINGS

In the July 2019 *G Magazine*, the following categories of voicers are represented (see Figure 15.1): (a) the organization Grundfos as a collective; (b) different management levels and particularly CEO Mads Nipper; (c) employees; and finally (d) partners, that is, suppliers, customers and other stakeholders (Grundfos, 2020a).

The first voicer, the organization as a collective, is present throughout the magazine and is the most widespread voicer. The organization is communicatively constructed via the assumed 'we' /'our' (Cheney, 1983) 'where a common bond among members of the organization is taken for granted' (154), but rarely questioned, which makes it a very powerful way of identity regulation. In the magazine (Grundfos, 2019) we find examples like:

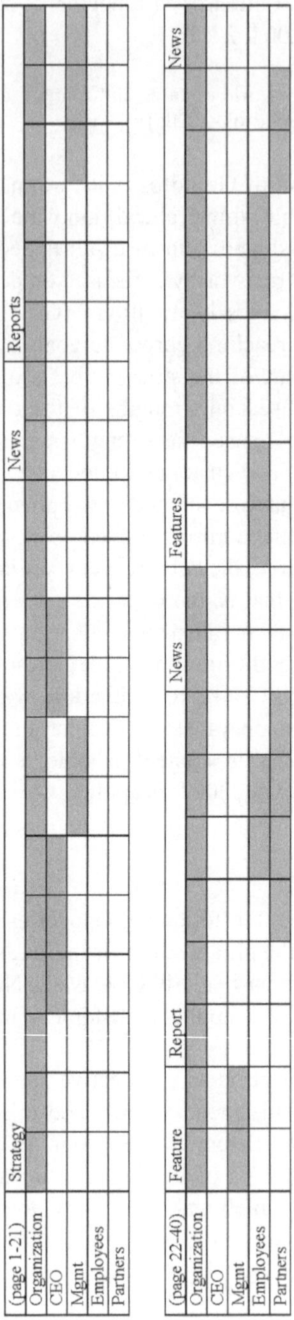

(page 1-21)	Strategy					News					Reports					News
Organization																
CEO																
Mgmt																
Employees																
Partners																

(page 22-40)	Feature					Report					News					Features					News
Organization																					
CEO																					
Mgmt																					
Employees																					
Partners																					

Figure 15.1   Voicers in G Magazine, July 2019

- We pioneer the future. (title page)
- Our top managers from around the world met at the Grundfos Leadership Conference. (3)
- We are continuing to grow more than our market, and our earnings are satisfactory, even though we still need to work on getting our margins fully on track. (4)
- We rolled out our strongest innovations at LSH in Frankfurt. (16)

Grundfos as a collective is supported visually by the extensive use of the Grundfos logo; the appearance of pumps and other products; the use of the corporate color, that is, blue; photos of items with 'Grundfos' and/or logo (e.g., signboards, packaging, T-shirts); and buildings and sculptures from the headquarters in Bjerringbro and other locations. In this way Grundfos becomes the hub of the employee magazine's universe and due to the absence of critical content (see above) it serves as a medium of classical positive self-presentation (Koch et al., 2018).

The second category of voicers is that of management, incl. CEO Mads Nipper – the most widespread individual voice of the first 11 pages of the magazine. Mads Nipper's voice is strongest in the CEO-letter (4) in which he introduces the main topic of the July issue by presenting and explaining the new strategy. In the rest of the first third of the magazine, he is the voicer of relatively long testimonial quotes regarding new members of Group Management Team and strategic choices. His role as voicer is strengthened visually through a close-up 'demand' portrait-photo (Kress and van Leeuwen, 1996) of him on the title page and another 'demand' photo of him in connection with the CEO-letter (4). As the most prominent individual voicer in general and in relation to strategic topics in particular, Mads Nipper acts as the personification of Grundfos.

Other managerial voicers are related to lower management levels. Three voicers are particularly salient: Gustavo Arriba, Vice President Quality, is interviewed on the understanding of quality that is 'essential in everything we do' (9); Venkataramanan Viswanathan, Associate Vice President, DBS, Grundfos India, is used as a voicer regarding the presentation and explanation of successful partnership building approaches on the market for Domestic Building Services in India (21); and finally, Catherine Yang, Regional Managing Director, China, is the main voicer in a portrait article about herself (22). The employees at Grundfos appear as dedicated, skilled, highly qualified and Grundfos is constructed as an employer supporting diversity, gender equality, and career possibilities for women. All voicers contribute to supporting the strategic goals of the employee magazine and of Grundfos: quality is one of the organization's strengths and part of the corporate value to be relentlessly ambitious; partnership is one of the corporate values and an integral part of Grundfos' purpose; and finally the people perspective is one of the corporate values and part of Grundfos' purpose (see above). They all form part of the first or the second part of the employee magazine, and all three voicers are the main voicers of the respective articles, which emphasizes the importance of the voicers.

The third category of voicers relates to employees. Employees are present in almost all parts of the employee magazine. However, they are only given a voice in a few texts in the last third of the magazine. Zhu Fu Quan, Sales Engineer, gives a small, but important statement in relation to a prestige project in China regarding customers' trust in the Grundfos brand and the opportunities for Grundfos to show its qualifications (27–28); Ehab Saad Edin, Senior Project Coordinator, Future Lab, Innovation Management, tells a personal story of his journey as a refugee from Syria to Denmark, not as an employee, but as a human being (32); and finally, Giovanni Luca Di Muoio, Alexander Mawer, and Simon Rosenberg Bolmgrenas, representatives of AME Digital Development and Innovation, explain the technical, competitive and financial advantages of simulation as a tool in innovation processes (36–37). Like the managerial voicers, the employee voicers contribute to supporting the strategic goals of the employee magazine and of Grundfos by showing (a) the strengths and qualities of the Grundfos brand and of Grundfos as a partner, (b) Grundfos as a responsible, inclusive organization, celebrating diversity, and (c) Grundfos as a digital frontrunner that thinks ahead and innovates. In this sense the voicers can be seen as propagators of corporate values like sustainability, focus on people, partnership, being relentlessly ambitious; for the overall purpose; for their promise to 'be think innovate'; and finally for the identified strengths regarding products, innovation, and quality.

The fourth and final category of voicers relates to partners, which resonates very well with the view that 'Grundfos and our partners are seen as a strong collective' (Grundfos, 2020a). Although the partners – and especially the customers – are present in many articles, they only appear as voicers in two. Customers Fei Wang, Vice General Manager, Zhengzhou Dongxing Environmental Energy, and Chang Hong Tao, Powerchina Henan Engineering, and Sun Yu Qiang, General Manager of the distribution partner DLG in Zhengzhou, are voicers in the longest article of the issue – a report on the Zhengzhou project in China that appears in the second half of the magazine. The voicers express that 'Grundfos and their partners fully meet all [the customers'] parameters' (27), how 'pleased' they are 'with [their] close partnership with Grundfos' (29), and finally, more indirectly, they praise the qualities of Grundfos products and solutions by, for example, stating that '[their] most important task is to find a sustainable and effective solution for managing the city's large volumes of waste' (27). The final partner voicer in the employee magazine belongs to Derek Johansson, CEO of Delta-Q, a US Grundfos representative. The feature article describes a prestige project in California, namely the construction of the

LA Stadium. However, it is dominantly a presentation of Delta-Q as a partner, a propagator for persistence and good teamwork as foundation for the successful construction of the LA Stadium, and finally a testimony to the qualities of Grundfos as a partner. In this way, the partner voicers of Grundfos support the corporate value of sustainability and partnership, and the identified strengths re. product, innovation, and quality.

To sum up, all voicers play a strategic role in the employee magazine and support the strategic goals of both the employee magazine and of Grundfos. The organization as a collective acts as the backcloth, CEO Mads Nipper sets the scene, and the rest of the voicers contribute to playing out the strategic managerial game on the organizational stage. If we extract from the above findings some of the major empirical indications, it is obvious that who has a voice in the magazine is strictly regulated, what an actor is allowed to give voice to equally so, and finally, that the amount of space allocated for any given voicer as well the distribution of voicers over the course of the magazine is indicative of its stipulated strategic importance.

CRITICAL REFLECTIONS AND CONCLUDING REMARKS

Voice, in sum, is assigned or not; and content voiced is strategically preselected, tailored, and distributed according to strategic considerations making it a clear-cut management-centric view on voice (section 2). Of the 19,280 Grundfos employees in 56 countries, a mere fraction of them are constituted as having a voice in the magazine. That, needless to say, is also attributed to the media format and its affordances. Even if we allow for that, it is telling that only organizationally speaking ideal actors from within the four categories of voicers are constituted as having a voice in the magazine. If we compare this to the idea that communication constitutes social reality (section 2), this gives rise to yet another layer of reflection. For a lack of voice (Kuhn and Deetz, 2009, 188) or pervasive employee silence (van Dyne et al., 2003, 1363) is constituted equally as much as being assigned a voice. It counts as a further insight that not only does communication constitute the social reality of Grundfos in general, communication also constitutes participation (Kuhn and Deetz, 2009, 187) – or the lack of it – in particular. In a critical reading, this is especially important since participation *in* communication in the first place is the very condition upon which any notion of communicating ethically must rest (Mumby, 2013, 49). We will return to communication ethics, but before we do so we would like to link participation – or the lack of it – to identity regulation (section 2) as well. Based on the assumption that the strict selection of actors, as well as what issues they are allowed to voice, are indicative of how Grundfos would like to present itself, it follows that the magazine as a strategic instrument of management is actively used in order to regulate employee identity. The identity regulation in question, however, is pursued covertly. According to social identification theory (e.g., Tajfel and Turner, 1979), any group socialization process, in our case: organizational socialization, goes through a number of phases. The first being social categorization: for an employee this corresponds to being onboarded into the company, including its mission, values, and strategies. If successful (from the point of view of the inductor's intention), this kind of overt identity regulation results in social identification proper. That is, that an employee adopts the identity of the company and – in the process – attaches not only professional but also emotional significance to his/her identification with, in our case, Grundfos. Having achieved that the employee's self-esteem is bound up with group membership, the final phase is referred to as social comparison. That, in turn, is the phase in which one's social identity is pitted against that of other social identities. In the extant literature this is typically seen as the cause for (socially unwanted) us vs. them dichotomies of various kinds. However, Grundfos avoids falling into the trap of an us vs. them discourse, that is, of, say, explicitly pitting the prowess of Grundfos and its employees against those of other companies. Instead, the *G Magazine* lets it be up to its readers to draw any comparisons, letting the social force inherent in the social comparison phase find its outlet not in spurring group-external animosity, but employing it in the service of explicating group-internal conformity. Because the voicers present in the *G Magazine* appear in their capacity as highly successful stakeholders of Grundfos, they are in effect idealizing the type of stakeholders that employees (and other relevant stakeholders) should aspire to resemble or, indeed, to become.

Even if these are quite interesting observations in and of themselves, as critical scholars documenting this does not suffice. From the above presentations, analyses, and discussions it is easily inferable that the *G Magazine* serves dominant interests at Grundfos in as much as it uses the magazine format's 'communicative resources to shape organizational reality in a way that supports those interests' (Mumby and Kuhn, 2019, 53). As critical scholars we are keenly 'interested in identifying the underlying interests, values and assumptions that make some forms of organizational reality [...] possible and foreclose the possibility of other [...] realities' (Mumby and Kuhn, 2019, 52). It is obvious that not only has a strategic agenda been set and followed, content-wise. It is equally obvious that, framing-wise, all content selected is portrayed in a manor deprived of conflict, negativity, or misgivings. Not only are potential other voicers and their potential other realities effectively silenced, so is content not conforming to the corporate mission, values, and strategies. Among the other realities that the *G Magazine* could have been instrumental in constituting, but was not, would be, say, genuine inter-stakeholder dialogue, the acknowledgement of conflicting stakeholder interests, participatory decision-making processes, and so on (e.g., Mumby, 2013, 49).

Being critical scholars, however, does not imply that we would (naïvely) deem all processes of employee control and identity regulation problematic in and of themselves. We are quite aware of and accept that to a large degree 'members' identification with an organization [is] necessary for that organization to thrive' (Mumby and Kuhn, 2019, 52). But as long as organizations – whatever else they are doing – are also 'continuously in the process of making decisions that affect people's lives in fundamental ways' (Mumby, 2013, 49), there is a just cause for critical evaluations of organizations' constitutive communicative practices. And it seems that the phenomena of voice and voicer would be a fruitful prism through which to begin exploring empirical instantiations of real-life organizational communication ethics. The ur-point of departure for future critical investigations along these lines being that *not* having a voice bars any attempt at participatory communication from the get go.

REFERENCES

Alvesson, M. and Willmott, H. (2002), Identity regulation as organizational control: Producing the appropriate individual. *Journal of Management Studies*, 39(5), 619–644.

Ashcraft, K. L., Kuhn, T. R. and Cooren, F. (2009), Constitutional amendments: 'Materializing' organizational communication. *The Academy of Management Annals*, 3(1), 1–64.

Bashshur, M. R. and Oc, B. (2015), When voice matters: A multilevel review of the impact of voice in organizations. *Journal of Management*, 41(5), 1530–1554.

Berger, P. L. and Luckmann, T. (1996 [1966]), *The social construction of reality: A treatise in the sociology of knowledge*. Penguin.

Boussebaa, M. and Brown, A. D. (2017), Englishization, identity regulation and imperialism. *Organization Studies*, 38(1), 7–29.

Bowen, F. and Blackmon, K. (2003), Spirals of silence: The dynamic effects of diversity on organizational voice. *Journal of Management Studies*, 40(6), 1393–1417.

Bowen, S. A. (2018), Mission and vision. In Heath, R. L. and Johansen, W. (eds.), *The international encyclopedia of strategic communication*. John Wiley and Sons. DOI: 10.1002/9781119010722.iesc0111.

Cheney, G. (1983), The rhetoric of identification and the study of organizational communication. *Quarterly Journal of Speech*, 69, 143–158.

Cheney, G., Christensen, L. T., Zorn, T. E. and Ganesh, S. (2011), *Organizational communication in an age of globalization* (2nd edition). Waveland Press.

Clampitt, P. G., Crevcoure, J. M. and Hartel, R. L. (1986), Exploratory research on employee publications. *The Journal of Business Communication*, 23(3), 5–17.

Cooren, F., Kuhn, T. R., Cornelissen, J. P. and Clark, T. (2011), Communication, organizing and organization: An overview and introduction to the special issue. *Organization Studies*, 32(9), 1–22.

Cornelissen, J. P. (2004), *Corporate communications: Theory and practice* (1st edition). Sage.

Cornelissen, J. P. (2011), *Corporate communication. A guide to theory and practice* (3rd edition). Sage.

Deetz, S. A. (1992), *Democracy in an age of corporate colonization: Developments in communication and the politics of everyday life*. State University of New York Press.

DiSanza, J. R. and Bullis, C. (1999), 'Everybody identifies with Smokey the Bear': Employee responses to newsletter identification inducements at the U.S. Forest Service. *Management Communication Quarterly*, 12, 347–399.

Ditlevsen, M. G., Engberg, J., Kastberg, P. and Nielsen, M. (2007), *Sprog på arbejde [Language at work]*. Samfundslitteratur.

FitzPatrick, L. (2016), Internal communications. In Theaker, A. (ed.), *The public relations handbook*. Routledge, 295–335.

Foucault, M. (1974), *The archeology of knowledge*. Tavistock.

Gambarotto, F. and Cammozzo, A. (2010), Dreams of silence: Employee voice and innovation in a public sector community of practice. *Innovation*, 12(2), 166–179.

Gehman, J., Lefsrud, L. M. and Fast, S. (2017), Social license to operate: Legitimacy by another name? *Canadian Public Administration / Administration Publique du Canada*, 60(2), 293–317.

Grabuschnig, M. and Vizgirdaité, J. (2015), The role of employee magazines as an internal communication tool in international organisations (Case of Automotive Industry in Germany and South Africa). *Informacijos Mokslai*, 72, 33–55.

Grundfos (2019), *G Magazine*, July 2019.

Grundfos (2020a), *Our values and purpose*. Retrieved from https://www.grundfos .com/about-us/Our%20company/our-values-and-purpose.html, 14 August 2020.

Grundfos (2020b), *be think innovate*. Retrieved from https://www.grundfos.com/about -us/Our%20company/be-think-innovate.html, 14 August 2020.

Hirschman, A. O. (1970), *Exit, voice, and loyalty*. Harvard University Press.

Kastberg, P. (2020), Medarbejdermagasinet – et udtryk for strategic corporate journalism [The employee magazine – instantiation of strategic corporate journalism]. In Aggerholm, H., Asmuß, B., Ditlevsen, M. G., Frandsen, F., Johansen, W., Kastberg, P., Nielsen, A. E. and Thomsen, C. (eds.), *Intern kommunikation under forandring*. Samfundslitteratur, 199–225.

Koch, T., Vogel, J., Denner, N. and Encarnacao, S. (2018), Voice of the management or employee advocate? How editors of employee magazines see their professional role. *Corporate Communications: An International Journal*, 23(1), 51–65.

Konrad, A. M., Prasad, P. and Pringle, J. K. (eds) (2006), *Handbook of workplace diversity*. Sage.

Kounalakis, M., Banks, D. and Daus, K. (1999), *Beyond spin: The power of strategic corporate journalism*. John Wiley and Sons.

Kress, G. and van Leeuwen, T. (1996), *Reading images: The grammar of visual design*. Routledge.

Kuhn, T. and Deetz, S. (2009), Critical theory and corporate social responsibility. Can/should we get beyond cynical reasoning? In Crane, A., Matten, D., McWilliams, A., Moon, J. and Siegel, D. S. (eds.), *The Oxford handbook of corporate social responsibility*. Oxford University Press, 173–196.

Law, J. (2004), *After method: Mess in social science research*. Routledge.

Ledin, P. and Machin, D. (2020), *Introduction to multimodal analysis*. Bloomsbury Academic.

Li, H. and Yamanishi, K. (2000), Topic analysis using a Finite Mixture Model. *Proceedings of the 2000 Joint SIGDAT Conference on Empirical Methods in Natural Language Processing and Very Large Corpora*, 35–44.

Logan, N. and Tindall, N. (2018), Voice. In Heath, R. L. and Johansen, W. (eds.), *The international encyclopedia of strategic communication*. John Wiley and Sons.

Morrison, E. W. and Milliken, F. J. (2003), Speaking up, remaining silent: The dynamics of voice and silence in organizations. *Journal of Management Studies*, 6, 1353–1358.

Morsing, M. and Schultz, M. (2006), Corporate social responsibility communication: Stakeholder information, response and involvement strategies. *Business Ethics: A European Review*, 15(4), 323–338.

Mumby, D. K. (2013), *Organizational communication. A critical approach*. Sage.

Mumby, D. K. and Kuhn, T. R. (2019), *Organizational communication. A critical introduction* (2nd edition). Sage.

Nicotera, A. M. (2009), Constitutive view of communication. In Littlejohn, S. W. and Foss, K. A. (eds.), *Encyclopedia of communication theory*. Sage, 176–179.

Putnam, L. L. and Fairhurst, G. T. (2015), Revisiting 'Organizations as discursive constructions': 10 years later. *Communication Theory*, 25, 375–392.

Putnam, L., Nicotera, A. M. and McPhee, R. D. (2008), Introduction: Communication constitutes organization. In Putnam, L. and Nicotera, A. M. (eds.), *Building theories of organizations: The constitutive role of communication*. Routledge, 1–19.

Rorty, R. M. (1992 [1967]), *The linguistic turn – essays in philosophical method*. University of Chicago Press.

Ruck, K. (2015), Informed employee voice. In Ruck, K., *Exploring internal communication. Towards informed employee voice* (3rd edition). Gower, 47–55.

Ruck, K., Welch, M. and Menara, B. (2017), Employee voice: An antecedent to organisational engagement? *Public Relations Review*, 43, 904–914.

Seeger, M. W. and Seeger, H. S. (2018), Core values. In Heath, R. L. and Johansen, W. (eds.), *The international encyclopedia of strategic communication*. John Wiley and Sons.

Solomon, J. (2007), *Corporate governance and accountability*. John Wiley and Sons.

Tajfel, H. and Turner, J. C. (1979), An integrative theory of inter-group conflict. In Austin, W. G. and Worchel, S. (eds.), *The social psychology of inter-group relations*. Brooks/Cole, 33–47.

Taylor, J. R. and Cooren, F. (1997), What makes communication 'organizational'? How the many voices of a collectivity become one voice of an organization. *Journal of Pragmatics*, 27, 409–438.

van Dyne, L., Ang, S. and Botero, I. C. (2003), Conceptualizing employee silence and employee voice as multidimensional constructs. *Journal of Management Studies*, 40(6), 1359–1392.

van Leeuwen, T. (2005), *Introducing social semiotics*. Routledge.

Wanberg, C. R. (2012), Facilitating organizational socialization: An introduction. In Wanberg, C. R. (ed.), *The Oxford handbook of organizational socialization*. Oxford University Press, 3–7.

Weick, K. E. (1974), Middle range theories of social systems. *Behavioral Science*, 19, 357–367.

Wilkinson, A. and Fay, C. (2011), New times for employee voice? *Human Resource Management*, 50(1), 65–74.

16. Let us (not) speak Finnish! On language, power relations and ambivalence

Janne Tienari

INTRODUCTION

Let us all speak Finnish! Let us make Finnish into the global lingua franca of business and international business studies! Just kidding, of course… we Finnish speakers are painfully aware of the irrelevance of our language in the grand scheme of things. Finnish is a miniscule language. It is a secret language, which we can use over the heads of others. Although most kids in Finland speak it, the Finnish language has proven difficult for adults to learn. It is not connected to any other languages apart from Estonian, which is an even smaller language. That is why we embrace bad English as a global communication tool. It offers us Finns something of a level field with others.

This approach to language is very different from, for example, speakers of French or Spanish. It is very different from English, too. We do not pretend to elevate our humble tongue into a world language. For starters, we were never real colonizers (although the Sámi up north in Lapland may disagree). We were colonized for a long time, first by the Kingdom of Sweden and then by Imperial Russia. The Swedish and Russian languages were imposed on us. We do not expect others to bother to learn our language, but we like to defend it. I just wanted to get your attention and, hopefully, make language scholars and linguistic colonizers out there pay attention. Please reflect. Language issues are much more complicated and ambivalent than you ever dreamed. They are contextual and embedded in power relations.

I approach language(s) from this vantage point, and I join an exciting conversation. Natural languages have received increasing attention by international business studies scholars (Piekkari et al., 2014) and a 'language-sensitive' research agenda is taking shape (Beeler et al., 2017). This is long overdue, given the important role of multinational corporations in the contemporary global order, and considering the crucial significance of languages in the functioning of these organizations. A focus on language is also necessary for scrutinizing knowledge production in universities, which is increasingly carried out in a single language, English, our own lingua franca (Boussebaa and Brown, 2017; Boussebaa and Tienari, 2021).

Language is intimately connected to power and resistance, and we must labor to unravel these connections. A focus on how languages operate separately and together in different contexts gives us opportunities to dwell on the in-built tensions created by multiple languages in complex organizations such as multinational corporations and universities. It also allows us to pinpoint the varied solutions through which organizations operate beyond, or despite, these tensions—and how they find common ways forward.

In this chapter, I argue that meaningful language-sensitive analysis in international business studies entails that we acknowledge the ambivalence that characterizes language relations in the world today. This means that we take tensions, uncertainties, and mixed feelings regarding languages seriously.

Next, I introduce my take on power and resistance in relation to language(s). Using this power relations lens, I elucidate problematics of strategy and strategic decisions in multinational organizations. I move on to the individual level and consider languages as a question of identity for international business studies scholars in business schools. The linguistic set-up in my two examples is the same—it involves Swedish, Finnish, and English—but the context and power relations that condition languages and linguistic relations are different. Finally, I offer some ideas to take the debate on international business and languages forward.

LANGUAGE, POWER, AND RESISTANCE

Language is linked with power and resistance—what I refer to as power relations—in and around organizations. While power is of crucial importance for social analyses, it is understood in a variety of ways (Clegg et al., 2006). A basic distinction can be made between those who understand power as a resource, as something held and used, and those who argue for a relational view of power. I build on the latter, post-structuralist conception that challenges the established traditions. It grew out of Michel Foucault's (1977, 1984) work where he conceptualized social actors as controlled and disciplined by practices and discourses, which construct subject positions and identities. In this view, power is in relations, which are understood to be multifaceted. For example, those conventionally seen as powerless also exercise power. Central to Foucault's ideas on power is that it is productive and transformative as well as exacting and limiting (Foucault, 1980). Power is fundamentally relational and it modifies, directs, and guides rather than dominates.

The question of resistance is crucial for understanding power. When power is viewed as a resource to be held and used, resistance acquires specific meanings. It is often presented as a hindrance to organizational development and something to be overcome by means of management. Interestingly, however, resistance can also be celebrated as a potential contribution to meaningful organizational change (Thomas and Hardy, 2011). In contrast, research on the 'labor process' has concentrated on the collective, conscious, concerted, and organized responses to owner and managerial power. Building on Marxist understandings, power and resistance are presented as antithetical, and related to management and employees and their tense relationships in organizations (Braverman, 1974). Critical analyses of management extend this and typically address how cultural traditions and the acts of powerful agents contribute to 'freezing' social reality for the benefit of specific interests at the expense of others (Alvesson and Deetz, 2000). Resistance becomes a 'natural' element of human social relations and interaction, and hence power, too.

I build on critical scholarship where power and resistance are viewed as complex issues that cannot be reduced to tensions between managers and employees. While the mainstream literature continues to embrace power as a resource, more critical work slides toward processual and relational understandings. In the Foucauldian view, acts of resistance—conventionally seen as a counterforce to power—are an inherent part of power relations. Resistance is not considered as separate from power. It is inherent in exercising power (Knights and Vurdubakis, 1994). In fact, some claim that resistance can be conceptualized to constitute a form of power (Collinson, 1994).

For me, the key question (to study) is how and why a particular version of social reality on language(s), carrying specific meanings, becomes accepted and normalized as 'truth' at a given time and place, and what opportunities for alternatives and resistance this opens up (Tienari and Vaara, 2012). From the point of view of language, I find the implications of power relations in terms of strategies and identities to be particularly intriguing and relevant. Language— or languages, in the plural—emerges as a central concern for making sense of these constructs, but it is too seldom considered as such. It seems to me that the international business studies literature epitomizes a lack of serious concern for understanding languages, power, and resistance from a relational perspective.

Of course, power and resistance remain a contested terrain for researchers. Both views—power as resources and power as relations—have been criticized (Tienari and Vaara, 2012). On the one hand, to understand power as a resource runs the risk of simplification. Power can be reduced to qualities and possessions of individuals and groups and the positions they hold. On the other hand, post-structuralist conceptions of power relations can promote a deterministic view that gives limited significance to individual subjects and selves. By questioning the existence of 'stable' structures, post-structuralists also run the risk of relativism where critiquing structural inequalities and subordination is limited (Tienari and Vaara, 2012). Taking some sort of middle ground is tempting, but difficult to operationalize in research practice.

There are some recent contributions on language in international business studies, which are sensitive to questions of power relations. Beeler and Lecomte (2017) studied linguistic hegemony and language-based in-group behavior in cross-cultural encounters. They applied Mikhail Bakhtin's dialogical perspective to conceptualize sensemaking as the co-construction of meaning. Dialogical practices that they focused on include interconnected utterances ('addressivity' and 'responsivity'), multivoicedness ('polyphony'), and multiple speaking styles ('heteroglossia'). These practices and the dialogues they engendered proved for some to be effective in fostering cross-cultural collaboration in multicultural teams. Unfortunately, Beeler and Lecomte (2017) point out, many teams that they studied failed in this respect.

Following Michel Foucault, in turn, Gaibrois and Steyaert (2017) sought to understand how intra-organizational power relations are defined and redefined through language use. They explored power from a discursive perspective and defined it as an effect of speaking acts. Their analysis enables us to see how people contribute to the creation of power relations in the multilingual organization by adopting a multiplicity of subject positions when they talk about their own and others' experiences. Gaibrois and Steyaert (2017) consider power as productive in a general sense and point out that this productivity engenders competition as well as cooperation in the multilingual organization.

Understanding how language plays into power and resistance—or power relations—in organizations forms the basis for my argument. I am interested in how power relations engender a sense of ambivalence—tensions and uncertainty—around questions of language. It seems to me that ambivalence is the outcome of the fact that we view power relations in organizations from different vantage points and perspectives or, in Michel Foucault's words, in and through different subject positions. In the following, I offer two examples to elucidate this. The first example, strategy, operates on the organizational level where language choice viewed as a strategic question becomes central. The second example, identity, takes the discussion to the level of individual experience in organizations, and unravels how language and power relations condition our ambivalent experiences at work.

LANGUAGE AND ORGANIZATION: A QUESTION OF STRATEGY?

Language is a strategic matter in, and for, organizations. A cross-border merger involving two parties that have different mother tongues is a case in point. In these circumstances, language—and language choice—becomes a far-reaching question that sets the direction and tone for merger integration and future operations. It also illustrates the power implications of languages in organizations. Language issues come to the fore when negotiating communication and decision-making practices and when confronting the 'Other' in the reality of the post-merger context (Vaara et al., 2005).

On the one hand, from the perspective of corporate strategy, different natural languages pose a need to agree upon and control communication and decision-making practices so that the language differences do not hamper 'effective' functioning of the new post-merger corporation. On the other hand, the merger process is likely to be characterized by cultural confrontation where natural languages are concrete examples, signifiers, and emblems of organizational and national identification.

Vaara et al. (2005) studied the language choice in a cross-border merger in the financial services industry from the perspective of power relations. They built on Stewart Clegg's (1989) 'circuits of power' framework, which is an example of multidimensional conceptualizations of power (and resistance). Clegg brings together three levels of analysis in his framework. First, he discusses episodic power relationships manifested in concrete situations where different social actors interact. Second, he considers rules of practice that fix relations of meaning and membership that both define identities and subjectivities for the actors interacting in specific episodes and are affected by these interactions. Third, Clegg (1989) specifies structures of domination constituted by social practices and techniques empowering or disempowering actors. The term 'circuit' refers to the co-existence and connections between all three levels.

Drawing on Clegg's ideas, Vaara et al. (2005) studied in-depth the language choice in the cross-border merger. They elucidated how power operates in three interconnected circuits in the merging organization. First, Vaara et al. (2005) argue that in observable social interaction, language skills facilitate understanding and communication and thereby have many kinds of power implications. Among other things, this means contributing to the creation of language-based networks for accessing information and knowledge in the post-merger organization. Second, the selected language (re)constructs and defines meanings and membership categories in the merging multinational corporation, implying complex identity and subjectivity constructions. Third, the institutionalization and normalization of specific identities and practices leads to the reification of structures of domination, that is, relatively fixed social power relationships between the merger parties (and the nation-states they 'represent') in the specific context.

These ideas have implications for our understandings of 'doing' strategy in MNCs in the light of language(s) and power relations. I was part of the research initiative and took part in writing the text. As we stressed in the article, we could not make sense of the 'drama' in the language choice in the multinational corporation without setting it against the backdrop of a specific socio-historically constituted linguistic context and the relations of the 'nations' in question. The company we studied was the outcome of a merger between a Finnish and a Swedish (or Swedish and Finnish) financial services company. The choice of joint corporate language for the post-merger organization was Swedish. Hell broke loose.

Simply, most Finns in the organization not only had mixed feelings; they were very annoyed when they found out what the 'official corporate language' was going to be. They were not happy about the pressure put on them to learn or brush up their Swedish, which was to be on top of their daily duties and all the merger-related extra integration hassle. Most Swedes were happily ignorant of all the drama. In fact, some of our key informants in Sweden said that they would have been comfortable with choosing English as the corporate language. They told us that it was some key Finnish decision-makers who came up with the idea of choosing Swedish. Of course, these particular Finns could communicate fluently in both Swedish and Finnish.

This language choice is not as strange as it may sound. Finland was part of the Kingdom of Sweden from 1323 until 1809. Many of the institutional arrangements and cultural conventions in Finland were adopted from Sweden. Swedish colonization is also the reason for the continued presence of Swedish language in Finnish society. Finland is officially bilingual, with around 6 percent of the population speaking Swedish as their mother tongue. All state institutions and public services in Finland are available in two languages. In Helsinki, the Finnish capital city, Swedish speakers are in popular discourse portrayed as affluent. Businesses owned by Swedish-speaking families remain relatively powerful in the Finnish economy and society. At the same time, all Finns must study a certain amount of mandatory Swedish at school. Many do this reluctantly and are very unsure about their modest Swedish language skills. Some embrace the opportunity.

Beyond the more practical challenges in operating in a 'foreign' language, then, Finns in the post-merger MNC organization resisted what to them amounted to old-school colonialism, especially given the global nature of financial services where the common language across the world is English. The Swedish-speaking Finns in the company were in a specific position. You may think that they as a 'group' benefited from the language choice. Their reality was complicated. In many ways, Swedish-speaking Finns were comfortable with the opportunity to work in their mother tongue. However, they soon found themselves doing a fair bit of translation work on documents and other materials on top of their other duties and responsibilities. It was annoying when they found out that the 'real' Swedes in Stockholm did not appreciate their efforts and developed a habit of correcting their language. Swedes openly joked about the old-fashioned nature of the Swedish language spoken in Finland.

Overall, it turned out that language really was a strategic question for the new organization, and an inherent part of the unfolding power relations in the sensitive post-merger setting. The question was notably multifaceted and ambivalent. When the Swedish–Finnish (or Finnish–Swedish) financial services company merged with a Danish company sometime later, the resistance by Finns was acknowledged. Already in the first letter to the stakeholders—and the 'merger prospectus'—it was clearly stated that the corporate language in the new Swedish–Finnish–Danish organization was English.

Questions of language and power relations take different forms. In my next example, the Swedish language attains different meanings and it proves to be an even more complicated question. The three languages involved are still the same—Swedish, Finnish, and English—but the power relations in the focal organization and its operating environment differ. My example shows how language and power intertwine with self-identities of individuals in organizations.

LANGUAGE AND INDIVIDUALS: A QUESTION OF IDENTITY?

Language does not only operate on the level of organizations or multi-linguistic teams. I offer myself as an example of how language matters for individuals, how it plays into our identities and identity work, and how this is related to power relations and ambivalence in and beyond organizations (Tienari, 2019). My focus is not on 'organizational identity' as a collective construct (Pratt et al., 2016), but on self-identities that are our subjectively but socially construed understandings of who we were, are, and desire to become as individuals (Brown, 2015).

In 2016, I moved from a Finnish-speaking business school to a Swedish-speaking one in Helsinki, Finland. I am a Finnish speaker who has always worked in English. With my move into a new environment I discovered something new about myself. In the Finnish-speaking business school—Aalto University School of Business—I was part of the dominant group and I was in many ways an insider; connected and informed. In the Swedish-speaking business school, I am in some ways on the margins due to my lack of Swedish language skills. I continue to work in English. This has enabled me to enact an outsider identity in my work community. I am comfortable with this, but I have also developed a sense of lack and guilt for not contributing in Swedish. As such, my argument is that professional—here, academic—identity is based on language, and once that foundation is shaken, it can trigger self-reflection that shows how language is inevitably tied in with power relations (Tienari, 2019).

The question of Swedish language—the history of which was described above—in contemporary Finland is complex and contested. Mandatory Swedish for all Finns at school is debated in media and social media, and there are occasional challenges to its status from the nationalist political right. The Swedish-speaking business school in Helsinki—Hanken School of Economics—has a specific mission in society and a mandate in offering business studies education in the Swedish language. It cherishes its (linguistic) mission, mandate, and independence. However, it is also an international and accredited business school, and it hosts many faculty and students who speak neither Swedish nor Finnish. The business school must embrace the global discourse of academic excellence and English as its lingua franca. It must engage in balancing acts between its mission and mandate related to the Swedish language and the hegemonic discourse. The situation is more ambivalent than a shallow analysis would suggest, especially from the point of view of individual academics such as myself.

Language shapes social practices and knowledge flows in organizations (Piekkari et al., 2014) such as universities (Tietze and Dick, 2013) and it is evident in my experiences. Language, power, and identity are central to academic work, which is to a significant extent about research, writing, and publishing. 'Englishization,' or the normalization of English as the language of academic writing and publishing worldwide, is in many ways problematic (Boussebaa and Brown, 2017; Boussebaa and Tienari, 2021). Language is a crucial source of boundaries in globalized academia as careers in national academic contexts are conditioned by the dual challenge to master English and the local language(s) (Pudelko and Tenzer, 2019). For non-native speakers in universities, Englishization may lead to feelings of vulnerability and frustration, but it is also 'contested, complained about and appropriated in the creative identity work of those subject to it' (Boussebaa and Brown, 2017, 7). For me, it is the other way around. English is my escape. My ability to be productive in terms of publications in English is at the core of my sense of self as an academic. However, it leads to ambivalence in my work.

My story shows that language in academia is not only about English. In countries such as Finland it never can be. In my case, it is about juggling English, Swedish, and Finnish. Steyaert and Janssens (2012, 133) argue that 'power, domination, negotiation and forms of resistance are core ingredients of the way language is performed' but they also suggest that research on political processes of language use 'need to be conducted in situ, focusing on how the multiplicity of languages is enacted as a negotiated multilingualism'. My insistence to work in English is justified against the backdrop of the global discourse of excellence in business schools and the fact that our many foreign students and faculty appreciate it. However, my story also elucidates how 'even if we mainly use English in our research and writing practices, we still operate in a multilingual context which needs to be made visible and reflected upon' (Steyaert and Janssens, 2012, 132; see also Tietze, 2017).

Following the Foucauldian tradition, this leads me to consider whether my reluctance to engage with Swedish is a way to resist a subject position and identity that is imposed on me: to mimic the Swedish speakers and seek to become one of them (which I know I can never do). Foldy (2002) urges us to explore identity as a key site for power relations where resistance is a continuous process of adaptation and reinscription of the dominant discourses. Resistance creates new types of practice and discourse-level responses to challenging social situations (Thomas and Davies, 2005). By questioning the dominant local discourse of Swedish at the level of subjectivity, I respond to dominant articulations of what I ought to be (Holmer-Nadesan, 1996). However, I am sure that my actions do not count as resistance. I am not actively standing up for anything or taking a real risk of any sort (Contu, 2008). I am entangled in power relations around language that generate a sense of guilt and lack as well as a sense of being an outsider. I feel tensions and uncertainty. Ambivalence.

When we introduce the Finnish language into the equation, my experiences get even more ambivalent. In the Swedish-speaking business school where I am currently employed, I speak Finnish with some of my colleagues who are either Finnish speakers or bilingual Swedish-speaking Finns. As the administrative languages at Hanken are Swedish and English, I am careful not to turn to Finnish in any official communications. If I were to impose Finnish on the committees that I am a member of, it would be seen as a provocation, and it would be meaningless anyway. I stick to English and encourage others to use Swedish. Having studied Swedish at school, I can read it and understand it when spoken by Swedish-speaking Finns (in my ears they have a clear accent, in contrast to 'real' Swedes in Sweden). However, I find constant switching between languages difficult and tiresome.

The English language stirs emotions in all Finnish universities that I know of. We had heated discussions about English and Finnish languages at Aalto University, my previous employer. Some colleagues were offended by having to work solely in the English language. They made a point of turning to Finnish whenever they could. Yet, the reality is that an increasing number of their colleagues today are not Finnish speakers. So, I can fully understand and appreciate that Hanken is Swedish-speaking at its core, but in current global academia we cannot escape English. Tensions and uncertainty continue to characterize our experiences as academics.

My lack of Swedish skills brings a sense of ambivalence to my work and it is changing my identity as an academic. My sense of ambivalence is self-inflicted, however, as I 'enact the self I am trying to describe' (Butler, 2005, 66). One outcome is that through my work and my choices I contribute to Englishization—the normalization of English as the language of writing and publishing—in academic knowledge production (Boussebaa and Brown, 2017; Boussebaa and Tienari, 2021). English is my escape from Swedish. At the same time, I am against Englishization as a matter of course. Dealing with this ambivalence—or paradox—of language use is a significant part of my identity work right now, because I am contributing to something with which I am not fully comfortable, yet I cannot find a viable alternative for it in my work.

Working on my outsider identity helps me deal with the tensions and uncertainty I am experiencing. I feel guilty about my inability to contribute in Swedish, but by working in English I connect with my international colleagues. Working in English, I am not only ascribed an identity by myself and by others, but my identity work has consequences for those around me as I drift away from my Swedish-speaking colleagues. My sense of guilt is something that some of my international colleagues find hard to understand. It is very difficult for them to see the position of the Swedish-speaking minority in contemporary Finnish society, and they fail to comprehend how Swedish language is at the core of the Swedish speakers' identity and, thus, also their academic identities. In contemporary Finland, the Swedish language is far from being any sort of vehicle of (neo-)colonization. On the contrary, perhaps.

In this sense, I have a responsibility, which I do not fulfill. I am all for internationalization in academic work and I am always suspicious of parochialism. Nevertheless, for me, the Swedish language in Finnish society is something to be preserved and protected. It is a major part of my Finnishness to cherish the bilingual nature of my society, even if Swedish reminds us of our colonial past and even if I am not comfortable speaking it myself. In a nutshell, my identity as an academic is torn.

When I think of myself as a white male academic in a senior position, my guilt mounts. I am taking advantage of the opportunities available to me. Some of my junior Finnish-speaking colleagues have made efforts to brush up their Swedish to the extent that they can contribute in teaching in Swedish. After all, our undergraduate program is run in the Swedish language. I doubt if they would say it to my face, but perhaps they view me as arrogant. Gendered and racialized hierarchies remain strong in Finnish business schools and I am positioned in these power relations in a way that enables me to continue working as I have always done. The question of language at Hanken no doubt looks different when viewed in and from different subject positions.

My story could also be understood in the light of other conceptual frameworks. For example, it can be made sense of through the idea of 'layers of language' as argued by Welch et al. (2005). These authors distinguish between everyday spoken and written language in the workplace, 'company speak,' and professional and industry-specific language. My current employer, the Swedish-speaking business school in Helsinki, embraces the Swedish language in all its daily operations because that is its mission and mandate. However, the 'company speak' is a mix of this identification as a key provider of Swedish language business education in Finland *and* the hegemonic global discourse of academic excellence produced in English. The business school must cater for both audiences and engage with both discourses. The professional 'global' language in business studies is English. There is no way people like me could ever dream of making an academic career without a solid publication record in highly regarded international journals published in English. All this contributes to a sense of ambivalence, which is reflected in my experience and self-identity where the everyday 'reality' in the organization and the discourse of global academic meritocracy clash at times.

You may think that my experience is idiosyncratic. Yet I would argue that Swedish, Finnish, and English languages in contemporary Finnish society bring to the fore something important that I assume remains more hidden in many other contexts. The question of French language in academia, for example, plays out differently because it is embedded in a different history of nation-building, colonialism, and language relations. The French State apparatus actively promotes and sustains what is known as 'Le Monde Francophone' or the French-speaking world, which in many fields continues to challenge English as the global lingua franca (sic). Many French speakers are reluctant to give up their privilege in speaking their own language when they interact with others. The European Union is an acute example.

In French business schools today, this plays out as identity clashes for individuals and groups (Boussebaa and Brown, 2017). Language and power relations reveal their complexity and, I would argue, ambivalence. The English language for the French represents a competitor for linguistic dominance. Dynamics of power and resistance play out in specific ways. This appears very different from the perspective of Finns who embrace English as a more level playing field, or as an escape from other languages, as I described in my own experience above. Nevertheless, language and power relations are fundamentally important for us all.

CONCLUSION

In this chapter, I have joined the conversation on natural languages in international business studies (Piekkari et al., 2014; Beeler et al., 2017). I have considered language(s) in the light of power relations in and beyond organizations and suggested that we must labor to unravel connections between language, power, and resistance in their multiplicity. A perspective that is sensitive to power relations helps us appreciate and make sense of the ambivalence—tensions, uncertainty, and mixed feelings—that characterizes language relations and experiences today. Ambivalence is the outcome of the fact that we view power relations in organizations from different vantage points, perspectives and, in Michel Foucault's words, subject positions. One example of this is that members of the dominant language group in a given organization are usually collectively unaware of the forms and consequences of their dominance. They (unconsciously) reproduce established power relations and the status quo. In the eyes of those who are not part of the dominant group, in contrast, domination and subordination as well as inclusion and exclusion play out differently. They are very visible. Co-existence of these different experiences and views is what sustains the ambivalence.

I have argued that meaningful language-sensitive analysis in international business studies entails that we acknowledge the ambivalence that characterizes languages and linguistic relations in the world today. With my examples of strategy and identity, organizations and individuals, I have attempted to shed light on the various aspects and dimensions of this ambivalence. The 'language-sensitive' research agenda in international business studies is very welcome (Piekkari et al., 2014; Beeler et al., 2017). There is a lot to be researched. Beeler et al. (2017, 4) argue that we must acknowledge the 'positive role of the interplay between the different languages.' This is a lovely thought. But it depends. I hope that my examples elucidate the ambivalence in languages and language relations. So maybe we really should all speak Finnish. Except Swedish-speakers. And maybe the English and the French. And all others. I am faced with ambivalence again. Kiitos ja anteeksi.

REFERENCES

Alvesson, M. and Deetz, S. (2000), *Doing critical management research*. London: Sage.

Beeler, B., Cohen, L., de Vecchi, D., Kassis-Henderson, J. and Lecomte, P. (2017), Special issue on language in global management and business. *International Journal of Cross Cultural Management*, 17(1), 3–6.

Beeler, B. and Lecomte, P. (2017), Shedding light on the darker side of language: A dialogical approach to cross-cultural collaboration. *International Journal of Cross Cultural Management*, 17(1), 53–67.

Boussebaa, M. and Brown, A.D. (2017), Englishization, identity regulation and imperialism. *Organization Studies*, 38(1), 7–29.

Boussebaa, M. and Tienari, J. (2021), Englishization and the politics of knowledge production in management studies. *Journal of Management Inquiry*, 30(1), 50–67.

Braverman, H. (1974), *Labor and monopoly capital: The degradation of work in the twentieth century*. New York: Monthly Review Press.

Brown, A.D. (2015), Identities and identity work in organizations. *International Journal of Management Reviews*, 17(1), 20–40.

Butler, J. (2005), *Giving an account of oneself*. New York: Fordham University Press.

Clegg, S.R. (1989), *Frameworks of power*. London: Sage.

Clegg, S.R., Courpasson, D. and Phillips, N. (2006), *Power and organizations*. London: Sage.

Collinson, D. (1994), Strategies of resistance, in J. Jermier, D. Knights and W.E. Nord (eds.), *Resistance and power in organizations*. London: Routledge, 25–68.

Contu, A. (2008), Decaf resistance: On misbehaviour, cynicism, and desire in liberal workplaces. *Management Communication Quarterly*, 21(3), 364–379.

Foldy, E.G. (2002), 'Managing' diversity: Identity and power in organizations, in I. Aaltio and A.J. Mills (eds.), *Gender, identity and the culture of organizations*. London: Routledge, 92–112.

Foucault, M. (1977), *Discipline and punish: The birth of the prison*. Harmondsworth: Penguin.

Foucault, M. (1980), *Power/knowledge: Selected interviews and other writings 1972–1974*. ed. C. Gordon. Brighton: Harvester Press.

Foucault, M. (1984), *The history of sexuality: An introduction*. Harmondsworth: Penguin.

Gaibrois, C. and Steyaert, C. (2017), Beyond possession and competition: Investigating cooperative aspects of power in multilingual organizations. *International Journal of Cross Cultural Management*, 17(1), 69–84.

Holmer-Nadesan, M. (1996), Organizational identity and space of action. *Organization Studies*, 17(1), 49–81.

Knights, D. and Vurdubakis, T. (1994), Foucault, power, resistance and all that, in J. Jermier, D. Knights and W.E. Nord (eds.), *Resistance and power in organizations*. London: Routledge, 167–198.

Piekkari, R., Welch, D. and Welch, L. (2014), *Language in international business: The multilingual reality of global business expansion*. Cheltenham, UK and Northampton, MA, USA: Edward Elgar Publishing.

Pratt, M., Schultz, M., Ashforth, B. and Ravasi, D. (eds.) (2016), *The Oxford handbook of organizational identity*. Oxford: Oxford University Press.

Pudelko, M. and Tenzer, H. (2019), Boundaryless careers or career boundaries? The impact of language barriers on academic careers in international business schools. *Academy of Management Learning and Education*, 18(2), 213–240.

Steyaert, C. and Janssens, M. (2012), Multilingual scholarship and the paradox of translation and language in management and organization studies. *Organization*, 20(1), 131–142.

Thomas, R. and Davies, A. (2005), Theorizing the micro-politics of resistance: New Public Management and managerial identities in the UK public services. *Organization Studies*, 26 (5), 683–706.

Thomas, R. and Hardy, C. (2011), Reframing resistance to organizational change. *Scandinavian Journal of Management*, 27(3), 322–331.

Tienari, J. (2019), One flew over the duck pond. Autoethnography, academic identity and language. *Management Learning*, 50(5), 576–590.

Tienari, J. and Vaara, E. (2012), Power and politics in mergers and acquisitions, in David Faulkner, Satu Teerikangas and Richard Joseph (eds.), *The handbook of mergers & acquisitions*. Oxford: Oxford University Press, 495–516.

Tietze, S. (2017), Multilingual research, monolingual publications: Management scholarship in English only? *European Journal of International Management*, 12(1–2), 28–45.

Tietze, S. and Dick, P. (2013), The victorious English language: Hegemonic practices in the management academy. *Journal of Management Inquiry*, 22(1), 122–134.

Vaara, E., Tienari, J., Piekkari, R. and Säntti, R. (2005), Language and the circuits of power in a merging multinational corporation. *Journal of Management Studies*, 42(3), 595–623.

Welch, D., Welch, L. and Piekkari, R. (2005), Speaking in tongues: The importance of language in international management processes. *International Studies of Management & Organization*, 35(1), 10–27.

Conclusion to *Understanding the Dynamics of Language and Multilingualism in Professional Contexts*

Claudine Gaibrois, Betty Beeler, Philippe Lecomte and Mary Vigier

When we came up with the idea of this volume, we set ourselves three over-arching goals. We aimed at providing researchers from inside and outside the language-sensitive Organisation Studies (OS) and International Business (IB) communities with fresh inspiration and novel insights into certain 'blind spots' in the field. Furthermore, we aspired to show how scholars at the forefront of language-sensitive research in management and organisational studies are advancing our understanding of the processes underlying collaboration across boundaries. In addition, we strived for a contribution to a greater dialogue between the disciplines.

We are convinced that this book offers many insights and inspirations that are relevant for both research and practice. On a conceptual level, it further encourages us to view language as social practice (Karhunen et al., 2018) in the multilingual reality of the workplace, thus moving beyond a functionalist understanding of language as a transmission tool for information. It also further problematises the notion of 'language' as a pre-defined set of structures; replacing it with the view that language and communication experience con-stitute a dynamic pattern of practices, potentially detached from pre-defined groups or speech communities and placed instead within emerging and evolv-ing networks of practice. As Cohen and Kassis-Henderson (Chapter 11) stress, a monolingual vision of communication with its linguistic norms and standard-ised practices fails to reflect the reality of who people are and what skills they actually have. In their study, Matras, Tipton and Gaiser (Chapter 4) provide an excellent example of such a multilingual reality. In general, urban settings are super-diverse environments (Busch, 2012; Blommaert and Backus, 2013). Taking the example of multilingual Manchester, Matras, Tipton and Gaiser study communication practices for interacting with patients in a bottom-up fashion based on their manifold language backgrounds. Importantly, this example also invites us to broaden our understanding of language diversity by considering 'community languages' and languages that are not highly valued languages as equally valuable language resources in a European or in a Western business context. It reminds us that languages are 'not equal in terms of socio-politico-economic value' (Hua, 2014, 236). In fact, as Erbil, Özbilgin and Bağlama (Chapter 12) show in the case of Turkey and Britain, the hierarchisation of languages today continues to reflect historical power relations, affecting opportunities for employment, marginalising employees along linguistic lines and perpetuating norms that fail to take into account the diversity of humanity.

The volume thus encourages us to move from the understanding of language diversity as an individual marker of difference to an understanding that views people as members of language groups, investigating reasons and effects of belonging to a certain language group. Several theoretical frameworks are proposed to support our analysis of how such language group memberships play out. Cohen and Kassis-Henderson (Chapter 11) suggest intersectionality (Crenshaw, 1991; Boogaard and Roggeband, 2010; Zander et al., 2010; Frame, 2016) as a lens for the analysis of how the multiple facets of our identity can be drawn on, depending on the context and the effect we wish to provoke. In Chapter 2, Johansson and Śliwa propose recognition theory for the analysis of relations and hierarchies of power in multilingual contexts. Recognition work encompasses individual and organisational acts of bestowal or denial of recognition, to account for how recognition does not only take place between individuals but, significantly, also involves institutions such as the workplace (Cox, 2012). Several authors remind us of the potential agency of individuals and language groups. Drawing on Foucault (1974), Tienari (Chapter 16) also calls for recognition of a less valued language such as Finnish and highlights the ambiguity of power, thus proposing that power includes both the power to decide and the power to resist. On another note, the volume introduces subjectivity and emotionality in the analysis of practices of language use at the workplace. For instance, Fiset's study (Chapter 8) reveals solidarity, a shared identity and making a positive impression as possible motives to explain organisational members' desire to use a non-mutually understood language. Several chapters propose the notion of 'voice' inspired by Bakhtin's research on heteroglossia (Bakhtin, 1981), which highlighted the diversity of 'voice' as the essence of verbal performance, for the analysis of language practices in multilingual workplaces. In their critical study of voices in the employee magazine, Kastberg and Ditlevsen (Chapter 15) show who has a voice and who counts as a legitimate organisational voicer, in order to identify which actors of the organisation contribute to shaping employee identity formation. Räisänen and Kankaanranta (Chapter 6) remind us to include written communication in multilingual organisations when considering language diversity in professional contexts.

The book has also explored the potential for cross-pollination between discourse-oriented OS (Organisation Studies) scholars who study the way multiple voices combine and compete within an organisation, on the one hand, and language-oriented IB (and some OS) scholars who focus on the way multiple languages compete and combine within an organisation, on the other (Janssens et al., 2004; Tietze, 2008; Brannen et al., 2014; Angouri and Piekkari, 2018; Karhunen et al., 2018). In fact, as Janssens and Steyaert (2013) point out, there is a gaping inconsistency in the idea of exploring the increasingly multilingual workplace from a monolingual world view. Johansson and Barner-Rasmussen (Chapter 10) propose paths of exploration that could be shared by both streams, and in particular, the combining of IB findings on multilingual issues with the theory developed by OS researchers on the Communicative Constitution of Organisations (Cooren et al., 2011). According to the authors, the epistemological and ontological implications of managing people of diverse origins should not be ignored in organisational studies.

On a methodological level, the volume invites us to open up our understanding of language diversity in the workplace beyond the white collar and managerial realm. In her study on the role of language in initiatives to integrate refugees on the labour market, Lønsmann (Chapter 3) encourages us to include refugees in research on language diversity. How pressing this call is, was sadly illustrated by the refugee wave caused by war in Ukraine that was going on at the time of finalising this book. The volume also encourages us to adopt the perspective of the various actors involved in complex multilingual workplace settings, and to understand how language practices are intertwined with institutional logics, as Johansson and Śliwa's chapter on non-native English speaking international staff at universities in the UK, or Lønsmann's study on refugees on the Danish labour market illustrate. This also includes seeking to understand the motives for choosing a language. In Chapter 8, for example, Fiset explores the reasons for speaking a non-mutually understood language in the workplace. Furthermore, the volume encourages us to venture into underexplored methods of data collection. Räisänen and Kankaanranta (Chapter 6) as well as Humonen and Angouri (Chapter 7) propose ethnography as a seldomly used method in the field of language-sensitive International Business. In their call for reflexivity in analysing language data, Humonen and Angouri point out that the researcher's subjectivities can impact the reading of the data. By so doing, the authors aim at enhancing our awareness of the co-existence of multiple truths and interpretations.

The practical implications of this book are manifold. Räisänen and Kankaanranta's analysis of practices of language use in written communication, and Fiset's study of the motives underlying the engagement in speaking a non-mutually understood language in the workplace, provide human resource professionals with valuable suggestions for effectively meeting the multifaceted requirements of linguistically diverse organisations. Erbil, Özbilgin and Bağlama (Chapter 12) propose the creation of a polyphonic workplace, beginning with recruitment and promotion that favours those with multiple language skills and human resource practices that encourage language learning within the institution. The case of the healthcare employees in the multilingual city of Manchester shows how creative staff can become when it comes to making communication possible, which encourages leaders to trust in their employees' capabilities to make things work, rather than developing language policies in a top-down manner. Our book shows that attempting to solve language issues by designing top-down language policies often fails to do justice to the complexity of today's multilingual workplace. Indeed, several chapters demonstrate how employees resist language policies or develop their own practices of language use. Sanden (Chapter 14) points out the discrepancy between language policies and practices and the correlated opposition between micro and macro language management processes. Importantly, however, as Tienari reminds us, resistance is not necessarily always problematic. Instead of viewing it as a hindrance to managerial decisions, the author proposes to view it positively and dynamically as a driver of organisational change.

The world was a different one when we started work on this book. Few people could have imagined that two years after a pandemic threatened lives and livelihoods all over the world, the invasion of Ukraine by a powerful neighbouring nation would shake up the stability of Eastern European borders and highlight once again the plight of refugees. It is our hope that this book may contribute to a greater awareness of the importance of an inclusive approach to language practices, one which recognises the value of diversity in the workplace and the international arena.

REFERENCES

Angouri, J. and Piekkari, R. (2018), 'Organising multilingually: Setting an agenda for studying language at work', *European Journal of International Management*, **12** (1/2), 8–27.

Bakhtin, M. (1981), *The Dialogic Imagination: Four Essays*, Michael Holquist (ed.), Austin, TX: University of Texas Press.

Blommaert, J. and Backus, A. (2013), 'Superdiverse repertoires and the individual', in Ingrid de Saint-Georges and Jean-Jacques Weber (eds), *Multilingualism and Multimodality: The Future of Education Research*, Rotterdam: Sense Publishers, pp. 11–32.

Boogaard, B. and Roggeband, C. (2010), 'Paradoxes of intersectionality: Theorizing inequality in the Dutch police force through structure and agency', *Organization*, **17** (1), 53–75.

Brannen, M.Y., Piekkari, R. and Tietze, S. (2014), 'The multifaceted role of language in international business: Unpacking the forms, functions and features of a critical challenge to MNC theory and performance', *Journal of International Business Studies*, **45** (5), 495–507.

Busch, B. (2012), 'The linguistic repertoire revisited', *Applied Linguistics*, **33** (5), 503–523.

Cooren, F., Kuhn, T., Cornelissen, J.P. and Clark, T. (2011), 'Communication, organizing and organization: An overview and introduction to the special issue', *Organization Studies*, **32** (9), 1149–1170.

Cox, R. (2012), 'Recognition and immigration', in Shane O'Neill and Nicholas H. Smith (eds), *Recognition Theory as Social Research: Investigating the Dynamics of Social Conflict*, Basingstoke, UK: Palgrave, pp. 192–212.

Crenshaw, K. (1991), 'Mapping the margins: Intersectionality, identity politics, and violence against women of color', *Stanford Law Review*, **43** (6), 1241–1299.

Foucault, M. (1974), *The Archeology of Knowledge*, London: Tavistock.

Frame, A. (2016), 'Intersectional identities in interpersonal communication', in Kamila Ciepiela (ed.), *Studying Identity in Communicative Contexts*, Frankfurt: Peter Lang, pp. 21–38.

Hua, Z. (2014), 'Piecing together the "workplace multilingualism" jigsaw puzzle', *Multilingua*, **33** (1–2), 233–242.

Janssens, M., Lambert, J. and Steyaert, C. (2004), 'Developing language strategies for international companies: The contribution of translation studies', *Journal of World Business*, **39** (4), 414–430.

Janssens, M. and Steyaert, C. (2013), 'Multilingual scholarship and the paradox of translation and language in management and organization studies', *Organization*, **20** (1), 131–142.

Karhunen, P., Kankaanranta, A., Louhiala-Salminen, L. and Piekkari, R. (2018), 'Let's talk about language: A review of language-sensitive research in international management', *Journal of Management Studies*, **55** (6), 980–1013.

Tietze, S. (2008), *International Management and Language*, London, UK: Routledge.

Zander, U., Zander, L., Gaffney, S. and Olsson, J. (2010), 'Intersectionality as a new perspective in international business research', *Scandinavian Journal of Management*, **26**, 457–466.

Index